SOCIAL MEDIA

Pedagogy and Practice

Edited by
Kehbuma Langmia
Tia C. M. Tyree
Pamela O'Brien
Ingrid Sturgis

University Press of America,® Inc.
Lanham · Boulder · New York · Toronto · Plymouth, UK

Copyright © 2014 by
University Press of America,® Inc.
4501 Forbes Boulevard
Suite 200
Lanham, Maryland 20706
UPA Acquisitions Department (301) 459-3366

10 Thornbury Road
Plymouth PL6 7PP
United Kingdom

Library of Congress Control Number: 2013952522
ISBN: 978-0-7618-6195-9 (paperback : alk. paper)
eISBN: 978-0-7618-6196-6

⊖™ The paper used in this publication meets the minimum
requirements of American National Standard for Information
Sciences—Permanence of Paper for Printed Library Materials,
ANSI Z39.48-1992

DEDICATION

This book is dedicated to all of the participants in the 2011 and 2012 Social Media Technology Conference and Workshops. The research presented at the conferences inspired the creation of this work.

TABLE OF CONTENTS

PREFACE

There has been explosive growth in the use of social media technology over the past decade with most students primarily using Facebook, YouTube, and Twitter, according to some studies. These digital natives have been born into a world in which technology forms the center of the way they learn, socialize, and communicate, spending hours a day on one form of social media or another. Although many faculty members have readily adopted the technology for personal and professional use, others remain wary of the academic benefits of the new technologies.

But as social media continue to influence all areas of our lives, it is important to examine and debate not only the use of various social media tools in different contexts, but also how they change the manner in which students, academics, business owners, and the governments make use of this medium. In the ensuing years, educators have sought to harness the intellectual power and curiosity to develop the first wave of first social media courses.

In order to synthesize their findings about what was being taught nationally and internationally, faculty at Bowie State University and Howard University conducted the first annual Social Media Technology Conference and Workshop in 2011, which convened scholars, professionals, and other experts in the area of social media to share their perspectives on the technical, ethical, economic, legal, political, and cultural implications of social media use.

The editors of *Social Media Pedagogy and Practice* believe it is critical to find the proper balance of technology, pedagogy, and content to develop college-level courses. This book seeks to enlighten educators, scholars, and practitioners about social media and provide them with the knowledge to create and effectively utilize social media in different contexts. It is anchored on the premise that information could immediately be incorporated into curricula to identify and build skills needed for students going into journalism, public relations, integrated marketing, and other communications fields. It focuses on the use of social media in educational settings and how social media is impacting and altering pedagogical thought. It provides opportunities for academics and scholars to incorporate social media practices into the learning environment that could potentially transform what has been a distraction into an enhancement of learning objectives.
— The Editors

ACKNOWLEDGMENTS

Creating a new academic conference is not an easy task. While the idea may generate from a few individuals, there are many others who must help make the idea a reality. In the case of the Social Media Technology Conference and Workshop, two Universities had to come together to bring the conference to life. Dr. Kehbuma Langmia, Dr. Pamela O'Brien, Dr. Tia Tyree, and Professor Ingrid Sturgis would like to thank the administrators at Bowie State University and Howard University, especially within the College of Arts and Sciences at Bowie State and the School of Communication at Howard, for providing the time and resources necessary to launch the annual conference in September 2011.

In addition, the conference relied on many colleagues, staff and students at both Universities. The editors of this book are grateful for all of the assistance. The continued success of the conference is a result of the dedication and hard work of everyone who has contributed to the first two conferences.

INTRODUCTION: SOCIAL MEDIA HISTORY AND USE
Pamela C. O'Brien

> ... nothing less than a new organization of society—a state of things in which every individual, however, secluded, will have at call every other individual in the community, to the saving of no end of social and business complications, of needless going to and fro, of disappointments, delays, and a countless host of those great and little evils and annoyances which go so far under present conditions to make life laborious and unsatisfactory.

While the above prediction regarding the impact of a new communication technology on the structure and functioning of society could be referencing the early days of the Internet or social media, it was actually written by the editors of *Scientific American* in 1880 about the potential influence of the telephone (Marvin, 1988, p. 65). Like the telegraph before it, the telephone ushered in a new era of information sharing and potential for instantaneous, global communication. While the influence and reach of the telephone was seen as revolutionary in the late 1800s, communication technology would continue to evolve and eventually converge with computers and the mass media to create a digital environment where consumers could use a single device to make phone calls (or VOIP), watch television, send emails, listen to music, play games, create documents, etc. from anywhere at any time. Smartphone and tablet devices (Android and iOS) have experienced worldwide adoption rates that have outpaced any previous consumer technology (Miot, 2012, Paragraph 2). Google has estimated that there are now more than 500 million Android devices worldwide with more than 1 million tablets and smartphones being activated daily (Bell, 2013). Apple outpaces those numbers with more than 600 million iOS devices sold worldwide (Whitney, 2013).

The technology itself, however, is not the driving force of change. In other words, without an active human element, the communication device does not have a purpose as there is a medium, but no message. As consumers have grown accustomed to being able to access all of their communication technologies at one time, a shift developed in the balance of power in the creation and control of content for these devices. Consumers want to be able to have some influence on the messages or content available to them on their computer, smartphones or tablets. For some users this translates to the ability to provide feedback to the content creators (be they large corporate entities or simply other individual users), to create levels of content themselves, or to control when and where they view the content. This philosophical change in relationship between the user and the media has developed, in part, from the prevalence of social media. As converged, communication devices have become more powerful, pervasive, and accessible worldwide, there is growing interest in who is using them and how these devices are currently being used, as well as how they could be used to influence those same communities that *Scientific American* wrote about more than 100 years ago. The purpose of this book is to explore how social media are being studied and taught within academic settings, but also how social media are being used to shape communities and influence world events.

Definition of Social Media

Before exploring the development, prevalence, and uses of social media, it is necessary to have an understanding of what social media encompasses. It should be noted that there is no universal agreement on a definition of social media or what social media encompasses. This is due in part to the continually evolving nature and role of social media. A strict dictionary definition, however, would describe social media as, "forms of electronic communication (as websites for social networking and microblogging) through which users create online communities to share information, ideas, personal messages, and other content (as videos)" (merriamwebster.com, 2013). The format for a social media site can vary dramatically; blogs, microblogs, message boards, wikis, picture and video sharing, podcasts, and digital scrapbooking are all examples of social media.

But there is more to the actual use or influence of social media than is being conveyed by this definition, as it does not completely address the level of human interconnectivity that is a significant hallmark of contemporary social media networks. Boyd and Ellison (2007) better capture the human-technological connection with their definition of social network sites, which defines them ". . . as web-based services that allow individuals to (1) construct a public or semi-public profile within a bounded system, (2) articulate a list of other users with whom they share a connection, and (3) view and traverse their list of connections and those made by others within the system" (paragraph 4).

Social media sites, thus, allow potentially large groups of people, who are not bound by time and geography, a platform to express their thoughts, ideology, creativity, and professional goals within networks of individuals that might not otherwise have ever known each other. This is often accomplished through the creation of a user profile (which can either be public or restricted depending on the nature of the site or the privacy settings of the individual user) and the establishment of a group of Friends, Fans, or Followers who can then see each other and each other's profiles. Of course, meeting new people is not necessarily the primary goal of social media sites, but rather it is a way to allow others to see, comment on, and understand a person's interests and the network of individuals who share some or all of those interests (Boyd and Ellison, 2007, paragraph 6). Thus, social media, unlike other forms of mass communication, provide a platform for anyone who has access to a smartphone, computer, or tablet to share their voice, personality, and creativity with the world.

A Brief History of Social Media

While it may seem as if social media or social network sites are a new phenomenon, only developing in the last few years, that is not entirely the case. As occurs with many "revolutionary" technologies, the actual roots of the technology (and accompanying uses) can be traced decades, if not centuries, before their adoption by a widespread public. This is due not only to the often long research and development time involved in the creation of a new communication technology, but also due to remediation. Remediation occurs when aspects of one medium or technology are utilized or are visible in a different medium or technology. Remediation is a crucial concept when evaluating new digital media, as many elements of digital media are drawn from earlier media such as television, print journalism, radio, photography, the telegraph, etc. The components of the old media do not always look identical when they are used by the new media, but are rather a repurposing. In other words, the myth of modernity creates the assumption that all new forms of media must be distinct from what has come before. However, these new forms of media rely on their predecessors to help create the cultural significance of the new media (Bolter and Grusin, 2000).

Social media are no exception to the process of remediation, and thus, its history could be seen as beginning as far back as 550 B.C. when the first postal service was created, because written communication (in this case letters) being sent across distances represents part of the definition of social media (Hendricks, 2013). Placing the beginnings of social media this far in the past may seem farfetched, but each historical step helps to set the stage for what will come next and each step seems more revolutionary than the one before it to the audience.

It may be easier to see how social media are tied to the two next historical milestones. In 1792, the first telegraph was sent, thus increasing the speed and reliability of communication and communication technology. In many ways, the electronic connections in the world wide web look and function in a similar fashion to the wires of the telegraph. In addition, communication over the Internet uses a computer code that must be encoded by the sender and then decoded by the receiver just as Morse Code is used to encode and decode telegraph messages. It is interesting to note that the telegraph was still being used in India, the last country to do so, until July 13, 2013. So important was the telegraph in modern India that a telegram could be used as a legally binding document in some cases (Brown, 2013).

As mentioned earlier, the invention of the telephone, itself a remediation of the telegraph, in 1890 helped to show how communication technologies could link communities together, right in their own homes or businesses, and solve problems that resulted from an inability to communicate quickly and efficiently. With the telegraph, messages had to be decoded and then delivered to the receiver. There was an additional time delay if the receiver wanted to reply to the message. The telephone removed those obstacles, although in the early days of the telephone an operator was required to be able to connect a call. Radio signals, first used in 1891, would take the concept of point-to-point communication and expand message delivery to mass communication. However, with radio and television the communication was one way. Receivers did not have an easy method to respond to what they were hearing or seeing (unless they took the time to write a letter to the network or station). While all of these technologies evolved and improved over time, they each were limited. A technology's limitations often create the impetus for the development of a new technology that takes the best of the previous ideas to develop something new and without the same limitations. In terms of the mass media and interpersonal communication, the possibility for such convergence would require a different delivery mechanism than any of the analog models: the computer.

Not only were these early forms of communication technologies analog rather than digital, they also did not contain the key characteristics of social media, such as a public profile shared within an electronic system or the use of multimedia elements such as text, pictures, and videos. The beginning of the platform to allow such functionality can be seen in ARPANET (Advanced Research Projects Agency Network), a packet switching network funded by the Department of Defense to be used by its researchers at the University of California, Los Angeles; University of California, Santa Barbara; University of Utah; and Stanford Research Institute. First deployed in 1969, ARPANET utilized TCP/IP and would become the basic prototype for the Internet.

Computer networks began to proliferate in the early 1970s, but many aimed toward either researchers or business. CompuServe Network Inc., which began as a dial-up computer processor sharing service aimed at businesses, was the first major commercial online service. CompuServe, which would be a dominate player in the industry through the mid-1990s, allowed users to share processor time during business hours, but also to share data and send emails (the first of which was sent in 1971) (Goble, 2012). In the late 1980s, CompuServe shifted its focus to the public realm as the Internet began to proliferate into the consumer market (Goble, 2012). CompuServe, and services like it, allowed for communication interaction through discussion forums and email exchange, as well as file sharing (Goble, 2012).

A major development toward social media sites occurred in 1978: the Bulletin Board System. The first Bulletin Board System (BBS) was created by two hobbyists in Chicago who wanted a way to inform friends about meetings, post announcements, and share interesting information. It was the electronic version of a community bulletin board found in many apartment or housing complexes in the United States (The brief history of social media, 2013). By 1979, UseNet, a BBS that connected Duke University and the University of North Carolina, offered a virtual newsletter for its users to stay connected (The brief history of social media, 2013).

The home computer revolution in the 1980s, as well as the growing use of Internet relay chats (IRCs), set the stage, technologically and socially, for what is currently recognized as social media. In 1984, Prodigy began offering online services for the Internet that included news, shopping BBSs, games, banking, stocks, weather, and travel services—all in one portal. The services were represented by a graphic user interface. In 1994, Prodigy offered access to the World Wide Web, and by 1997 it became a true Internet Service Provider (ISP) (Banks, 2008). Prodigy was followed by America Online in 1985, which allowed users to search member profiles within its member created communities (Goble, 2012).

The most significant development, however, occurred at the end of the 1980s when Tim Berners-Lee's work with CERN (the European Organization for Nuclear Research) in Switzerland would lead to the creation of the World Wide Web (WWW). CERN permitted universal access to the WWW technology in 1993, and, that same year, Mosaic, the first graphical browser, allowed for the creation of web pages that are similar in user interface to what is available today. By the end of 1993, there were more than 200 web servers online (The brief history of social media, 2013).

The mid to late 1990s would mark rapid developments of online communities, Internet search tools, and social media sites. Geocities, debuting in 1994, allowed users to create websites based on types of urban areas. By 1994, there were 1,500 web servers online, and by 1997 there were more than a million web sites (The brief history of social media, 2013), but there was not anything that could be defined as a social media site, although there were many that had elements of a social media site. Websites were allowing users to blog, and AOL began its Instant Messenger service to allow its members to "chat" in real-time over the Internet. Classmates.com, a site designed for virtual class reunions, began in 1995 and quickly developed a significant user base. While users could not create a profile, Classmates.com is one of the longest lasting social media forerunners, with more than 500 million accounts currently active (Goble, 2012). Educational institutions were looking to the Internet for ways to improve the learning environment and Blackboard learning management system was launched in 1997 (The brief history of social media, 2013).

The first true social network site was SixDegrees.com, which launched in 1997. SixDegrees offered users a chance to create a profile, organize groups, search other user's profiles, and make "friends." The site's name came from a popular Internet game that revolved around the concept that there were only six degrees of separation between any famous person and the actor Kevin Bacon (Goble, 2012). SixDegrees.com, however, did not find enough success to be sustainable, and it went offline just after 2000 (Goble, 2012).

By the end of the 1990s, the Internet bubble was ready to burst, and the business side of the Internet would change significantly. However, in 2000 there were seventy million computers connected to the Internet, so there was a significant base of users available to support what would come next (The brief history of social media, 2013). And what would come next would be a rush of social media sites fueled by the movement toward smartphones (the first, introduced by Palm, would reach the United States in 2001) and tablets. Wikipedia, the world's largest wiki, went online in 2001, and Friendster went public in 2002. Friendster built on the concept of separation started by SixDegrees and early dating sites, but altered the connections so that they became a graphic "circle of friends" to easily show how one person was linked to another in their friend group. In other words, the groups' common bonds were visible (Goble, 2012). In just three months, Friendster would have three million users (The brief history of social media, 2013). While Friendster is no longer a strong social media site in the United States, it is still extremely popular in Asia and the Philippines (Goble, 2012).

Clones of the most popular social media sites sprang up quickly. In 2003, MySpace, very similar to Friendster, launched, as did Linden Lab's Second Life, an online virtual community. MySpace was aimed at young adults and had a more contemporary feel than Friendster. MySpace became the dominant social media site until 2008, when it was replaced by Facebook. Also in 2003, iTunes was started by Apple and LinkedIn became the social media site for business professionals. There were now 3 billion web pages (The brief history of social media, 2013).

In 2004, niche social media sites, a social media site that is tailored to a more specific community or is limited to the types of media share, began to become more prevalent with Photobucket and Flickr. These two sites were developed specifically for photo sharing (niche social network sites are still popular and encompass Foursquare, Tumblr, Pinterest, etc). Flickr and Photobucket were not the first targeted, or niche, social media sites, however. Social media sites such as BlackPlanet, AsianAvenue, and MiGente were created for the African-American, Asian, and Hispanic communities in the late 1990s.

The most significant development in social media in 2004, however, was the creation of Facebook, which began as a social media site for Harvard students only. Facebook would not expand its offering to the general public until 2006, but by then it already had tremendous financial backing and public interest (Goble, 2012). While Facebook's success has recently been marred by legal and financial/stock controversies, its early success was due to smart advertising, easy-to-use features, and the ability of third parties (through Facebook's open API) to create applications usable on the site itself (Goble, 2012). In addition, Facebook developed the "Like" button that allowed for Internet cross-platform promotion. Very quickly the "Like" button became a ubiquitous feature across the World Wide Web. Similarly Twitter (the microblogging site), which launched in 2006, allowed users to "follow" other users, and allowed for cross-platform connectivity. Both Facebook and Twitter allow for instantaneous communication to large numbers of friends or followers without losing the intimate feel of direct person-to-person communication. This is one of the reasons they have become the two dominate social media sites worldwide.

The third most utilized social media site utilizes a different concept of social connectivity. YouTube, debuting in 2005, was a significant development for the spread of social media as individuals were able to experiment with creating user-generated content and sharing it with anyone who wanted to watch (Hendricks, 2013). Culturally, YouTube began the shift away from a mass media-controlled communication environment to a user-controlled communication environment. On YouTube, users can have channels and post comments on other videos, but the primary purpose is to share videos rather than to create a network of like-minded individuals. However, by linking YouTube videos with Facebook pages or Twitter feeds, the videos can provide compelling support for an individual or group's point of view, or the delivery of information. As will be discussed in a later chapter, YouTube videos were an essential component for helping to frame the events that occurred during the Arab Spring revolutions. Such cross-posting thus furthers the reach and/or impact of a message (Hendricks, 2013).

By the end of 2006, Google (which started in 1998 as a search engine) had indexed more than 25 billion web pages and more than a billion images, and saw more than 400 million queries a day (The brief history of social media, 2013). With the release of the Apple iPhone in 2007, the social media landscape would change from being locked into a person's desktop or laptop computer to being accessible anywhere at any time. In addition, smartphones and tablets (the iPad was first sold in 2010) further the evolution of the use of social media to the point where average citizens could be become journalists (Twitter broke the story of the 2009 plane crash in the Hudson River), U.S. presidential candidates could generate funds and visibility (Barak Obama's campaign in 2008), movies could be funded by fans (Veronica Mars movie raised its capital through Kickstarter), or political revolutionaries could mobilize similar to overthrow governments (the Arab Spring in 2010).

Social Media Use

Social media have become a dominate force in the lives of millions of people worldwide. It is often the first thing people check when they wake up in the morning and the last thing they look at before they go to bed. And social media is not just limited to teenagers and young adults. While it is not the purpose of this introduction to explore all of the use aspects of social media (that will come in later chapters of this book), it is important to have an overall sense of who is using social media, what sites are being used the most, and how much time is being spent with social media.

If there is any doubt about the rise of mobile communication technology, the prevalence of social media, or the dominance of social media over traditional media, just download Gary Hayes' Social Media Counts app. Compiling data from more than a dozen sources, which is then estimated into a linear form, this app tracks information such as how many mobile phones have shipped worldwide, how much money is made from mobile music and videos, how many comments have been made on Facebook, or how many tweets have been sent over the last year, month, day, or seconds. It is an almost addictive running count of our social and technological lives. The following year-to-date figures were taken from the Social Media Counts app on July 5th, 2013:

- 269,002,833,920 comments made on Facebook
- 7,320,644.096 apps installed on Facebook
- $626,128,512 earned in ad revenue on Facebook
- 366,002,176,000 pieces of content shared on Facebook
- 18,973,592 hours of video uploaded to YouTube
- 732,005,859,328 videos watched on YouTube
- 32,939,735,040 tweets sent on Twitter
- 144,395,354,112 minutes of Skype calls
- $5,514,990,592 spent on virtual goods globally
- 732,005,859, 328 searches made on Google
- 121,524,195,426,304 emails sent globally
- 790,566,272 images uploaded to Flickr
- 1,242,784,896 new mobile phones shipped
- 132,816,704 new users of mobile social networks
- 8,184,038,400 logged onto the web using mobile
- $341,942,248,608 global TV revenue
- 1,404,066,816 single music track downloads
- 12,339,344,384 people tuning into a U.S. radio station

It is clear from the above statistics that there is significant time and money being spent with social media, but which sites are the dominant social media sites and how are they being used? By June 2013, Facebook and YouTube both had more than one billion users worldwide, while Twitter had more than 500 million (The brief history of social media, 2013). A compilation of user statistics by Statistic Brain in 2012 found that of all social media users, 56% maintained at least one social media profile and 54% said they had a Facebook profile ("Social networking statistics," 2012). This makes Facebook the dominant social media site regardless of the age of the user (Webster, 2012). Of individuals 18-24, 98% reported being users of social media, and they further indicated that they log onto Facebook more than ten times per day ("Social networking statistics," 2012). In the United States, the average user of Facebook checks in five times a day (Webster, 2012). And social media users are not single taskers when it comes to media use. More than 62% of people in a 2012 study conducted by Ericsson reported using social media while they watch television. That is an 18% increase over the previous year's study. However, they are not using social media to talk about what they are watching: only 25% of respondents talk about the show they are watching while on social media (Bergman, 2012).

These numbers are staggering on their own, but take on further significance when the amount of time devoted to each of these activities is tracked. Every month, the 11% of the world population that uses Facebook spends 700 billion minutes on the site. This amounts to an average of 15 hours and 33 minutes spent on Facebook per user per month. For YouTube, the monthly time spent viewing totaled 2.9 billion hours ("Social networking statistics," 2012). Since the average user of social networking sites frequents more than one, these statistics do not show the true time spent using picture. The average American, aged 18-64, spends 3.2 hours per day on social media sites. Women are heavier users than men, with women spending 3.6 hours per day compared to men, who spend 2.6 hours. The most staggering statistic, however, is that one in five social media users aged 18-34 say that they spend six hours or more per day on social media (Social networking eats up 3+ hours per day for the average American user, 2013).

But who are these people spending so much of their time online and why? Overall, women are heavier users of social media than men, not an uncommon statistic for use of traditional media as well (Lunden, 2012), but the use is a bit more pronounced with social media. A 2012 study conducted by Arbitron and Edison found that in the United States, female users of social media skewed slightly higher than the general population (54% to 51%) (Webster, 2012). The study also found that while over half of social media users are in the 12-34 age bracket, more than 15% of users are older than 55. Social media may have reached somewhat of a saturation point with younger age groups as the most significant growth in social media uses from 2011 to 2012 occurred in the ages of 45 or older, with a 10% increase (Webster, 2012).

Additional studies have offered greater detail in terms of time spent online based on age and geographic location. Across all age groups worldwide, the majority of users spend 0-3 hours per day online. However, individuals age 31 or older are more likely than younger age groups to spend five hours or more online each day (Vannozzi and Bridgestock, 2013). In terms of geographic influence, Latin American and African citizens spend more than five hours per day online, while Europe and Asia report three hours or less. The countries showing the highest hours spent per day online are Indonesia and Saudi Arabia (both with 5.1), while France and Japan had the lowest levels (2.3 hours). Saudi Arabia and Mexico had the highest percentage of their populations on social media at 91%. In the United States the percentage is 75% ("Social networking eats up to 3+ hours per day for the average American user," 2013).

In terms of education, social media users mirror that of the general population, which indicates that social media access is not limited in terms of age or education. Individuals with low education levels, as well as individuals with low household income, do spend more time online than their counterparts with higher education and income. The differences are not dramatic, with low income and education users only spending a half-hour more per day ("Social networking eats up to 3+ hours per day for the average American user," 2013). However, certain social media do skew to certain audiences. Not surprisingly, more than 70% of LinkedIn users have at least a four-year degree, while on Facebook that number drops to 41% (Webster, 2012). LinkedIn tends to have more users who are older than 31 than younger age groups, while YouTube and Pinterest skew to the youngest audiences (Vannozzi and Bridgestock, 2013). Business owners and executives spend significantly more time online, up to 50%, than non-business owners ("Social networking eats up to 3+ hours per day for the average American user," 2013). On Twitter, 40% of monthly users identify themselves as belonging to the Democratic Party, which is 10% more than in the general population (Webster, 2012). This could help explain why social media was such an important factor for Barack Obama in both of his presidential election bids.

When people think of social media users, they may have the perception that everyone on social media sites is actively posting their thoughts and videos, but this is not the case. One-third of all social media users are silent, i.e., they do not post status updates. However, a different third of social media users update their status/profile at least once every day (Baer, 2012). But some social media sites have even less active users than others. For example, overall Twitter's registered users are some of the least active. More than half of all Twitter users report that they only read tweets by others and do not send any tweets of their own (Baer, 2012).

While being a registered user of a social media site does not mean that a person is an active participant on the site, being active does indicate that a person is more likely to own a smartphone than the general population and that the person is more likely to stay in touch when he or she is not face-to-face by texting rather than talking on the phone. Social media users are also more likely to watch television on the computer or smart device than the general population. Social media use influences more than technology purchases and use, however. More than one-third of social media users responded that they actively follow some brand through social media, often due to coupons or discounts, while 47% indicate that Facebook influences their purchasing decisions (Webster, 2012).

As can be seen from the previous discussion, people are clearly using social media in large numbers, and social media demonstrates an influence over those users in certain areas. But why do billions of people worldwide spend so much time on social media? Regardless of age, ethnicity, or socio-economic status, the most common reason given for joining a social media site is for the individual to "keep up to date." This is followed closely by wanting to make or keep connections with other people and finding interesting content. Younger users also express a desire to use social media so they can have a place to express their opinions and be heard (Vannozzi and Bridgestock, 2013).

Book Overview

Clearly, in just a few short years, social media has changed the socio-cultural landscape. But the reach is beyond just interpersonal connections, and now encompasses advertising, politics, economics, education, etc. It is these aspects of social media on which this book will focus. The book is divided into three sections to help guide the reader through the key aspects of social media pedagogy and practice.

Section I explores the pedagogy associated with teaching or using social media in an academic setting. In chapter one, Tia C. M. Tyree explores how educators can effectively incorporate social media into the classroom. She examines best practices for use, as well as tips for seamless integration. Jennifer Cox, in chapter two, expands on the topics raised in chapter one, but looks specifically at social media sites and app sharing in the classroom. She discusses the pros and cons of using social media sites such as Facebook and Twitter. Chapter three studies an aspect of social media that has not been covered yet in the book. Ingrid Sturgis and Todd Shurn explore how game design can be used to teach computation literacy at the collegiate level. In chapter four, Kehbuma Langmia and Stella-Monica Mpande begin a discussion regarding critical pedagogy and social media. In other words, how can instructors respond to the unique challenges and opportunities faced by the presence of social media in the classroom? Can instructors use social media to improve critical thinking and cognitive ability rather than deriding it as a drain on a student's attention? Chapters five and six, turn the attention away from classroom use of social media to social media as a research tool. William Hart and Erica Taylor provide an overview in chapter five of the ways in which scholars can use social media as a platform for conducting research. Jamie Cohen and Paul Mihailidis, in chapter six, look more specifically at best practices for conducting research using social media, with a specific focus on Storify.

Section II is dedicated to practical issues surrounding social media in the United States. Jayne Cubbage begins this section with an in-depth look at how African Americans are using social media for social and political activism. In chapter eight, Yanick Rice Lamb and Kendra Desrosiers study the digital content of seven leading women's magazines, McCall's, Ladies Home Journal, Good Housekeeping, Redbook, Better Homes and Gardens, Woman's Day, and Family Circle, and how they have reacted to the change in user dynamics due to social media. Jamila Cupid and S. Lenise Wallace, in chapter nine, discuss how college students can brand themselves using social media when they are looking for employment. They explore both the pros and the cons of a student's social media presence in terms of its potential impact on a prospective employer. Chapter ten raises crucial questions regarding the intersection of social media practice and the law. Angela Minor provides compelling arguments for why it is vital for anyone using social media to understand the legal issues relating to social media, especially privacy.

The final section of the book addresses international social media practices. Chapter eleven, by Adam Klein, explores how social media created a platform for participatory media in the events of the Arab Spring. Klein shows how young adults especially utilized social media to organize the protests and share information with each other and the world. Nikesia Gordon, in chapter twelve, focuses on social media and participatory development. Gordon questions the dominant development paradigm and shows how social media can allow for greater individual participation through a case study analysis of two public social media pages maintained by the United Nations Development Program. The final chapter in the book, by Kehbuma Langmia, explores the role that social media played in the 2013 presidential election in Kenya. Utilizing textual analysis, Langmia explores the questions of how Kenyan citizens utilize verbal and nonverbal elements within YouTube postings during the election, and how Kenyan citizens utilize the "texts/comments and likes" features on their YouTube postings during this time.

It is apparent from this overview that social media is being explored and utilized in a remarkable number of ways by very diverse groups of individuals. There is no one use for social media, and its true influence may yet be seen, but globally it is a platform for discussion and individual idea sharing. While there are limits on the conversations, most notably government restrictions or censorship of the Internet or specific social media sites, the ways in which social media are being used is truly revolutionary. What can be accomplished through and with social media has brought to fruition, in a way perhaps more significant than could have been fathomed, what *The Electrical Review* predicted in 1889, "Possibly the time will come when so far as seeing objects are concerned, one can make a tour of Europe without going out of his own house" (Marvin, 1988, p. 200).

References

Banks, M. (December 18, 2008). Prodigy: The pre-Internet online service that didn't live up to its name. *TechRepublic.* Retrieved from

http://www.techrepublic.com/blog/classic-tech/prodigy-the-pre-Internet-online-service-that-didnt-live-up-to-its-name/214

Bell, L. (January 11, 2013). Outdated Android devices are exposing 400 million users to security threats. *The Inquirer.* Retrieved from http://www.theinquirer.net/inquirer/feature/2235734/outdated-android-are-exposing-400-million-users-to-security-threats

Bergman, C. (August 31, 2012). 62 percent of TV viewers use social media while watching. *Lost Remote.* Retrieved from http://lostremote.com/social-media-use-in-front-of-tv-jumps-18-percent_b33562

Bolton, J.D., and Grusin, R. (2000). *Remediation: Understanding New Media.* Boston, MA: The M.I.T Press.

Boyd, D.M. and Ellison, N.B. (2007). Social network sites: Definition, history scholarship. *Journal of Computer-Mediated Communication*, 13(1), article 11. Retrieved from http://jcmc.indiana.edu/vol13/issue1/boyd.ellison.html

The brief history of social media. (n.d.) Retrieved from http://www.uncp.edu/home/acurtis/NewMedia/SocialMedia/SocialMediaHistory.html

Brown, R. (June 15, 2013). World's last telegram to be sent next month. *USA Today.com.* Retrieved from http://www.usatoday.com/story/news/world 2013/06/15/last-telegram/2426373

Goble, G. (September 6, 2012). The history of social networking. *Digital Trends.*
Retrieved from www.digitaltrends.com/features/the-history-of-social-networking/

Hayes, G. (2013). *Social Media Counts* (1.1) [Mobile application software]. Retrieved from http://itunes.apple.com

Hendricks, D. (May 8, 2013). Complete history of social media: Then and now. *Small Business Trends.* Retrieved from http://smallbiztrends.com/2013/05/the-complete-history-of-social-media-infographic.html

Lunden, I. (October 5, 2012). Nielsen: Women watch more TV than men, but connected games consoles are changing that. *TechCrunch.* Retrieved www.techcrunch.com/2012/10/05/nielsen-gaming-tv-console/

Marvin, C. (1988). *When Old Technologies Were New: Thinking About Electric Communication in the Late Nineteenth Century.* USA: Oxford University Press.

Miot, S. (August 27, 2012). Smartphone adoption rate fastest in tech history. PCMag.com. Retrieved from www.pcmag.com/article2/0, 2817,2408960,00.asp

Social media. (n.d.). Retrieved from www.merriam-webster.com/dictionary/social% 20media

Social networking eats up 3+ hours per day for the average American user. (January 9, 2013). Retrieved from http://www.marketingcharts.com/wp/ Interactive/social-networking-eats-up-3-hours-per-day-for-the-average-American-user-26049

Social networking statistics. (November 12, 2012). *Statistic Brain.com.* Retrieved from www.statisticbrain.com/social-networking-statistics/

Vannozzi, M. and Bridgestock, L. (2013). Students' online usage global market trends report. *QS Top Universities.com.* Retrieved from

http://www.topuniversities.com/publications/students-online-usage-global-trends-report-2013

Webster, T. (June 2012). The social habit: 2012. *Arbitron and Edison Research.* Retrieved from http://socialhabit.com/secure/wp-content/uploads/2012/07/The-Social-Habit-2012-by-Edison-Research

Whitney, L. (June 10, 2013). Apple by the numbers, from WWDC 2013. *c/net*.com. Retrieved from http://news.cnet.com/8301-13579_3-57588547-37/apple-by-the-numbers-from-wwdc-2013/

Section I: Pedagogy
Chapter 1
Using Social Media and Creating Social Media Courses
Tia C. M. Tyree

In June 2010, I attended the New Media Academic Summit in New York, New York. It was hosted by Edelman, the largest public relations firm with a global reach and commitment to fostering the ethical, mutually beneficial, and quality practice of public relations. In 2007, it brought marketers, journalists, and educators together for the first time to discuss the "tectonic shift the Internet is causing in business communications." Three years later, I came with the sole purpose of harnessing the intellectual power and curiosity at the summit to develop Howard University School of Communications' first social media course set for fall 2010. Sessions were anchored around the premise that information could immediately be incorporated into curricula to identify and build skills needed for students to enter the communications and integrated marketing fields.

What was sure to be the highlight was the syllabus exchange. It was an opportunity for professors using social media in the classroom or teaching social media courses to share information, swap syllabi, and share their successes and challenges in the classroom. I was excited to have the ability to review the syllabi of others who used and taught social media. However, when it was time to begin my course preparation ritual, I soon realized the task would be more difficult than usual. As I began to sift through the pages, I quickly realized the approaches, content, assignments, required textbooks, readings, and objectives were so varied that it became more confusing than helpful. I decided to complete an informal content analysis to really obtain what could be the "best practices" and "common texts" within the syllabi. I even decided to search the Internet for additional ones. In total, I had 50 syllabi, but the issue remained the same.

I later developed my course by utilizing what I learned through my informal research. At the time, I saw it as a cutting edge menagerie of social media promise. The students, graduate and undergraduate, excelled in the course, appreciated the approach and content, and enjoyed the challenge of learning about social media in a structured manner. After consultations with my other sequence faculty, efforts were made to teach the history, development, and utilization of social media throughout all of our skills courses. Yet, the experience and challenge of bringing in the proper content was one that carried forward in all of my classes, and I believe is worth sharing with academic colleagues.

Ultimately, it is critical to find the proper balance of technology, pedagogy, and content for courses. Therefore, I am offering tips to create social media courses and to use social media in courses. While it is difficult to offer a complete guide, I do offer several key ideas to consider, including setting a historical foundation; understanding students and their connections to technology; knowing and respecting the learning environment; learning how to select the appropriate social media sites for assignments, making content relevant to students; and knowing the importance of bringing in experts to enhance the teaching of course content as well being an "expert" of the social media used in the course. These are not expected to be all-inclusive topics, but if taken into consideration, these ideas may help create the necessary foundation to assist instructors in incorporating social media or teaching social media courses.

Set a Historical Foundation

With social media revolutionizing the manner in which humans communicate, interact, and conduct business, it is necessary for instructors to place social media in the proper perspective. Whether starting from the development of the Internet or simply explaining why subscribing to a specific blog is essential to course content, instructors should work to help students understand the importance of social media. Students may come to the course using social media, but be ignorant of how they developed, the types and purposes of each as well as ways to use them outside of recreational purposes. Instructors should provide students a chance to see social media through different lenses, starting with a historical one. The biggest foundational building blocks students need to grasp are defining social media, understanding how they became the communication forces they are in the 21st century, and the necessary and proper uses of them for personal and professional purposes. What follows are some key historical ideas and information to teach students and understand as instructors.

The Internet is an undeniably powerful force with the ability to connect, influence, and mobilize people (Cabral, 2011). In formal and informal settings, web-based environments are a natural part of everyday life and used to distribute information (Salavuo, 2008). The "renaissance stimulated by the World Wide Web" worked to incubate numerous formats and channels of communication and creativity (Bull, Thompson, Searson, Garofalo, Park, Young and Lee, 2008, p. 100). With advances in technology, Internet users changed the manner in which it was initially used. The World Wide Web changed from a "read only" media into a "read/write" media (Salavuo, 2008), which was a critical pivot. This change helped create a sense of ownership and connectedness with the users of Internet and the content on it.

The term "Web 2.0" was developed in 2004 to describe the move from read-only Web 1.0 to "read and write Web 2.0" (McManus, 2005, ¶1). Web 2.0 supported "participatory," "collaborative," and "distributed" practices within informal and formal areas in everyday activities (Lankshear and Knobel, 2006, p. 38). Web 2.0 should be understood as a platform where innovative technologies are created as well as a space users can upload and share content (Cormode and Krishnamurthy, 2008). Bull et. al. (2008) note the presence of "dynamic media," which, from a technical sense, is interactive and multilayered and mobile, and, from a cultural sense, is remixable, sharable, and a catalyst for social interactions (p. 103). The coupling of users taking a more active role in Internet content creation, as well as the advances in software and technological devices, created the perfect stage for the explosion of what is now the social media takeover of everyday communication.

Many define social media in different ways, and Kaplan and Haenlin argue there is no systematic way to categorize social media applications (2010). Kaplan et. al. (2010, p. 61-62) define social media as "a group of Internet-based applications that build on the ideological and technological foundations of Web 2.0, which allows the creation and exchange of user-generated content," and they further classify them as virtual social worlds, virtual games, social networking sites, collaborative projects, content communities, and blogs. Greenhow (2009) provides several categories for Web 2.0, including creative works; collaborative knowledge development through wikis; social networks; social bookmarking; content aggregation and organization; media sharing; and remixes or mash-up content. However, social media usually utilize tools often seen as second generation or Web 2.0 software or website functionalities, and most importantly, individuals use them to share opinions, insights, experiences, content, perspectives, and other types of media (Wilcox and Cameron, 2009).

Instructors who wish to help students understand and study the types of social media should require the reading of *The Social Media Bible* written by Lob Safko. It offers one of the simplest definitions of social media. Safko defines social media as "the media we use to be social" (2012, p. 3). Expanding on the definition, social is described as the instinctual human need to connect with others, and the term media is defined as what humans use to make those connections. Safko "attempts" to categorize social media into the following categories: virtual worlds, gaming, audio, video, social networking, photo sharing, microblogging, livecasting, RSS and aggregators, search, mobile, and interpersonal (2012, pp. 9-10).

Setting the proper historical background is essential to help students understand why social media are so pervasive in everyday communication as well as why it is central to the course or assignment. This is the time for instructors to define terms, such as Web 2.0 and social media, that students often hear, but do not know the proper definitions. Ultimately, with myriad definitions and possible uses, social media are omnipresent in our lives, but the challenge is to determine how best to teach them or utilize them as teaching tools.

Understanding Students and Their Connections to Technology

Students currently in college and high school are known as Generation Y and were born between the mid-1970s and the early 2000s. While past differences in generations were "incrementally" marked by changes in such things as slang, clothes, body adornments, and styles, Generation Y may have a singular "discontinuity" of fundamental proportions that differentiates it from past generations (Prensky, 2001, p. 1). The "singularity" was the development and speedy dissemination of digital technology in the later part of the 20th century (Ibid). Generation Y is the first generation entirely immersed in digital technologies (Bull et. al., 2008). This generation goes by several other names, including "digital natives" (Prenksy, 2001) and "net generation" (Cabral, 2011). They are "'native speakers' of the digital language of computers, video games, and the Internet" (Prensky, 2001, p. 1). Other key digital influences include digital music players, video cameras, cell phones, computer games, email, instant messaging, texting, blogs, and social media (Bull et. al., 2008; Prensky, 2001).

Generation Y constitutes the highest number of social media users, and they are said to be "unconsciously addicted" to them (Cabral, 2011, p. 5). They constantly feel pressured to connect with peers by maintaining an attachment with technology, and this "connectedness is creating new kinds of peer-to-peer relationships that are considerably different from previous generations" (Cabral, 2011, p. 6). A survey of more than 1,000 American college students found:

> 64 percent of students use social media to 'connect with classmates' to study or work on class assignments at least several times per month. Forty-one percent use social media to 'study or work on class assignments' at least several times per month. Twenty-seven percent use social media to 'connect with faculty to study or work' on class assignments, at least several times per month (Caraher & Braselman, 2010, p. 13).

It is important to understand students' attitudes toward their academic and social lives in order to engage them effectively (McCarthy, 2010). Through a survey of the technology usages of 11–16 years, researchers coined the term "digital dissonance," which labels the existing tension between learners' in- and out-of-school use of social media and related technologies (Clark, Logan, Luckin, Mee and Oliver, 2009). Jones and Czerniewicz (2010) argue students identify a clear separation between their learning and personal spaces, and instructors must identify student's preferences to understand how spaces should be merged or separated. In 2009, Greenhow examined how learning and teaching are influenced by the unique capabilities of Web 2.0 and youth proclivities. Two themes emerged from the analysis, which were learner participation and creativity as well as online identity formation (Greenhow, 2009). Others argue students come to campuses and classrooms with the intention of using their online identities as well as capitalizing on their social network connections in the learning process. They view the Internet as a space where they add to and tap into knowledge, which contradicts traditional pedagogical models that position the instructor as the sole authoritative source for submission and feedback as well as students' tendencies to expect peer evaluation and feedback (Baird and Fisher, 2005; Barnes, Marateo, and Ferris 2007). Further, these students prefer to receive information swiftly and can then quickly process it; they prefer multitasking and nonlinear access to information; they prefer active learning rather than passive learning and lectures; and they deeply depend on social media for information retrieval as well as social and professional interactions (McCarthy, 2010).

It is critical for instructors of any course to know their students. If instructors are aware of who is sitting in their courses – literally and figuratively – then they can adjust teaching styles and content to suit their students' needs. (See also Jennifer Cox's views in Chapter 2.) In addition, how they experience social media is important, as attitudes, skills, and personal experiences vary between students and can impact instruction.

Respect and Teach in the Proper Learning Environment

How we explain our existence in the teaching realm has changed. Years ago, it was understood that teaching meant standing in front of students in a classroom. Web 2.0 changed teaching forever. With the advent of online classes, the teaching environment changed, as some students never come to campuses to earn degrees. Still there are other gray areas or what is now termed "hybrid" courses, in which teachers use a combination of both online and offline interactions to meet course objectives. Ultimately, while much can be said regarding the way teachers should interact with students "in person," there is also much to be learned and adhered to in e-learning situations. By understanding the learning environment, instructors can better structure courses and work to utilize the best technologies that enhance student comprehension and their ability to acquire new skills.

In the new millennium, students have increased opportunities to determine the time and manner in which learning occurs. Students can be engaged in formal and informal learning in a cross section of contexts, and they can exercise substantial influence over when, how, and with whom they learn (Greenhow et. al., 2009). Barron works to place learning in context by defining a learning ecology as a set of contexts, in virtual or physical spaces, that offers learning opportunities, and each context encompasses a distinctive configuration of relationships, activities, interactions, and material resources. (Barron, 2004;

Barron, 2006). Greenhow et. al. (2009) summarized Barron's (2006, pp. 199-201) concept of a learning ecology as follows:

> (a) individuals are simultaneously involved in many settings, (b) individuals create learning contexts for themselves within and across settings, (c) the boundaries among settings can be permeable, and (d) interest-driven activities can span contextual boundaries and be self-sustaining given adequate time, freedom, and resources.

The Internet has transformed how learning occurs, and the collaborative and social nature of Web 2.0 technologies, such as social media, can be in opposition to traditional educational pedagogy. When learning happens in a traditional educational setting, these traditional practices emphasize acquiring information, which is obtained through factual knowledge and not new knowledge built in the community (Bereiter, 2002). Traditional learning practices have a strong legacy and are proven to be effective in many ways. Saluvoa (2008) asserts the collaborative processing of knowledge, coupled with an environment supported by the contributions of a person's creative ideas and works, run contrary to traditional educational practices and are often foreign to the existing learning culture. Ultimately, Web 2.0 technologies created a rift in how knowledge is created, and it is relayed from instructors to students.

Perhaps one of the most intriguing connections between Web 2.0 and hybrid learning was Chao, Parker, and Fontana's development of an interactive social media-based learning environment. The "web-based tool embraces social media and other Web 2.0 technologies to provide a new experience for interactive learning, and is designed to encourage student interaction, engagement, and participation in a dynamic lecture classroom" (Chao et. al., 2001, p. 323). It was also described as a software system that offers a "social media classroom experience for interactive learning" (Chao et.al., 2001, p. 323). In an effort to circumvent complications of commercial learning tools, the system was built using open source technologies and utilized Application Programming Interface to synch platforms, such as Google Docs, Twitter, and Facebook. Students in a classroom setting accessed the system, and they logged in using various mobile devices, iPads, laptops, tablets, or smartphones. They had the ability to view lecture slides, chat online with other students, send tweets to their Twitter followers, post items to their Facebook pages, and collaborate. Students could also answer, ask, and rate questions online; instructors could also administer quizzes and display visual results.

While Chao et. al.'s (2001) tool was a useful blend of the use of social media in the classroom, what happens when students must interact completely using computer mediated communications? Understanding the e-learning environment and how certain learning interactions change with the various technologies is worthy of discussion. Hrastinski (2008) acknowledged the debate over the practicality of asynchronous versus synchronous e-learning. The concept of cognitive participation noted by increased reflection and the ability to process information is associated with asynchronous e-learning; the concept of personal participation marked by motivation, increased arousal, and convergence of meanings is connected to synchronous e-learning. With its flexibility, asynchronous e-learning supports work relationships among learners and teachers and is assisted by media, such as email and discussion boards. Asynchronous e-learning often affords students the opportunity to more easily combine education, family, work, and other commitments; provides open access to the e-learning environment to download documents or communicate; and allows more thoughtful contributions. Marked by its social aspects, synchronous e-learning is most often sustained by media, such as chatting and videoconferencing (Hrastinski, 2008). Synchronous e-learning eases frustration as students can ask and instructors can answer questions in real time (Hrastinski, 2008). Synchronous learners feel less isolated and more like a member of a community (Haythronthwaite and Kazmer, 2002). To refine the issues, Hrastinski (2008) argues there should not be a question of which is better, but rather the questions of when, how, and why each should be used.

Knowledge-building environments are often referred to as computer-supported collaborative learning, but they are different as they focus more on the processes of idea improvement and knowledge creation. Several familiar tools are tied to them, including email, chat technologies, and electronic bulletin boards. Scardamalia and Bereiter (2003) addressed the issue of a "knowledge-building environment," and they rightfully asked whether it is a learning environment or a tool. At the core of the issue is the often-overlooked need to define what is knowledge building. Within an educational setting, it was originally referred to as the development and improvement of ideas within the world that are up for social processing of evaluation, revision, and application. It is best defined as: "any environment (virtual or otherwise) that enhances collaborative efforts to create and continually improve ideas" (Scardamalia et. al., 2003, p. 2). Regardless of the use of old or new technologies, knowledge-building opportunities are most effective when they are flexible and supportive of knowledge creation and not overly rigid (Scardamalia et. al., 2003).

Many educational institutions utilize Learning Management Systems (LMS), Virtual Learning Environments and Course Management Systems to support face-to-face or "in-person" instruction. The connection is often referred to as hybrid or blended learning. Vaughan (2008) defines blended learning as "the thoughtful fusion of face-to-face and online learning experiences" (p. 5). These systems are designed to enable, manage, and offer platforms and content relevant to a course, and they include popular tools, such as content discussion forums and production tools. These systems are social constructivist in nature and designed to engage students in collaborative knowledge-building activities, with several main goals to expand the possibilities of collaboration outside of the classrooms meetings, eliminate email, track student progress, and provide an easier way to share lecture notes (Salavuo, 2008). Blended courses provide more opportunities for student-teacher interactions, increased student engagement, better flexibility in the teaching and learning environment, and more opportunities for improvement (Vaughn, 2007).

There are some cautions regarding the degrees to which a successful blend between traditional and online learning is achieved. While blended courses offer more participant engagement and sense of community, a strong blend between the two environments is important (Garrison and Kanuka (2004). Institutionally, there must be the proper infrastructure to ensure sufficient technical resources, proper student feedback channels, organizational readiness, and motivated faculty (Tabor, 2007). Ultimately, institutions can initiate blended learning as a transformative process designed to restructure a course, instead of merely inserting technology (Sharpe, Benfield, Robert and Francis, 2006: Littlejohn and Pegler, 2007; Garrison and Vaughan, 2008).

When developing social media courses, it is important to first ask what type of learning environment will be used. Traditional learning environments, online courses, and blended courses all have specific benefits and challenges, and it is necessary for instructors to take those into consideration before developing their syllabi. Further, students in online learning environments come with diverse backgrounds, skills, learning styles, and critical thinking abilities (Gan and Zhu, 2007). Therefore, a one-size-fits-all approach to teaching students may not work well. Understanding what technological equipment students have to bring to the classroom or complete course assignments as well as their overall social media behaviors, including frequented platforms, skills, and comfort levels, is important. From an institutional standpoint, instructors must ensure there is a supportive e-learning culture and the proper infrastructures exist that allow the technologies utilized in the course to enhance, not hinder, learning.

Selecting the Appropriate Social Media Sites for Assignments

When it comes to social media in the classroom, important questions to ask are what works best and what is most used in the teaching environment? There are entire books dedicated to selecting the perfect social media sites for courses, and this chapter cannot comprehensively outline all sites and all uses for them in the classroom. Instead, a few of the more popular sites and uses are highlighted in this chapter. (See also Chapter 2 for additional ideas.)

First, there are several issues to take into consideration when bringing social media into the classroom. In the past, developing interactive and rich learning activities were difficult for instructors using online and blended courses, because traditional online learning activities were asynchronous. However, with more instructors using social media and scholars investigating social media uses in the classroom, much is being learned and shared in academic and scholarly settings (Stoerger and Joosten, 2012). Perhaps, the biggest caution for connecting social media to the classroom is relatively simple: unless a user knows why a technology is being used, implementation is never effective (Joosten, 2012). Therefore, when developing course learning activities, instructors can take the following into consideration: 1) identify the proper uses of selected social media, 2) justify the use based on pedagogical needs, 3) explore the characteristics of social media based on specific course need, and 4) readily highlight the considerations and benefits of the selected method (Joosten, 2012).

Despite being labeled as digital immigrants, faculty are "big users" and believers in social media, both personally and professionally, and according to a study by Moran, Seaman, and Tinti-Kane (2011), nearly all higher education teaching faculty know the major social media sites (p. 3). Faculty also believe in the value social media sites have for teaching and collaborative learning, and a large majority reported wikis, video, and podcasts were valuable tools for teaching. Almost two-thirds surveyed used social media in a class session, 30% posted content for students to view or read outside class, more than 40% required students to read or view social media as part of a course assignment, and 20% gave students an assignment to comment or post to social media sites. Overall, 80% of faculty reported using some type of social media as a part of teaching, with those purely teaching online courses more likely to assign students to read, view, or comment on social media sites (Moran et. al., 2011). Therefore, the idea that faculty are "digital immigrants" seems to be less accurate as time passes (Prensky, 2001, p.1).

An investigation into the uses of Web 2.0 and virtual world technologies in information systems classes offers several practices and ideas that can translate into other educational settings. Wikis, a collection of online pages designed to enable anyone to contribute or modify content, and blogs or weblogs, maintained by an individual or entity with entries, event descriptions, or other materials, are often used in educational settings (Harris and Rea, 2009). Harris et. al. note wikis can be used as a group authoring tool, a method to track a group project as well as to collect data. Further, they note wikis can be used for "knowledge building over the course of a term through the use of versions and groups critically reading and responding in a constructive and public way to others' work, progressive problem-solving (especially valuable for open-ended problems), and problem redefinition" (p. 139). Watson, Boudreau, York, Greiner and Wynn (2008) support the use of these tools and assert an "open classroom" model using wikis, blogs, and other "open" technologies to create ". . . enduring 'knowledge products' that more completely engage the students and provide value to society" (p. 75).

Blogs can benefit students either by writing them or reading them. Blogs can be used to facilitate knowledge and experience sharing, act as a group coordination, offer annotated links to readings and references, create content-related to professional practices, read discipline specific content, and provide instructional tips for students and course announcements (Baker, 2003; Scott, 2003; Bloulos, 2006).

Kietzmann, Hermkens, McCarthy, and Silvestre rightfully acknowledge the diverse choices and varied scopes and functionalities of social media sites as well as how cumbersome it is to stay abreast of the number of social media platforms available (2011). They offer a very useful "honeycomb" to assist with understanding the various levels of social media functionality, and how it might be used as a tool to evaluate the ever-changing social media ecology. It also works to help analyze specific aspects of the social media user's experience and those impacts on a firm. The seven functional building blocks are identity, conversations, sharing, presence, relationships, reputation, and groups. The building blocks are not mutually exclusive or designed to represent all social media activities (Kietzman et. al., 2011).

When bringing in social media, instructors must know whether to alter the approach of teaching, writing, or developing an assignment. Students should not simply be instructed to duplicate the same projects done in a traditional brick and mortar classroom on the Internet. For example, it is not beneficial to have a student develop a ten-page research paper and upload it on a wiki for other students to read, edit, and discuss. It is not functional. Bull et. al.. (2008) note content presented on the web changed the way people read, think, and process information. While print technology supports "forms of concentrated and sustained attention and thought," Internet technology is a "more distributed and plastic form of thinking," which shifts how people read (Bull et. al., 2008, p. 101). Instructors must be forwarded thinking and understand the purpose of the assignment, feasibility of the use of social media and adjust or abandon the use of social media for a particular assignment.

Prensky (2007) argues many students prefer familiar technologies be used as a part of their instruction, because they have mastered these tools, use them on a daily basis, and recognize their usefulness. Since users can create, exchange, and alter information in different ways instantaneously on Twitter and Facebook, these are great tools for instructors to use for communication with students. For example, an instructor can create a Facebook group, invite students to post information, and chat with them. The benefits of using this technology is that it encourages an open dialogue, works well with students who have a disability, creates less of a time constraint for those with internships or jobs, gives students more time to develop responses, provides a level of comfort for student too shy to speak in front of peers, and offers a nonthreatening environment (Moody, 2010). Other examples can be found in Ferris and Wilder's (2013) book titled *The Plugged-In Professor: Tips and Techniques for Teaching with Social Media*. The book is described as a resource to provide an effective way for academics and practitioners to reach students through social media; provide several teaching strategies that capitalize on the net generation's learning styles and habits; inform students how technologies can assist them in their personal and professional lives; and supports students' growth as 21st century citizens. An assignment example is one by Tyree (2013) designed to teach students how to use Twitter to enhance their understanding and creation of a nutgraph, which is a paragraph that summarizes a news story and highlights its significance. Students have a specific formula to create a nutgraph in 140 characters, and the assignment provides a step-by-step guide for instructors and students to live blog using the formula. See Table 1.1 for top social media to use in the classroom.

10 Popular Social Media Activities for the Classroom
1. Live blog
2. Hashtag chat using Twitter
3. Use Google hangouts
4. Use Second Life as the virtual classroom
5. Create a wiki
6. Watch and discuss YouTube videos
7. Use any one of the many tools on Diigo
8. Use storytelling abilities with Storify
9. Review and discuss what the teacher has on Delicious
10. Be content sharers and creators on Facebook

Table 1.1 – Using social media in the classroom

Rubrics

The syllabus is the obvious document to outline the course objectives and assignments, and it is the appropriate place to identify the social media used in the course and benefits. Yet, rubrics can be distributed or uploaded to provide more specific requirements for assignments. Rubrics are tools used to identify elements of proficiency, and they assist the teacher and student in outlining what is needed to meet a specific performance level (Skillings and Ferrel, 2000). Rubrics support student learning, development of sophisticated thinking skills, and support evaluation and accountability (Andrade, 2000). They, too, assist instructors in not only assessing work quicker and more efficiently, but also justifying student grades (Andrade, 2000). Truly, the rubric is one of the best measures for all parties – students, teachers and parents – to understand what is required of an assignment and to have a blueprint to help guide grading. It is also important to update rubrics after assignments are completed. By reflecting on and correcting what may have caused confusion or been troublesome to students, teachers can better gauge and grade future classroom and homework activities.

For example, Bryer and Chen (2010) interviewed an instructor who had students use LinkedIn for an assignment, which entailed students summarizing and reflecting their assigned LinkedIn activities and posting those reflections on the university's content management systems. With school and Family Education Rights and Privacy Act (FERPA) restrictions, the instructor could not grade the LinkedIn activities directly, but could do so on the content management systems. The rubric criteria allowed the instructor to assess the discussion posts on clarity, comprehension, writing, and original thinking, but none actually directly guided students' LinkedIn activities (Bryer & Chen, 2010).

Other Tips

Finally, what you do not do is as important as what you do. Moody outlined numerous pitfalls to avoid when using social media in traditional courses, which are: 1) Do not sacrifice old tactics for new ones, as traditional content has value. 2) Do not show too many videos. 3) Do not rely too much on a social media textbook, but supplement with course packets. 4) Do not use a top-down approach, but instead, support a friendly, collaborative atmosphere. 5) Do not be afraid to ask students about their social media for course ideas. Other challenges exist, including ensuring content matches learning objectives, time constraints, complexities technology brings to classroom management, access to Internet in schools, limited models of effective integration of media in teaching, and examples of best practices (Bull et. al., 2008).

Make It Relevant

This section intentionally steered cleared of leaning specifically toward a certain topic or field. The idea was to provide a baseline to help bring in social media or teach social media. However, it is essential to be relevant to the field of choice as well as the most relevant social media channels in the course. For the former, instructors should be sure to include online content from trade, business, political, news, and social media entities and influencers. Similarly, depending on the most relevant social media channels, instructors ought to require students to "like," follow, subscribe or read, listen, and see the content of the same types of individuals and companies that support course content.

Be an Expert or Bring in the Experts

Every instructor is not a digital immigrant; some are knowledgeable of cutting-edge social media innovations. Regardless, all should try to be an expert in the social media content covered or utilized in their classrooms. Instructors cannot expect students to master and utilize social media, while they simultaneously sit on the proverbial sidelines cheering them. Greenhow et. al. (2009) posit "new standards emphasize the learner, his or her experiences and choices, and the cognitive, social, and cultural dimensions of how technology is used in various settings" (p. 248). Further, in an effort to oversee and assist students, teachers must "co-learn, model, and facilitate the development of such competencies" (Greenhow et. al., p. 248).

While the article by Greenhow et. al. is a call to education researchers to understand Web 2.0 changes and establish online lives and identities as a part of their professional development, it is worth using one of the article's concepts for instructors engaging in the use of social media in their courses by "modeling, mentoring, and engaging." As a model, instructors should set the example and be the social media gurus or active social media users they expect to teach and create in their courses. It would be wise for instructors to follow the "M.O.B." mentality for social media ethics outlined by Tyree (2011, ¶ 2). The rules provide a structure for those utilizing social media to think in advance of the reactions of their mothers, offspring, and bosses, before posting, uploading, or engaging in certain online activities. By mentoring, the instructor should be a source of information and training, which means they may have to obtain training to be a trainer. While most social media are user-friendly and easy to master, there is a need to understand students may come into the course with varying skill levels. Instructors must lead by example and be able to answer questions and show students what to do, if necessary. Finally, engagement can come in various forms, but instructors should at least have active accounts on the social media platforms used in their courses and interact with students, when appropriate.

Bringing experts into the classroom is very beneficial to students and a longstanding practice. Instructors know the value guest speakers have to reinforce class lessons (Moody, 2010). Therefore, when an instructor does not hold the knowledge base for a specific topic covered in the course, it is wise to seek the assistance of experts who can speak to the content. If instructors want to reinforce course content, experts, too, are beneficial. Instructors can use the guest lecture as a chance to facilitate learning and student engagement in a different way. Credible guests speakers with a specialized area of expertise can better communicate the intricacies of a topic with authority to students, and they can also offer current, real world information and alternative perspectives not present in textbooks (Mullins, 2001). Guest speakers can also put a "face" to a specific abstract idea, act as role models, be catalysts to inspire students, and "demystify" subject matter (Agha-Jaffar, 2000).

Felder and Brent (2003) note learning is enhanced when undergraduate students perceive the significance of course content to their career goals, and their instructors did not take the "trust me" approach to learning. This style contends students might not see the relevance of content at the time, but will do so later (Felder and Brent, 2004, p. 11). This approach is ineffective and connected to poor learning, low motivation, high levels of attrition, and negative attitudes toward subject matter (Tobias, 1990). A bridge – guest speaker – could act as a tangible medium to connect theory and praxis (Agha-Jaffar, 2000).

Conclusion

With respect to the influence of social media in the classroom, resistance is futile. Social media cannot be ignored as passing fads or short-lived communication mediums. With the pervasive and intrusive nature of social media in the everyday lives of humans and businesses, it is clear all must work to function using them. Social media provide opportunities to integrate activities and possibilities to be constructors of knowledge, and they could play an essential role in everyday teaching and learning (Salavuo, 2009). It is necessary to think strategically about the selection of social media and the approach used to teach it. Salavuo (2009) asserts the key to the successful implementation in formal learning settings is to let students self-select their tools or utilize popular and familiar tools. These are important ideas, but the overall assignment and course objectives, learning environment, student population, and course content are equally important. All play a role in how instructors can maximize social media use in the classroom or select the correct approach to teaching social media's origins and social, economic, and cultural impacts.

Admittedly, instructors have problems with the incorporation of social media into courses, including time constraints as well as privacy and integrity issues (Moran, Seaman, and Tinti-Kane, 2011). Instructors must check FERPA, student handbooks and university social media policies to ensure course assignments do not violate rules. While teaching the "what is social media" class and module might not pose a problem, it is critical for instructors to weigh the pros and cons of utilizing social media in courses. Clearly, social media are inescapable in everyday life and in the classroom. Striking the perfect balance between respecting classroom practices and pedagogical needs is what instructors must strive to achieve.

References

Andrade, H. (2000). *Using Rubrics to Promote Thinking and Learning. Educational Leadership*, 57(5),13-18.

Agha-Jaffar, T. (2000). From Theory to Praxis in Women's Studies: Guest Speakers and Service-Learning As Pedagogy. *Feminist Teacher*, 13(1), 1-11.

Bargh, J., McKenna, K., & Fitzsimons, G. (2002). Can you see the real me? Activation and expression of the "true self" on the Internet. *Journal of Social Issues*, 58(1), 33-48.

Baird, D. E., & Fisher, M. (2005). Neomillenial user experience design strategies: Utilizing social networking media to support "always on" learning styles. *Journal of Educational Technology*, 34(1), 5-32.

Baker, J. H. (2003) The Learning Log, *Journal of Information Systems Education*, 14(1), 11-13.

Bloluos, M.N.K., (2006) Retrieved from http://www.biomedcentral.com/content/supplementary/1472-6920-6- 4 1-s2 .pdf

Barnes, K., Marateo, R. C, & Ferris, S. P. (2007, April/May). Teaching and learning with the net generation. *Innovate*, 3(4). Retrieved from http://www.innovateonline.info/index .php?view=article&id=382

Barron, B. (2004). Learning ecologies for technological fluency in a technology-rich community. *Journal of Educational Computing Research*, 31, 1–37.

Barron, B. (2006). Interest and self-sustained learning as catalysts of development: A Learning Ecology Perspective Brigid Barron. *Human Development*, 49, 193–224.

Bereiter, C. (2002). *Education and Mind in the Knowledge Age*. New Jersey: Erlbaum.

Bereiter, C., & Scardamalia, M. (1989). Intentional learning as a goal of instruction. In L. B.Resnick (Ed.), Knowing, Learning, and Instruction: Essays in Honor of Robert Glaser (pp. 361-392). Hillsdale, NJ: Lawrence Erlbaum Associates.

Bull, G., Thompson, A., Searson, M., Garofalo, J., Park, J., Young, C., & Lee, J (2008). Connecting informal and formal learning: Experiences in the age of participatory media. *Contemporary Issues in Technology and Teacher Education*, 8(2), 100-107.

Bryer, T. A., & Chen, B. (2010). Using social networks in teaching public administration. In C. Wankel, (Ed.), *Cutting-edge Social Media Approaches to Business Education: Teaching with LinkedIn, Facebook, Twitter, Second Life, and Blogs* (pp. 241-268). Charlotte, NC: Information Age Publishing.

Cabral, J. (2011). Is Generation Y Addicted to Social Media? *The Elon Journal of Undergraduate Research in Communications*, 2(1), 5-14.

Chao, J., Parker, K. & Fontana, A. (2011). Developing an interactive social media based learning environment. *Issues in Informing Science and Information Technology*, 8, 323-334.

Caraher, K., & Braselman, M. (2010). The 2010 21st-Century Campus Report: Campus 2.0. 2010 CDW Government LLC. Retrieved from http://webobjects.cdw.com/webobjects/media/pdf/newsroom/CDWG-21st-Century-Campus-Report-0710.pdf

Clark, W., Logan, K., Luckin, R., Mee, A., & Oliver, M. (2009). Beyond Web 2.0: mapping the technology landscapes of young learners. *Journal of Computer Assisted Learning*, 25(1), 56–69.

Cormode, G., & Krishnamurthy, B. (2008). Key differences between Web 1.0 and Web 2.0. *First Monday*, 13(6).

Felder, R., & Brent, R. (2005). Death by PowerPoint. *Chemical Engineering Education,* 39(1), 28-29.

Felder, R. M., & Brent, R. (2003). Learning by doing. *Chemical Engineering Education*, 37(4), 282–283.

Felder, R. & Brent, R. (2004). The intellectual development of science and engineering students teaching to promote growth. *Journal of Engineering Education*, 93(4), 279–291.

Ferris, S. & Wilder, H. (2013). *The Plugged-in Professor: Tips and Techniques for Teaching with Social Media*. Chandos Publishing: Cambridge, UK.

Garrison, R., & Kanuka, H. (2004). Blended learning: Uncovering its transformative potential in higher education. *Internet and Higher Education*, 7, 95-105.

Garrison, R., & Vaughan, H. (2008). *Blended Learning in Higher Education: Framework, Principles and Guidelines*. San Francisco: Jossey-Bass.

Greenhow, G., Robelia , R. & Hughes., J. (May, 2009). Learning, teaching, and scholarship in a digital age: Web 2.0 and classroom research: What path should we take now? *Educational Researcher*, 38(4), 246-259.

Gan, Y., & Zhu, Z. (2007). A learning framework for knowledge building and collective wisdom advancement in virtual learning communities. *Educational Technology & Society*, 10(1), 206-226.

Harris, A. & Rea, A. (2009). Web 2.0 and virtual world technologies: A growing impact on education. *Journal of Information Systems Education*, Vol. 20(2) 137-144.

Hrastinski. S. (2008). Asynchronous and synchronous e-learning. *Educause Quarterly*, 31(4), 51-55.

Hrastinski, S. (2007). The potential of synchronous communication to enhance participation. Paper presented at the 28th International Conference on Information Systems. Montreal, Canada, December 9-12, 2007.

Haythronthwaite, C. & Kazmer, M. (2002). Bringing the Internet home: Adult distance learners and their Internet, home, and work worlds. In Barry Wellman and Caroline Haythornthwaite (Ed.), *The Internet in Everyday Life*. Blackwell Publishing: Malden, MA, 431-463.

Joosten, T. (2012). *Social Media for Educators: Strategies and Best Practices.* John Wiley & Sons: San Francisco, CA.

Kaplan, A. M., & Haenlein, M. (2010). Users of the world, unite! The challenges and opportunities of Social Media. *Business Horizons,* 53(1), 59–68.

Kietzmann, J., Hermkens, K, McCarthy, I, & Silvester, B. (2011). Social media? Get serious! Understanding the functional building blocks of social media. *Business Horizons,* 54, 241-251.

Joosten, T. (2012). *Social Media for Educators: Strategies and Best Practices.* John Wiley & Sons: San Francisco, CA.

Jones, C., & Czerniewicz, L. (2010). Describing or debunking? The net generation and digital natives. *Journal of Computer Assisted Learning,* 26(5), 317–320.

Littlejohn, A., & Pegler, C. (2007). *Preparing for Blended e-Learning.* London: Routledge.

Lankshear, C, & Knobel, M. (2006). *New literacies: Everyday Practices and Classroom Learning* (2nd ed.). Maidenhead, UK: Open University Press.

McCarthy, J. (2008). Utilizing Facebook: Immersing Generation Y students into first year university. Education Research Group of Adelaide Conference 2008, 1(2), 39-49.

McCarthy, J. (2010). Blended learning environments: Using social networking sites to enhance the first year experience. *Australasian Journal of Educational Technology,* 26(6), 729-740.

McManus, R (2005, August 6). Web 2.0 is not about version numbers or betas. *Read/WriteWeb.* Retrieved October 2, 2008, from http://www.readwriteweb.com/archives/web_20_is_not_a.php

Moody, M. (2010). Teaching Twitter and beyond: Tips for incorporating social media in traditional courses. *Journal of Magazine & New Media Research,* 11(2), 1-9.

Moran, M., Seaman, J. & Tinti-Kane, H. (April 2011). *Teaching, Learning, and Sharing: How Today's Higher Education Faculty Use Social Media.* Retrieved from   http://www.pearsonlearningsolutions.com/educators/pearson-social-media-survey-2011-bw.pdf

Mullins, P. (2001). Using outside speakers in the classroom. *APS Observer*, 14, 8.

New   Media   Academic   Summit.   Retrieved   from http://www.newmediaacademicsummit.com/documents/EdelmanNMAS2007.pdf

Pew Research Center. (2011). *The Digital Revolution and Higher Education College Presidents, Public Differ on Value of Online Learning.* Retrieved from http://alexa.pewinternet.com/~/media/Files/Reports/2011/PIP-Online-Learning.pdf

Prensky, M. (2001). Digital natives, digital immigrants. *On the Horizon*, 9 (5). Retrieved from http://www.marcprensky.com/writing/Prensky%20-%20Digital%20Natives,%20Digital%20Immigrants%20-%20Part1.pdf

Prensky, M. (2007). How to teach with technology: Keeping both teachers and students comfortable in an era of exponential change. *Emerging Technologies for Learning*, 2, 40-46.

Safko, L. (2012). *The Social Media Bible: Tactics, Tools, and Strategies for Business Success* (3rd Ed.). Wiley: Hoboken, New Jersey.

Salavuo, M. (2006), Open and informal online communities as forums of collaborative musical activities and learning, *British Journal of Music Education*, 23(3), 253-271.

Salavuo, M. (2008). Social media as an opportunity for pedagogical change in music education. *Journal of Music Education and Technology*, 1-20.

Scott, L. (2003). *Matrix of Some Uses of Blogs In Education.* Retrieved from http://www.edtechpost.ca/wordpress/2003/10/09/matrix-of-some-uses-of-blogs-in-education/

Sharpe, R., Benfield, G., Roberts, G. & Francis, R. (2006). The undergraduate experience of blended e-learning: a review of UK literature and practice. Retrieved from http://www.heacademy.ac.uk/assets/York/documents/ourwork/research/literaturereviews/blendedelearningexecsummary1.pdf

Skillings, M. & Ferrell, R. (2000). Student-generated rubrics: Bringing students into the assessment process. *The Reading Teacher*, 53(6), 452-455.

Snurb's Blog, (2005). Blogs And Wikis In Teaching At Qut, Retrieved from http://Snurb.Info/Node/166

Snurb's Blog, (2006). Blogs And Wikis In Teaching At Qut – Update. Retrieved from http://Snurb.Info/Node/472

Sterling, R. (2008, April 29). Writing, technology, and teenagers. *Kojo Nnamdi Show*. Retrieved from http://wamu.org/programs/kn/08/04/29.php

Scardamalia, M., & Bereiter, C. (2003). Knowledge building environments: Extending the limits of the possible in education and knowledge work. In A. DiStefano, K.E. Rudestam, & R.Silverman (Eds.). Encyclopedia of Distributed Learning. Thousand Oaks, CA: Sage Publications.

Stoerger, S., & Joosten, T. (2012). Faculty Development and the Impact on Education in Virtual Worlds. 28th Annual Conference on Distance Teaching & Learning.

Tabor, S. (2007). Narrowing the distance: Implementing a hybrid learning model for information security education. *The Quarterly Review of Distance Education*, 8(1), 47-57.

Tobias, S. (1990). *They're Not Dumb, They're Different: Stalking the Second Tier*. Research Corporation: Tucson, AZ.

Tyree, T. (2013). Using Twitter to assist students in writing a concise nut graph. In S. Ferris & H. Wilder, H. (Eds). The Plugged-in Professor: Tips and Techniques for Teaching with Social Media. Chandos Publishing: Cambridge, UK.

Tyree, Tia. (April 18, 2011). M. O. B. Mentality for Social Media Ethics [Blog Post]. Retrieved from http://drtiatyree.blogspot.com/2011/04/mob-mentality-for-social-media-ethics.html

Vaughan, N. (2007). Perspectives on blended learning in higher education. *International Journal on E-Learning*, 6(1), 81-94.

Watson, R. T., Boudreau, M., York, P. T., Greiner, M. & Wynn, D. E. (2008). Opening the classroom. *Journal of Information Systems Education*, 19(1), 75-85.

Wilcox, D. & Cameron, G. (2009). *Public Relations Strategies and Tactics* (9th Ed). Pearson: Boston.

Chapter 2
Twitter, Facebook, Blogs, and Media-Sharing Sites in the
Classroom
Jennifer B. Cox

- How has the acceptance of social media as a pedagogical tool evolved?
- What are some practical applications for using social media as a
  teaching tool?
- What are the social and legal issues involved with using social media in
  the classroom?

Social media is everywhere – in peoples' homes, cars, workplaces, and on their
phones. Yet, scholars have pointed to one glaring hole in the sphere of social
media acceptability: the classroom. Make no mistake, college students are on
social media sites during class, hiding their smartphones beneath their desks, or
using lab computers to access platforms like Twitter and Facebook. However,
many professors fail to recognize opportunities to incorporate social media
practices into the learning environment that could potentially transform the
distraction into an enhancement of learning objectives.

The need to include social media in college curriculums occurred seemingly
overnight, leaving many professors and scholars scrambling for ways to
incorporate popular networking applications into their courses effectively. In its
brief history in the classroom, social media usage has evolved rapidly, with
professors first prohibiting the practice, and then begrudgingly accepting it as an
unavoidable competitor for students' attention. For some teachers who recognize
the need to reach students on modern platforms, that evolution has continued,
featuring the integration of social media as a way to connect with students and
prepare them for their professional paths. However, how did that evolution come
about? How can professors achieve high-impact learning goals without students

getting distracted? What are the potential social and legal issues involved with adopting social media in the classroom?

Several recent studies have illustrated how previous reluctance to incorporate social media in college classrooms is beginning to give way to new opportunities for interaction, learning, and critical thinking in a variety of fields (McEachern, 2011; Moran, Seaman, and Tinti-Kane, 2012; Plopper and Conaway, 2013; Thomas, 2010). Other studies have emphasized the need to integrate social media into college learning given the demand for savvy users in most professional fields (Holmes, 2012; Lewis, 2009); some have elaborated on the practical application of social media techniques in the classroom (Cardon and Okoro, 2010; Domizi , 2013; Kelm, 2011), and some analyze the social and legal challenges associated with social media adoption (Sacks and Graves, 2012; Veltsos and Veltsos, 2010).

Taken together, these studies illuminate trends in social media pedagogy that can aid professors in identifying challenges and best practices for incorporating networking platforms into their own classrooms and assist researchers in their continued study of the fast-evolving field. While scholars have repeatedly noted the need to reach students where they are, using social media platforms to communicate and engage them in learning, higher education institutions have been slow to adopt the practice, in part due to a lack of understanding and willingness to embrace change (Holmes, 2012; Kelm, 2011). This chapter will examine existing research to offer a broad perspective of the opportunities and challenges to adopting social media in the classroom and the imperative need to do so in an effort to best prepare students for future careers and social interactions.

History

Professors have traditionally been reluctant to adopt social media as a teaching tool for a variety of reasons. Although so-called Millenials – those born between the early 1980s and late 1990s – have been quick to embrace social networking and are very comfortable with the technologies required to share information online, their instructors have lagged behind (Vie, 2008). A 2006 study comparing the social networking use between undergraduates and college composition instructors revealed a vast majority of students had social networking accounts on MySpace, Facebook, or both, while the majority of instructors did not have accounts on either, leading students to believe their professors were woefully behind and were unlikely to engage in any new technology (Vie, 2008).

The reluctance of college professors to use social media has been based largely on a lack of understanding of its educational value. A 2010 survey of college faculty and students found significantly more students were open to the idea of using social networking sites for educational purposes in the classroom than were instructors, many of whom felt sites like Facebook were better suited for recreational use (Roblyer et. al., 2010). Some institutions have gone so far as to censor online networking in the classroom, using blocking software to prohibit students from using social media in the classroom (Thomas, 2012). Instructors have considered these sites to be distractions rather than opportunities for learning, and they are not without good cause. Many Millenials have a difficult time seeing social networking as a tool for critical thinking, using online tools as a means to an end rather than a didactic journey. For example, when online users have a question, they simply type key terms into a search engine, find the answer, and move on to the next activity. They rarely use the tools at their disposal to gain deeper understanding of a topic or to discover and consider new issues and perspectives (Anderson and Rainie, 2012).

A lack of time and funding may also be to blame for professors' resistance to incorporating social media into the classroom. The demands on professors' time can be staggering, with many responsible for teaching, research, service, and advising, among other endeavors. Learning new technologies and adapting teaching styles create new demands that many professors just do not have time to accommodate (Vie, 2008). Similarly, in spite of charges from political and educational institutions to incorporate more social networking tools into the classroom, little funding has been made available to train teachers and provide them with the new technologies needed to implement social media elements into their curricula (Plopper and Conaway, 2013).

However, as new information about demand for social media education and its useful applications in academia has come to the forefront, the need for valuable instruction on the topic has become nearly impossible to ignore. As the economy struggled to recover from recession in 2012, and unemployment in the U.S. lingered around 8%, job postings mandating applicants must possess social media skills rose 87% from the previous year (Holmes, 2012).

The usefulness of social media technologies has evolved with the demand. Early social networking iterations, such as Friends Reunited and SixDegrees, were created primarily as tools for people searching rather than conversing and collaborating. In the early 2000s, social networking expanded to include the modern interactive features users are familiar with today, with early sites, such as Friendster and MySpace, to more modern ones, including Facebook and Twitter. As the capabilities for real interaction expanded, so too did the need for higher-level attention and instruction (Vie, 2008). Although students are comfortable with social media, they lack the knowledge needed to apply their networking skills in professional settings (McEachern, 2011).

Recently, faculty members have begun to acknowledge the value of social media for personal use, though educational use – while gaining momentum – is still lagging behind. A 2012 study of college professors in the U.S. revealed nearly two-thirds visited a social media site within the past month for personal use, with the youngest faculty – those younger than age 35 – leading the charge (Moran, Seaman, and Tinti-Kane, 2012). In spite of their personal acceptance of social networking, only about one-third of those surveyed reported using Facebook, Twitter, and LinkedIn for teaching purposes, pointing to concerns with privacy and the integrity of student submissions as barriers to their adoption. Still, the hesitancy among faculty members regarding social media usage in the classroom has decreased from year to year, with more and more professors recognizing the need for increased instruction as demand for networking skills in every field continues to grow (Moran, Seaman, and Tinti-Kane, 2012).

Practical Applications

Although the adoption of social media has been slow in the classroom, some professors have incorporated networking tools into their curriculum with positive results. Kelm (2011) applied social constructivism theory to tout the advantages of using social media to achieve learning outcomes. Social constructivists believe knowledge is constructed in social contexts, with emphasis on collaboration among learners over traditional lecturing (Koohang et. al., 2009). Researchers believe opportunities for students to network and collaborate using social media tools can help learners construct knowledge by promoting engagement, encouraging group work, providing opportunities for group feedback, and connecting them with others whose strengths are different from their own (Fosnot, 2005; Kelm, 2011; Jonassen, Peck, and Wilson, 1998). Kelm (2011) argued social media have the ability to "transform large class lecture teaching to small group interaction" (p. 508), allowing students to learn more collectively rather than limiting education to each individual's own capacity for absorption.

Among the most commonly used tools in the classroom in recent years are blogs; Facebook; Twitter; social media video platforms, such as YouTube; and professional networking sites, such as LinkedIn. This section will explore each of these tools and their practical applications in the classroom.

Blogs

Blogs, also known as "web logs," came into vogue in early 1990s, mostly in the form of online diaries (Williams and Jacobs, 2004). They allow anyone to publish information online using simple content management systems to organize and present text, pictures, videos, and other shared materials. Harvard University was the first U.S. higher education institution to embrace blogs as educational tools in 2003 (Williams and Jacobs, 2004). Administrators there created a network where students could form their own blogs on the Harvard server in hopes of promoting lifelong learning and connections and to build a community and image for the school and its students.

As other universities have begun to adopt blogs as a means of communication in the classroom, professors employing them have remarked on their capacity to enhance the learning experience. Ferdig and Trammell (2004) found blogs to be useful teaching tools, because they provide space for students to reflect on learning and publish their thoughts; they allow professors and students to exchange ideas and feedback; and they encourage knowledge that is relational and contextual through the use of hyperlinks to other pieces of information. Professors have also praised blogs for their encouragement of higher-level thinking and self-evaluation. Williams and Jacobs (2004) wrote: "Blogs have the potential, at least, to be a truly transformational technology in that they provide students with a high level of autonomy while simultaneously providing opportunity for greater interaction with peers" (p. 245).

Professors have used blogs in the classroom in several different ways. Kelm (2011) used blogs as a means of communication with and among Master of Business Education students headed from the U.S. to China for a study abroad experience. Prior to leaving the states, Kelm used a class blog to distribute essential instructions students would need to ensure their success and safety on the trip. While overseas, Kelm used the blog as a tool for constant reflection among students, posting summaries of each day's activities, and requiring students to comment with their takeaways regarding Chinese culture. Upon their return, students continued to post on the class blog with critical analysis of the experience and thoughts regarding the long-term learning objectives attained. By requiring students to communicate with him and each other regularly, Kelm was able to use his blog as a tool to create a community when a physical classroom environment was not possible.

In his business communication class, Buechler (2010) used blogs to facilitate group work, helping students gather and store information and make group decisions on project components. Students were provided five companies to research in groups, and together, members were to make recommendations about the companies to the instructor and class using their blogs to communicate throughout the process. From the exercise, Buechler observed three learning outcomes that emphasized the effectiveness of the blogs: 1) blogs aided students in their group decision-making by providing a centralized location for the abundance of information and resources collected; 2) students were able to demonstrate proficiency with technology that will be of value to them as they seek post-graduate jobs; and 3) they forced students to take responsibility for their ideas, promoting a community dialogue that required blog authors to support their points in detail.

While many instructors believe incorporating the use of blogs and other forms of social media into their curriculum would be beneficial, some emphasize the need for caution before adopting those tools. A fair amount of planning and analysis is essential before requiring students to blog in class to distinguish fruitless online activity from applicable practices and skills. Cardon and Oroko (2010) suggested professors compare the use of various communication technologies they are thinking of employing in the classroom to those actually used in the field. Whatever the class or project, it is important for students to learn how social networking technologies are being used professionally so that they can parlay the knowledge and skills obtained into opportunities to make themselves more marketable in their careers. Professors should also ensure the networking technology they use promotes in-person interaction rather than turning the classroom experience into isolated independent studies (Cardon and

Oroko, 2010). Using blogs to prompt interpersonal interactions can better prepare students for the working world, where they will be expected to get out from behind their computer screens and form relationships and connections to further their organization's goals.

Twitter

Two of the most popular forms of online interaction today are Twitter and Facebook, especially among college-age users. As of October 2012, more than 1 billion people used Facebook, and the median age of those users is 22 years old (Ortutay, 2012). The number of Twitter accounts topped 500 million in late 2012, with three-quarters of those who reported their age to be between 15 and 25 years old (Telegraph, 2012). Most students are familiar with Facebook and Twitter, using both on their computers and mobile devices every day – if not every minute. However, many find it difficult to translate their social networking skills into professional and educational contexts (McEachern, 2011).

Although both Twitter and Facebook afford users opportunities to connect with people for both casual and business purposes, the two social media sites can be operated for completely different purposes which should be explored in classrooms. The ways in which connections are made on Facebook and Twitter have implications for their diverging uses. Facebook encourages participants to make connections with people they already know by requiring users to send and accept "friend requests" from one another or "like" organizations and groups in which they might be interested. Twitter allows users to find and "follow" people they don't know who might have shared interests, backgrounds, or professions. In this way, Twitter has more professional applications in that it encourages participants to reach beyond their physical connections and form virtual relationships with other professionals in their field. For example, a Twitter user who is studying to be a journalist might follow several news organizations, media groups, media personalities, and journalism scholars in order to keep a close watch on the industry into which they will soon enter.

Using Twitter to communicate is often referred to as microblogging, as the types of messages relayed often resemble shorter versions of blogs. Unlike Facebook, Twitter users are limited to 140 characters per tweet, making efficient, focused writing essential. Professors have used Twitter to aid students in identifying salient points in their writing. One instructor recommended teaching literature using Twitter, forcing students to focus on the most important aspects of what they were trying to say and the information they consumed (Doyne and Ojalvo, 2011). Researchers have found Twitter's unique opportunities for communicating can be helpful to both students and educators. Students can gain important feedback on their short reflections, and instructors can assess learning based on students' posting, allowing them to get a better impression of the learning environment (Ebner et. al., 2010).

Professors have used Twitter in the classroom in both passive and interactive ways, providing students with a better understanding of its professional functions. Many instructors require students to monitor current events in their field on the social media site using keyword searches and following industry leaders, and some even go a step farther, requiring students to incorporate the information gleaned into writing assignments with deeper analysis (Veltsos and Veltsos, 2010). Others use Twitter to build interactive communities both in and outside the classroom. One professor used Twitter in a graduate school class for multiple reasons, including fostering out-of-class discussion, communicating announcements to students, having students reflect on learning and reporting on self-learning goals, and sharing information relevant to their field of study (Domizi, 2013). Students in the class reported feeling more connected to one another and greater understanding of the content and expectations associated with the course.

However, using Twitter in the classroom can present professors with some challenges. Some professors require students to tweet throughout their lectures, posting questions and reflections on the topics being examined. While one professor found it helpful for fostering discussion without interrupting lecture, it can also be a distraction for students, who may get off topic and, in some cases, act inappropriately, with some feeling bold enough to make comments about professors and classmates that normally would not be said out loud in a classroom setting. Young (2009) observed "Opening up a Twitter-powered channel in class — which several professors at other universities are experimenting with as well — alters classroom power dynamics and signals to students that they're in control" (p. A1). Students in the class acknowledged getting sidetracked at times, but said they felt the tweeting did more good than harm as it allowed them to reflect on the lesson in real time rather than using notes and books later to cram in understanding just before an exam (Young, 2009).

Using Twitter for class purposes can also be overwhelming for students, as users send more than 400 million tweets each day (Tsukayama, 2013). Some strategies for dealing with information overload include the use of content managers such as Tweetdeck, which allows followers to organize their tweets and the people they are following into groups for easier access. Students can also use websites such as Storify to organize content into a narrative, which can help them to recall and reflect on the information they learned and tweeted during a class discussion. Having students use a shared hashtag for each tweet can also help students connect without too many distractions from other posts in students' Twitter feed. By having students open a search page for the hashtag during the discussion, they are only able to view other tweets with the same hashtag on that page.

Facebook

Facebook is used more frequently for personal connections and sharing pictures, videos, and memes (Mazer, Murphy, and Simonds, 2007). In spite of its reputation for being a tool for procrastination, Facebook can be a powerful tool for educators, many of whom have employed an array of strategies for using the social media site in the classroom, ranging from simple viewing and searching to heavy interaction. One professor used Facebook to provide examples of poor and unprofessional posts for students in hopes of helping them understand the importance of having strong writing skills (Decarie, 2010). Using samples of posts that were obscene, angry, poorly written, and even those in which students incriminated themselves in comments about skipping class, students were able to better understand the power of social media communication and its implications for their professional well-being.

One professor created an entire class around the use of social media, with Facebook being the primary focus (McEachern, 2011). Students in the course analyzed the use of social media among businesses and organizations to promote their missions and public personas. The exercises completed in the course lead to the creation of a "Facebook internship," during which time two students were hired to run communications among faculty, staff, students, and administrators for their university department using Facebook. Through their everyday use of Facebook for professional purposes, students learned valuable lessons on time management, how to publicize and promote their organization, and how to craft and control the image of their organization – skills which are easily applicable in most career fields.

Facebook also has its drawbacks for instructor-student communication that can lead to disruptions in the learning environment. The formation of informal relationships between teachers and their students on Facebook can also be problematic, as it may lead misconceptions regarding power dynamics in the classroom and favoritism among students, which is why many universities discourage or prohibit professors from "friending" students while they attend school (Matthews, 2012).

Despite these challenges, the need for proper instruction on professional Facebook use and its incorporation into college classrooms is essential. As more businesses and organizations around the world use Facebook as a medium for communicating images, promotions, information, and for building interactions and client bases, students need to understand the benefits and potentially career-ending consequences of posting on the social media site (Sacks and Graves, 2012). Furthermore, Facebook is where the students are, and professors need to be constantly adapting, searching for new ways to connect with and educate students to achieve course outcomes and promote lasting learning (Young, 2009).

In addition to Facebook and Twitter, which both have professional and personal applications, platforms for social networking designed exclusively for career connections have emerged. The professional networking site LinkedIn was created in 2003 as a platform for people working in an array of fields to connect with one another to promote possible job opportunities, collaboration efforts, and broader contact across specializations (LinkedIn, 2013). As of January 2013, LinkedIn reported having 200 million users in more than 200 countries (Nishar, 2013), making it the most-used social media site for professional networking in the world (Sacks and Graves, 2012). Other sites with similar purposes have since surfaced, including Biznik, a website connecting entrepreneurs and small business owners, Fast Pitch, where businesses can market their business plans and make connections with potential investors, and StartupNation, a site for beginning business owners to exchange ideas and information (Gregory, 2012).

While the educational benefits to using LinkedIn and other similar professional networking sites may seem obvious, professors have struggled with how best to instruct students on their use in a classroom setting. Two professors used LinkedIn to demonstrate the connectivity of working professionals all over the world, asking students to use the website to connect with well-known public figures (Sacks and Graves, 2012). Students were surprised to discover how easily connected they could be to people in high positions, prompting them to reflect on the professionalism of their own online behavior. Teaching students to search for jobs and connections on social networking business sites using various keywords and strategies may also help students gain a better understanding of the opportunities afforded them and get them thinking about ways to market themselves in professional settings (Crawford, 2012). In spite of their wide usage, strategies for teaching students to use these websites are sparse. With the expansion of opportunities of online image enhancement and destruction, more instruction on professionalism using LinkedIn and other professional networking tools is needed in the classroom and throughout students' college careers.

Social Media Videos

The video-sharing website YouTube is a preferred multimedia tool for college educators nearly since its creation in 2005 due to its searchability, the availability of material relevant to any topic, and its seemingly endless supply of footage uploaded at a rate of 48 hours of video per minute, or eight years' worth of video per day (YouTube, 2013). Recognizing YouTube's success as an educational tool, other sites have emerged to provide content suitable for the classroom, such as TED, a non-profit website containing lectures on a variety of topics from experts in those fields, Big Think, offering viewers access to presentations from professionals in fields ranging from poetry to politicians, and even YouTubeEDU, which divides educational presentations into various channels for academics to use in their classes (Gilroy, 2009). Seeking to reach college students who grew up in the Digital Age, where cellular phones, digital cameras, and online social networking platforms are not novelties but ways of life, professors have turned to these platforms to add appeal and zest to their lessons (Duffy, 2012). A 2012 survey of college educators revealed 88% used video in the classroom for teaching purposes, with 83% reporting they found the video material by searching online (Pearson, 2012).

However, some professors argue it is not enough to simply show a video clip at random; careful thought and strategy must be applied to maximize the value of social media videos as a learning tool. Duffy (2012) argued:

If we agree that there are changes occurring across the learning ecology and, that new conceptualizations are required to use these emerging technologies, then some care should be taken to think deeply about the impacts of Web 2.0 on the processes and practices of pedagogy (pp.49-50).

In order for social media videos to be effective vehicles for achieving learning objectives, instructors must take great care to ensure the viewed material is pertinent to their lesson and operates as a catalyst for further discussion, reflection, and analysis on the topic at hand (Duffy, 2012). The viewing of social media in classrooms ought to lead to active learning and engagement of students, rather than passive observation. Video-sharing can be used to create a community, giving a voice to students who might otherwise shy away from other types of classroom interaction and encouraging interaction and prolonged interest in topics long after the physical room has emptied (Skiba, 2007).

Some professors require their students to take social media viewing a step further by making them participants in the video-sharing process. Students in a communication ethics class were asked to get into groups to create a video demonstrating different types of unethical behavior (Lehman, DuFrene, and Lehman, 2010). The groups then loaded their presentations onto YouTube for the rest of the students to view and reflect on for in-class discussion and analysis of each of the scenarios. The professors found students not only enjoyed the assignment, but also emerged with a greater understanding of the various ethical violations, leading to deeper personal examination of and reflection on the content. Other professors have encouraged students to think beyond the classroom using YouTube to post self-produced video vignettes related to their career goals and work experience (Duffy, 2010; Skiba, 2007). Allowing students to explore their career options using technology and communication methods that are familiar for them may help enlighten and inspire them toward professional success.

Taxonomy of Practical Applications

The pedagogical strategies for incorporating social media into curricula fall into two categories: passive and active applications. Instructors just beginning with social media might feel comfortable with passive techniques, such as having students monitor local news or happenings pertaining to their fields of study on Facebook or Twitter. Students can easily scan the Internet or their social media feeds for projects that might further their understanding of and critical thinking about their studies in ways that are familiar and fun for them.

Figure 2-1 Taxonomy of practical social networking pedagogical applications

Once students and the instructor feel more at ease with social media use, lessons involving searches for items, people, and news outlets relevant to the course may be pursued. Students can experiment online in a risk-free environment, searching social media sites for possible connections and information without detection. For example, students can search for specific topics, individuals, and groups on sites including Twitter, YouTube, LinkedIn, Facebook, and Instagram without actually "following" or "friending" them, as long as their profiles are set to public rather than private.

Moving onward toward more rigorous engagement is recording. Professors sometimes encourage students to take notes using social media platforms, and some have even set up private Facebook accounts or blogs for their classes to provide students the opportunity to ask questions and make comments in a closed, safe online environment. Using social media to record and post class happenings can help students connect and share information both inside and outside the classroom.

Once the professor and students are comfortable moving beyond the barriers of the traditional classroom, active applications for interactive learning can begin. Once students have completed searches that might benefit their career goals and course learning objectives, they can begin connecting with those individuals and groups that might assist them in furthering their goals. Students can use LinkedIn to connect with professionals in their field and Twitter and Facebook to find and follow those connections daily.

Students can then begin to interact with their sources, asking them questions, beginning conversations, and making progress toward achieving their professional goals. Facilitating the start of these interactions may help students better assess their career goals and make lasting connections that could help them land internships and jobs in their field. These interactions can also be useful in reporting class-related projects that require outside reflection from expert sources. Students can begin with simple steps, such as commenting on someone's Facebook post, blog, or YouTube video. They can also get more direct, commenting on individual posts using professionals' Twitter handles to begin a conversation.

The ultimate goal for social media learning is community building. Whether using networking technologies to build a virtual classroom community or assisting students in the construction of their own professional communities, this step requires the processing of each of the previous levels of communication. Building online communities can facilitate long-term learning by connecting students with course materials, professionals, and classmates long after the semester concludes. The development of students' professional communities could also help them land career opportunities upon graduation. More importantly, learning about appropriate community building online could also alert students to behavior they have exhibited that is not appropriate and might prevent them from forming the professional communities they need to thrive, giving them the opportunity to adjust their online personas to facilitate more productive connections.

Social Implications

Researchers have explored the vast impact of social networking technologies on students' personal and professional lives, arguing more awareness of and education on these effects needs to be integrated into college curriculums. A 2005 study of students aged 8-18 revealed participants spent an average of one-quarter of each day interacting with various technologies, including computers, video games, and television (Roberts and Foehr, 2005). Without guidance and instruction, students' interactions with technology may lack purpose and critical reflection that could be valuable for furthering their personal and professional goals. Vie (2008) wrote, "For them, technology is a means to an end; with it, they can find information rapidly and move on to tackle their next hurdle" (p. 12). Essentially, social media is used more frequently to measure students' popularity and to demonstrate self-worth rather than as a tool for developing and maintaining beneficial relationships and seeking and sharing useful information and knowledge.

Researchers have found students tend not to think about their social media use, absentmindedly racking up friends or followers to build their networks without purpose, which could lead to sacrifices in network quality and information substance. Sacks and Graves (2012) mined social networking theories to explore the limits of having too many social media connections on students' networks, examining network size, network quality, social distance, network diffusion, and network complexity. Using Facebook as an example, the professors demonstrated ways in which more "friends" (network size) does not usually translate to a better understanding of more individuals (network quality). They found students with more in-class connections had faster access to information, but the number of channels those students had to go through lead to more rigorous relationship maintenance, whereas students with few in-class connections had more time to develop social ties outside of the classroom, ultimately freeing them up for more far-reaching interactions. The professors also demonstrated the concept of social distance using LinkedIn to show how many connections lose power the farther from personal interaction they get. For example, first-level connections are people a user knows personally, making it more likely that that user would do a favor for those connections rather than a friend of a friend (second-level connection) or a friend of a friend of a friend (third-level connection). Finally, the professors used Twitter to show how easily a simple message can be distributed via social media (network diffusion), but how difficult it is to find complex, meaningful information that can be helpful at a specific time (network complexity). Students were required to go on Twitter to find the weather in a far-away city, which they did with ease. However, they were unable to find more specific information, such as wind speed and future weather projections.

Most troubling is the addictive nature of social media, particularly when it distracts students from meaningful tasks, such as listening, learning, and processing. Pathological Internet use is especially common in college students and young children, who are psychologically at high risk for behavioral addictions such as this. One study of students at two universities found 4% of those surveyed displayed problematic Internet usage tendencies, and 70% reported they stay online longer than they intend to in many cases (Christakis, 2011). Researchers cited the vast availability of technologies that allow college students to access the Internet whenever and wherever, which many students do with regularity. In classrooms, many professors struggle to pull students' eyes from their mobile devices and claim their focus. It is largely due to this fear of distraction and addiction that many educators have been hesitant to introduce social networking into the curricula.

Students' heavy reliance on social media underscores the need for instructors to be savvy and competent with those mediums as well, teaching critical media literacy skills that can help learners move beyond passive use to engage in a deeper understanding of their online communication behaviors. Thomas (2010) wrote, "As students engage in social media frequently the use of these technologies in the classroom can be an effective way of encouraging students to be critical of the modes of communication with which they regularly interact and develop a kind of 'social media literacy'" (p. 23). Students who engage with technologies in the classroom similar to those for purposes outside academia can be taught to examine professional lessons in more personal contexts. By incorporating these technologies, students can relate their personal experiences to their studies to help them think critically about the social media messages they send and receive on a daily basis. Giving students a hands-on social media education could help elevate learning objectives based on Bloom's Taxonomy

(Anderson et. al., 2001) from simple knowing skills, including the ability to list, label, and identify, to higher-level evaluation skills that encourage students to give and seek critical feedback and be better equipped to support their work and ideas.

In teaching social media literacy, one of the main focuses must be on attention, which, coincidentally, seems to be one of the most problematic lesson for professors to teach and for students to learn. In spite of the many advantages to using social media technologies in the classroom, the biggest problem will always be keeping students on task while online. Internet surfing during class has become so problematic that some universities have gone so far as to ban laptops and Internet access in classrooms (Rheingold, 2010). While there does not appear to be a surefire way to eliminate online distractions when incorporating social media into the classroom, some professors feel it is their personal responsibility to keep students engaged (Cox, 2012; Rheingold, 2010). Cox (2012) wrote:

> I'm not proposing that we dance for our students or even attempt to meet their impossible standards for stimulation. What they want is an opportunity to connect with the professor and the material in a way that is meaningful and applicable to their lives and goals (p. B24).

By incorporating different time-tested teaching strategies into the lesson, such as discussion, group time, surveys, and personal anecdotes, professors can teach important social media lessons in ways that are fun yet informative to students.

Legal Issues

Professors wanting to use social media to connect with students in the classroom must exercise caution and develop a plan for communication that may involve some boundaries. Some professors use sites like Twitter to act as a liaison, connecting students with professionals in their fields of study by having them research and question experts online (Gilroy, 2009). Others take social networking in class a step farther, connecting with students on a personal level. One professor created class group sites on Facebook and encouraged students to join using their personal profiles. In addition to connecting the students with one another, the professor accessed his students' information to send birthday wishes, gain information for writing recommendations, and participate in their lives (Gilroy, 2009). While the instructor found students enjoyed the opportunity to engage both in and out of the classroom, others believe a separation of personal and professional information among students and teachers is more appropriate. Facebook encourages users to post details about their personal lives, including relationship statuses, which opponents of using social media in the classroom find inappropriate for students and teachers to share (Matthews, 2012).

Following the revelation of several cases of inappropriate social networking among teachers and students, often including sexual content, at least 40 school districts nationwide implemented social media policies prohibiting teachers from accepting friend requests from students (Matthews, 2012). Many universities have adopted policies restricting student-teacher relationships on social media, though most do not include an outright ban on "friending." Legislators have been careful not to enforce sweeping Facebook bans on instructors, fearing many would view the move as an infringement on their First Amendment rights (Matthews, 2012). However, many colleges and professors agree keeping classroom activities on Facebook within professional user groups, which restrict the amount of personal information that can be accessed among "non-friends," and saving students' friend requests until after they have graduated to be best practices for avoiding legal issues (Petronzio, 2012).

Similarly, professors have expressed concern over the nature of social media in general, citing student privacy as one of their top reasons for opposing use of the platforms in class (Moran, Seaman, and Tinti-Kane, 2012). The privacy of students' postings online has revolved largely around Facebook, with 59% of respondents to a CNBC poll reporting they had little to no trust that their information would be kept private by the site's administrators (Tauche and Bergman, 2012). Another study conducted by *Consumer Reports* (2012) found 28% of U.S. Facebook users share their wall posts with an audience wider than their friends, and about 13 million users either do not know or have not taken the time to adjust privacy settings for their account. Facebook also constantly changes its policies regarding information sharing, allowing administrators to legally sell user information to third parties without user's full comprehension or approval (Bilton, 2012).

Professors who shy away from using Facebook in the classroom out of concern for their students' overall privacy are encouraged to try Twitter, which has never made users' private information public. However, it should be noted that unless students' wish to set their accounts to private, their Twitter postings can be seen by all Twitter users, even those who don't follow them. Additionally, all tweets except those that have been deleted or locked using privacy settings, will be stored in the Library of Congress as part of a historical document for all to see (The Telegraph, 2013). Professors may also consider using closed services that allow the instructor to control settings and participants, such as PBWorks instead of Wikipedia, Jabber rather than Twitter, or Ning in lieu of Facebook (Veltsos and Veltsos, 2010). Even though those networking sites are less familiar to students, instructors may still incorporate them into lessons to teach similar networking principles in a more secure setting.

Other legal considerations instructors should take into account before integrating social media into a class include protections for both themselves and the works of others. While it is vital for professors to be able to communicate using social media platforms to successfully incorporate them into their curricula, it is even more important that they understand their students' right to confidentiality. One high school English teacher was fired after she reflected on a students' presentation on her personal blog (Hardy, 2010). Although she did not reveal the student's name or other identifying information, the student's parents complained their child's privacy had been compromised. Additionally, any information about students' grades or class performance should not be shared via social media so as not to violate their privacy (Veltsos and Veltsos, 2010).

Students and professors must also have a clear understanding of copyright laws when using materials produced by others, such as text, pictures, videos, and music. While the "fair use" doctrine often protects students and teachers who use copyrighted materials in the classroom, any material used for commercial purposes is not recognized and could land users in legal trouble (Veltsos and Veltsos, 2010). Professors can avoid issues with copyright laws by reviewing their institution's policies before incorporating social media into the classroom.

Conclusion

The need for social media instruction in college classrooms has never been greater. As more professions demand their applicants be social media savvy and vast amounts of personal information are made available online every day, students without proper training in social networking may find their classroom-based knowledge rendered obsolete and their hopes of getting hired dashed before they even set foot into the job market. Employers look to new hires as having the potential to propel their organizations farther into the Digital Age, giving recent graduates unprecedented opportunities for leadership roles and responsibilities early in their careers. However, students without a developed appreciation for the power and reach of social media may be their own obstacles, hindering chances to succeed with the click of a button. Teaching students acceptable social networking behavior is critical when nearly everything published is available in perpetuity for all to see. In this rapidly evolving technological society, social media searches on potential applicants have become as routine as checking references, making it imperative that students be prepared to account for themselves online.

The acceptance of social media as a pedagogical tool has evolved greatly in recent years, and it will likely continue to permeate college curricula in the years to come. Although professors have been slow to adopt social media in the classroom, its incorporation is unavoidable, as neither teachers nor students can cloister themselves from the World Wide Web. The application of social constructivism theory to social media practice has helped instructors recognize the value of networking in achieving learning outcomes. Social media have the ability to instill critical knowledge and promote engagement when used properly. Instructors can use networking tools to foster group interaction and connect students who otherwise may not engage in classroom settings.

As the technologies and platforms have evolved exponentially during the past few years, instructors have pioneered many practical applications for using social media as a teaching tool. Professors have developed useful strategies for integrating platforms, such as blogs, Facebook, Twitter, YouTube, and many others, into their classes to enhance learning and engage with students where they are. Activities range from passive engagement, including social media searches for topics and the reading of blogs and websites, to more active interaction, requiring students to break out of their comfort zones and make real connections with professionals in their fields. Students have found these activities to be fun and informative, and professors reported greater retention of the material and, in many cases, long-term interaction with the lessons following the conclusion of the class.

In spite of its many uses, new platforms for interactive online learning use should be approached with some level of planning and caution, as there are several social and legal issued involved with using social media in the classroom. The incorporation of social networking activities in the classroom may prove fruitless if lessons are not properly geared toward learning objectives. Instructors are cautioned to take great care to identify the goals and planned outcomes of each lesson before attaching social media components. If not, the results may likely be those assignments are regarded as "busy work" aimed at occupying students' time rather than enhancing the learning experience.

Similarly, examinations of social and legal ramifications are essential when considering the use of social networking platforms in the classroom. Although the opportunities for learning are abundant, the potential for distraction online is also great. Teaching students to be social media literate is essential to achieve educational objectives, so students know how to properly engage with the technologies in professional settings. Special emphasis could be placed on attentive learning, teaching students how not to be derailed by online temptations that could sap their productivity.

Professors are encouraged to pay close attention to social media policies at their institutions to ensure legal protection. By clearly defining classroom social media requirements and expectations with students and administrators, any potential issues can be considered and managed before they arise. Instructors could benefit from observing best practices in social networking in their personal adoptions, taking care not to violate the privacies of students and co-workers, as well as their own personal privacy.

The opportunities for social media adoption in the classroom are abundant, and students are eager to explore familiar platforms in professional, engaging ways. As more technologies for communicating online become available, the need for education will continue to grow. While more college classes have begun to explore social media exclusively, there is a real need for teachers in all fields to incorporate these lessons into their existing curricula to meet the challenges and opportunities facing graduates today. By offering social networking instruction in the classroom, professors can equip students with the tools and knowledge they need to compete and succeed in the modern job market.

References

Anderson, L.W. (Ed.), Krathwohl, D.R. (Ed.), Airasian, P.W., Cruikshank, K.A., Mayer, R.E., Pintrich, P.R., Raths, J., & Wittrock, M.C. (2001). *A Taxonomy for Learning, Teaching, and Assessing: A Revision of Bloom's Taxonomy of Educational Objectives (Complete Edition).* New York: Longman.

Anderson, J.Q., & Rainie, L. (2012). Millenials will benefit and suffer due to their hyperconnected lives. *Pew Research Center.* Retrieved from http://www/pewinternet.org/~/media/Files/Reports/2012/PIP_Future_of_Intern et_2012_Young_brains_PDF.pdf

Barber, L., & Pearce, K. (2008). The effects of instructor Facebook participation on student perceptions of teacher credibility and teacher attractiveness. *Conference Papers - International Communication Association,* 1-14.

Bilton, N. (2012, May 18). Facebook vs. Twitter. *The New York Times.* Retrieved from http://bits.blogs.nytimes.com/2012/05/18/facebook-vs-twitter/

Cardon, P.W., & Okoro, E. (2010). A measured approach to adopting new media in the business communication classroom. *Business Communication Quarterly,* 73(4), 434-438.

Consumer Reports. (2012). Facebook & your privacy. *Consumer Reports magazine.* Retrieved from http://www.consumerreports.org/cro/magazine/2012/06/facebook-your-privacy/index.htm

Christakis, D.A., Moreno, M.M., Jelenchick, L., Myaing, M.T., & Zhou, C. (2011). Problematic Internet usage in U.S. college students: A pilot study. *BMC Medicine,* 9(77), 1-6.

Christakis, J.B. (2012, April). Reclaiming the classroom with old-fashioned teaching. *Chronicle of Higher Education,* 58(24), B24-B24.

Crawford, M. (2012). Tips to use LinkedIn effectively for job hunting. American Society of Mechanical Engineers. Retrieved from https://www.asme.org/kb/news---articles/articles/job-hunting/tips-to-use-linkedin-effectively-for-job-hunting

Decarie, C. (2010). Facebook: Challenges and opportunities for business communication students. *Business Communication Quarterly,* 73(4), 449-452.

Domizi, D.P. (2013). Microblogging to foster connections and community in a weekly graduate seminar course. *TechTrends,* 57(1), 43-51.

Doyne, S., & Ojalvo, H.E. (2011). Less is more: Using social media to inspire concise writing. *The New York Times.* Retrieved from http://learning.blogs.nytimes.com/2011/03/28/less-is-more-using-social-media-to-inspire-concise-writing/

Duffy, P. (2012). Engaging the YouTube Google-eyed generation: Strategies for using Web 2.0 in teaching and learning. In M. Ciussi & E. G. Freitas (Eds.), *Leading Issues in e-Learning Research* (pp. 47-70). London: Good News Digital Books.

Ebner, M., Lienhardt, C., Rohs, M., & Meyer, I. (2010). Microblogs in higher education – A chance to facilitate informational and process-oriented learning? *Computers & Education,* 55(1), 92-100.

Ferdig, R.E., & Trammell, K.D. (2004). Content delivery in the "blogosphere." *Technological Horizons in Education Journal Online.* Retrieved from http://defiant.corban.edu/jjohnson/pages/Teaching/BloggingBlogosphere.pdf

Fosnot, C. T. (Ed.). (2005). *Constructivism: Theory, Perspectives and Practice* (2nd ed.). New York, NY: Teachers College Press.

Gilroy, M. (2009). Higher education migrates to YouTube and social networks. *Education Digest,* 75(7), 18-22.

Gregory, A. (2012, August 28). 20 social networking sites for business professionals. *SitePoint.* Retrieved from http://www.sitepoint.com/social-networking-sites-for-business/

Hardy, D. (2010, June 9). Ex-teacher learns the hard way: Watch what you put online. *The Philadelphia Inquirer.* Retrieved from http://www.philly.com/philly/education/95933539.html

Holmes, R. (2012). Universities are failing at teaching social media. *CNN Money.* Retrieved from http://tech.fortune.cnn.com/2012/09/26/universities-are-failing-at-teaching-social-media/

Jonassen, D. H., Peck, K. L., & Wilson, B. G. (1998). *Learning with Technology: A Constructivist Perspective.* Upper Saddle River, NJ: Merrill/Prentice Hall.

Kelm, O.R. (2011). Social media: It's what students do. *Business Communication Quarterly,* 74(4), 505-520.

Koohang, A., Riley, L., Smith, T. & Schreurs, J. (2009). E-learning and constructivism: From theory to application. *Interdisciplinary Journal of E-Learning & Learning Objects*, 5(1), 91-109.

Lehman, C., DuFrene, D.D., & Lehman, M.W. (2010). YouTube video project: A "cool" way to learn communication ethics. *Business Communication Quarterly*, 73(4), 444-449.

Lewis, B.K. (2009). *Social Media and Strategic Communications: Attitudes and Perceptions among College Students*. (Doctoral dissertation). Retrieved from http://139.78.48.197/utils/getfile/collection/Dissert/id/73777/filename/74468.pdf

LinkedIn. (2013). About us. Retrieved from http://www.linkedin.com/about-us

Matthews, K. (2012, April 18). Should teachers and students be Facebook friends? NBC News. Retrieved from http://www.today.com/id/47090194/ns/today-today_tech/t/should-teachers-students-be-facebook-friends/#.UX7RIoI3k9Y

Mazer, J.P., Murphy, R.E., & Simonds, C.J. (2007). I'll see you on "Facebook": The effects of computer-mediated teacher self-disclosure on student motivation, affective learning, and classroom climate. *Communication Education*, 56(1), 1-17.

McEachern, R.W. (2011). Experiencing a social network in an organizational context: The Facebook internship. *Business Communication Quarterly*, 74(4), 486-493.

Moran, M., Seaman, J., & Tinti-Kane, H. (2012). *How Today's Higher Education Faculty Use Social Media*. Boston, MA: Pearson.

Nishar, D. (2013, January 9). 200 million members! LinkedIn Blog. Retrieved from http://blog.linkedin.com/2013/01/09/linkedin-200-million/

Petronzio, M. (2012, October 29). The teacher's guide to Facebook. Mashable. Retrieved from http://mashable.com/2012/10/29/facebook-for-teachers/

Plopper, B.L., & Conaway, A.F. (2013). Scholastic journalism teacher use of digital devices and social networking tools in a poor, largely rural state. *Journalism & Mass Communication Educator*, 68(1), 50-68.

Ortutay, B. (2011, October 4). Facebook tops 1 billion users. *USA Today*. Retrieved from http://www.usatoday.com/story/tech/2012/10/04/facebook-tops-1-billion-users/1612613/

Roberts, D. F., & Foehr, U. J. (2005). Generation M: Media in the lives of 8–18 year-olds. *The Henry J. Kaiser Family Foundation.* Retrieved from http://www.kff.org/entmedia/7251.cfm

Roblyer, M.D., McDaniel, M., Webb, M., Herman, J., & Witty, J.V. (2010). Findings on Facebook in higher education: A comparison of college faculty and student uses and perceptions of social networking sites. *The Internet and Higher Education,* 13(3), 134-140.

Sacks, M.A., & Graves, N. (2012). How many "friends" do you need? Teaching students how to network using social media. *Business Communication Quarterly,* 75(1), 80-88.

Skiba, D. (2007). Nursing education 2.0: YouTube. *Nursing Education Perspectives,* 28(2), 100-102.

Tausche, K., & Bergman, J. (2012, May 15). As investors fawn over Facebook, poll finds user distrust, apathy. CNBC. Retrieved from http://www.cnbc.com/id/47413410

Telegraph, The. (2013, January 22). Library of Congress is archiving all of America's Tweets. *Business Insider.* Retrieved from http://www.businessinsider.com/library-of-congress-is-archiving-all-of-americas-tweets-2013-1

Telegraph, The. (2012, October 11). Average Twitter user is an American woman with an iPhone and 208 followers. Retrieved from http://www.telegraph.co.uk/technology/news/9601327/Average-Twitter-user-is-an-an-American-woman-with-an-iPhone-and-208-followers.html

Thomas, K. (2012). 'Status update': Using social media platforms as a tool for teaching political studies in senior school. *Ethos,* 20(1), 22-26.

Tsukayama, H. (2013, March 21). Twitter turns 7: Users send over 400 million tweets per day. *The Washington Post.* Retrieved from http://articles.washingtonpost.com/2013-0321/business/37889387_1_tweets-jack-dorsey-twitter

Veltsos, J.R., & Veltsos, C. (2010). Teaching responsibly with technology-mediated communication. *Business Communication Quarterly,* 73(4), 463-467.

Vie, S. (2008). Digital divide 2.0: "Generation M" and online social networking sites in the composition classroom. *Computers and Composition,* 25(1), 9-23.

Williams, J.B., & Jacobs, J. (2004). Exploring the use of blogs as learning spaces in the higher education sector. *Australasian Journal of Educational Technology*, 20(2), 232-247.

Young, J. R. (2009). Teaching with Twitter: Not for the faint of heart. *Chronicle of Higher Education*, 56(14), A1.

YouTube. (2013). Frequently asked questions. Retrieved from http://www.youtube.com/t/faq.

Chapter 3
Teaching Computational Literacy Through Game Design
Ingrid Sturgis & Todd Shurn

> The age of ubiquitous computing clearly has arrived, and computational thinking
> has become a valued and necessary intellectual commodity if one is to be literate in
> the 21st century (Way, Cassel, Pearson, Wolz, Tatar, and Harrison, 2010).

In today's pervasively connected world, it's imperative for journalists to develop computational literacy. For journalism students, it's even more critical to develop such competency because the digital revolution has demolished business models that have sustained the profession for more than a century. Despite this disruption, scholars, journalists, and computer scientists say the same technological advances can also empower a new generation of professional programmer-journalists and assist them to engage online news audiences in the process.

We address this reality by presenting an experiment in Cooperative Expertise in which Computer Science and Journalism faculty collaborate to share cross-discipline experiences and subject-matter expertise. It explores the challenge of this prototype for team-teaching cross-disciplinary game-design courses – one for journalism students and one for computer-science students. We describe the prototype collaboration, including the approach used, faculty analysis of the outcomes and the potential for future course collaborations.

The digital revolution has transformed the media, disrupting traditional methods of reporting, distribution, and news presentation. It has led to an environment where anyone can be a publisher, and where the barrier to entry for those publishers has greatly diminished. In addition, the development of high-speed Internet-connected tablets, smartphones, touch-screen displays, very large screens, and small monitors provide journalists with an evolving array of platforms to imagine, redesign, and create innovative multimedia news products.

One result of these changes is a call for schools to teach students to broaden their journalism skills to become "programmer-journalists" in order to take advantage of this ubiquitous self-publishing, technology-driven marketplace (Winer, 2011). One way to start, according to Winer, is for journalism schools to encourage students to manage their own publishing infrastructure, eventually making students more comfortable with infrastructure development.

Even now, it is clear that major and minor news organizations are tapping programmer-journalists to produce multimedia stories that incorporate reporting, analytical data, and relevant social media. For example, traditional news organizations like *The Washington Post* and *The New York Times* seek to hire journalists with computer-programming skills to develop tools that facilitate news aggregation, data visualization, human collaboration or crowdsourcing, and mobile computing.

Progressive journalism schools like Northwestern University's Medill School of Journalism, Media, Integrated Marketing Communications offer curriculum to train programmer to become journalists. Students admitted to these graduate programs have backgrounds in computer science, mathematics, quantitative sciences and sociology. Their common background thread is demonstrated problem-solving involving extensive data analysis. According to Flew, Spurgeon, Daniel, and Swift (2012), programmer-journalists are in demand because of several factors: Big data — the availability of large datasets released by the government, database query software, social media ubiquity, and a continually expanding digital economy. The programmer-journalist is establishing new media value, according to Francisco-Revilla (2012), by devising methods to analyze digital artifacts such as Twitter "tweets" and Facebook "likes," comments, and memes to explain complex ideas.

As a result of new media trends, today's journalism students must master traditional newsgathering skills as well as develop technical expertise to become literate in computational journalism, which involves using analytical techniques for real-time social-media parsing. Although technology has fundamentally altered the way journalists gather, create, and disseminate news, it doesn't change the central purpose of journalism, which is to provide citizens with what Kovach and Rosenstiel (2001) call the "accurate and reliable information they need to function in a free society." Consequently, programmer-developers are essential to the future of journalism.

Given the impact of these media trends on journalism careers, students can benefit from developing the logical thought patterns of computer scientists and from a better understanding of computer science's impact in the world today. In addition, researchers, scholars, and instructors must begin to define what is meant by computational fluency and how it can help improve journalism student outcomes.

This article explores an effort by two Howard University faculty members to collaborate to teach game-design to provide journalism students with a project-oriented programming experience. The class also exposed computer science and journalism students to collaborative cross-disciplinary problem solving that is prevalent in today's networked society. The course sought to incorporate techniques from technology innovation, game creation, and social media, which some scholars claim can improve student engagement (Heiberger and Junco, 2011). Through course topics, discussions, and assignments, students were immersed in the new media technology trends that have brought transformational change to journalism.

Several important takeaways can be gleaned from the outcomes of this relationship and applied to future courses and to areas of research. It is clear that this pilot can yield important results that benefit computer science and journalism students, including broadening the thinking of the instructors and their respective departments. This article describes our experience in introducing cross-disciplinary collaborative projects to nurture group innovation.

Cooperative Expertise

Cooperative Expertise is a one of three collaborative-teaching models that derive from the Distributed Expertise approach in which faculty from computer science collaborate with those from other disciplines to share knowledge and experiences that eliminate barriers to computational fluency. (Way, Cassel, Pearson, Wolz, Tatar, and Harrison, 2010). In an era when technology has had a transformative impact on disciplines from journalism to teaching to public affairs, there remains a shortage of computing expertise as enrollment has declined in computer science programs. In addition, students must learn to operate outside silos in a more matrixed environment in which teams may work on several goals.

The Distributed Expertise model can offer access to such expertise on campuses, particularly Historically Black Colleges and Universities and other colleges that may not be able to offer new courses because they experience limited resources. Those impediments may include weak course enrollment, shortage of experienced computer science faculty, or other specialized expertise. Today, faculty may be able to utilize electronic solutions to solve such limitations, including the use of course management systems or new media tools such as Skype or Google Hangouts to bring in specialized expertise (Way et. al., 2010).

Other models of collaboration in the Distributed Expertise approach include Remote Expert with Local Facilitator (RE), in which an expert faculty member who teaches at a one institution benefits the faculty and students at another institution. Special Resource (SR) is a format in which a faculty expert is brought in to guest lecture on a specialized topic in a regular class or through a recorded format.

According to Wolz, Cassel, Way, and Pearson (2011), the Cooperative Expertise model permits "faculty from two distinct courses identify and share expertise with faculty and students in other courses to support learning goals in both courses" (p. 333). Each instructor takes a turn serving as a facilitator, and students benefit from exposure to the concepts of the collaborative relationship as well as sharing subject matter expertise. All three models offer research and teaching innovation. Wolz et. al. acknowledged the trends in team teaching, interdisciplinary collaboration, and the expansion of computing into all disciplines, and offered a roadmap for faculty members to follow in introducing this concept to the Howard campus.

For the purpose of this chapter, the Cooperative Expertise example focused on two Howard University instructors who were on the same campus but in different disciplines and with different expertise. Two upper-level courses are described: A Game Engine Programming course for computer science majors and a multimedia News Game design course for communications students.

This project fit with Howard University's strategic planning efforts as outlined in its Presidential Commission on Academic Renewal (PCAR):

- To promote new interdisciplinary programs;
- To encourage all students to conduct research;
- To infuse technology thoroughly into its teaching and learning processes; and
- To enhance student learning by developing pedagogies that will take advantage of new and emerging technologies (Howard University, 2010).

The gaming course also dovetailed with a collaborative effort by Arts & Science, Communications, and Engineering faculty to develop a cutting-edge interactive media and gaming undergraduate curriculum. It would include a professional certificate training program and innovative research center for the study of interactive media and gaming.

Background

The project received support from a National Science Foundation CPATH: Distributed Expertise grant that is a collaboration with Villanova University, Virginia Tech, and The College of New Jersey (TCNJ). The CPATH Distributed Expertise Project started in 2008. Its goal was to diffuse computer expertise across disciplines, as well as to develop resources to support the exploration of computing and its impact on other disciplines. According to co-Principal Investigator Associate Professor Kim Pearson of The College of New Jersey:
Part of our vision is that this could be a way of providing CS expertise to disciplines that are becoming computing dependent, such as journalism, while helping CS students understand the nuances of working with content from different knowledge domains (Para. 4).

The CPATH support allowed Howard University faculty to plan and develop the Cooperative Expertise project. It was piloted as a directed study course in spring 2012, with a four-student subgroup. (Originally, the group included two journalism majors, one public relations major, and two computer science majors. One journalism student later dropped the course.) Each instructor was responsible for his or her course, including developing its content, assignments, and grades, and retained responsibility for syllabus and course administration. The instructors used separate syllabi appropriate for the accredited course descriptions.

The computer science students were enrolled in Game Engine Programming, a computer science course; and journalism students were enrolled in a course called News Game. The four-student interdisciplinary team worked collaboratively using Scratch, a visual-programming language developed by Massachusetts Institute of Technology to teach computing skills to middle school students. Scratch can be used to create computer games, interactive stories, graphic artwork, and computer animation with music and other sound effects.

The News Games class explored the emergence of games as a tool for journalistic storytelling. Students analyzed other games and learned to use the genre as a news storytelling technique. Students also examined how gaming techniques were being incorporated in public relations and marketing campaigns. The course ultimately focused on two things:

1. Discovering, documenting, and evaluating the design components of a variety of games in news, public relations, and education.
2. Learning to use Scratch to create a simple game based on the Associated Press Style Book.

The journalism team was tasked to develop an Associated Press style game for instructional use. The resulting game's story line featured a college-student band traveling to gigs during spring break. The Scratch characters moved from one place to the next on a map of the United States when a player successfully answered the AP style question. The journalism students also generated specific questions related to the theme, and researched design elements such as music, background images, and sprites. The computer science students were to help build it. The journalism students were to contribute 10 multiple-choice questions each, but the number was cut to five questions as it became clear that programming character movements in Scratch was more time consuming than expected. The class emphasized the value in journalism students being able to experience the type of thinking computer science requires — a very specific, step-by-step problem solving. The combined class met once each week for a 90-minute session. The computer science students were part of a larger class that was assigned to subgroups to complete various projects.

The goal of the project was not only to integrate emerging technologies into the journalism curriculum, but also to help journalism students become familiar with the culture of the computer science and to understand core computing concepts through the use of Scratch programming language. News Game also was conceived to help improve student engagement in learning to appropriately use Associated Press style. The project sought to test whether the use of gaming technology would motivate students to acquire and apply knowledge to become better editors and journalists. The ultimate goal was to improve student persistence, which would lead to mastery of AP style and more success in editing.

The Associated Press style was used because some faculty members have more or less discovered that some students did not learn the basics by the time they were enrolled in the upper-level copy-editing course taken by juniors and seniors. Although some publications, like *The New York Times* and *The Washington Post*, have developed their own guidelines, a basic knowledge of AP style is an important editorial skill required to work in most newsrooms, public relations, and advertising jobs. This knowledge gap could severely affect student outcomes in the copy-editing course as well as have a negative impact on the quality of student portfolios, resumés, and job applications prepared by seniors as they entered the journalism job market.

The course also endeavored to provide journalism and computer science students an opportunity to collaborate. The computer science students were to contribute technical guidance and programming expertise and the journalism students were to provide journalistic ideas, writing, research, editing, and promotional expertise. Neither journalism student had experience in developing games or writing code, nor prior knowledge of game design or programming. No prior knowledge of Associated Press style was required. This course was an intermediate option or elective for communications students.

As part of the course, journalism students had a number of assignments and deliverables that took them through the game creation process. They were required to keep a weekly game journal that described the features of various games that they researched and the game mechanics involved in creating the game. They developed directions for a board game as well as explored basic game-creation concepts. The final project proposal included a storyboard, directions, and sprite characters, as well as Associated Press rules in a multiple-choice format. They also developed a prototype for the final game.

Other student outcomes for the course included: being able to describe fundamental principles of game design; being able to discuss the ethical challenges related to the development of news games; and being able to develop a demonstrated ability to collaborate within a small, interdisciplinary team to design, implement, test, and evaluate small computer games to a degree appropriate to the student's academic background.

On the computer science team, participating students were part of a larger course called Game Engine Programming, which was a technical elective course emphasizing the coding constructs, framework, and assets necessary to create an original game. Course prerequisites for students included Computer Science III and junior standing. The students who enrolled were expected to be familiar with Java, C++, C#, Visual Studio, and Eclipse. The course curriculum contained ABET-accredited computer science core and advanced content for algorithms, data structures, programming languages, and software design.

Typically, Howard University computer science students graduate without ever enrolling in a course requiring software development as a member of a team with non-computer science students. This exclusively computer science perspective does not prepare students for the cross-disciplinary approach adopted by many successful, creative organizations. It is especially unrepresentative of the computer and video-game industry where programmers are just one element of a creative team.

In today's matrixed work environment, an employee may work on multiple projects at the same time as part of different teams that are managed by different project managers. Wolz et. al. (2011) said it is crucial that computer science students get out of their silos to gain experience working as part of a team to develop the soft skills needed for the complex organizational structure that requires employees who can effectively communicate with other members of the team.

Recognizing this reality, collaborative game projects were established with journalism students to develop scripted, story-driven games and interactive media. The class met for 90 minutes twice per week with typically one class per week conducted jointly with computer science and journalism students. There were six Game Engine Programming students. Four of whom were able programmers that had participated in programming competitions, while the other two were less capable. One was a struggling computer-science major, and the other was a senior mechanical-engineering student with limited programming skill. All the students were motivated to take the course because of their love of video games. The computer science students were responsible for three course assignments: game play review, an original game created for competition submission, and Kinect Sensor routine.

Students in both classes were required to participate in the game review event, the HU Roast and Toast, a scripted live event for students, faculty, and interested gamers conducted in the School of Communications screening room. The students reviewed selected console games (PS3, Wii, Xbox) for their story, graphics/audio, controller interface, and future extensions. Among games reviewed were Batman: Arkham City, Soul Caliber 5, Call of Duty: Modern Warfare 3, Elder Scrolls V: Skyrim, Dance Central 2 and Assassin's Creed: Revelations, Just Dance 3, and Dance Central 2. These game reviews were designed to help the computer science students to develop the skills of critique.

Game Engine students were assigned to create a game for submission to the Microsoft Imagine Cup or the ESA National STEM Video Game Challenge. They also were assigned to create an original routine using the Microsoft Kinect Sensor API. The routines were a sequence of motion-captured Kinect Sensors with associated scores, but not complete games or game concepts. Game Engine students were introduced to the Kinect Sensor API through Visual Studio using examples discussed in detail during class sessions. These examples were extended to become the basis for their Kinect Sensor routines.

Student outcomes for the computer science students in Game Engine Programming included:

- Recognizing the value in collaboration with journalism students.

- Working efficiently and creatively with students from other majors.
- Seeking students from relevant non-computer science majors to participate in game projects and competitions.
- Collaborating across disciplines to develop game and interactive products.

In order to begin planning for our Cooperative Expertise pilot project, the faculty members conducted two telephone meetings over winter break to define the goals of the collaboration. Admittedly, this pilot project was very ambitious. Not only did it seek to impart computational thinking and design skills in journalism students with no technology background, but it also sought to test the theory that the game created for the course would encourage more students to become proficient in AP style. In addition, it would seek collaboration between two groups of student with ordinarily little in common. Our over-arching objective was to examine how a journalism course and a computer science course could be coordinated to enhance learning and support faculty expertise in an interdisciplinary manner through the development of deliverables — a Scratch game that teaches Associated Press style and development of the scripted live event HU Roast and Toast.

As part of the planning, the faculty members collaborated on course activities for two separate classes. The Game Engine Programming course for computer science students and the News Game for journalism students met jointly each week during the spring 2012 semester. Course activities included computer science students mentoring and teaching Scratch to the journalism students. The journalism students researched and created the storyboard and script for the game. The four-person team worked collaboratively with Scratch programming language to develop a game. The journalism students were also charged with promoting the Roast and Toast event as well as editing videotape from the event.

At the end of the semester, we were anxious to synthesize our experiences in the pilot project. In post-mortem discussions and retrospective analysis, we discussed what we thought worked and what did not. We both emphasized the value of the journalism students experiencing the type of thinking computer science requires — very specific, step-by-step problem solving. The computer science students likewise had an opportunity to enhance their creativity and soft skills as well as gain experience working in a matrixed environment. Both groups of students benefited from learning more about how computational thinking has been infused in today's newsroom and in other areas of professional work.

In our assessment, a number of lessons were learned that could improve subsequent experiences in using the Cooperative Expertise model. What follows is what we feel are the most important lessons about team teaching, expectations, skill development, and student collaboration to deliver a successful cooperative expertise project.

Team Teaching and Expectations

The project course was planned over winter break and instructors communicated by phone but not in person. Both instructors conceded that a closer face-to-face collaboration to define parameters of the course, opportunities for enrichment, and articulation of combined goals would have resulted in better outcomes for student collaboration. Because neither instructor was familiar with the other's teaching style, nor each other's disciplines, it was difficult to anticipate ambiguous patches, and sometimes expectations were unmet. Our goals may have been too ambitious for the journalism students and the projects too complex for students who did not have a technology background. Similar to what Wolz, Ault, and Nakra discovered in their Cooperative Expertise project, perhaps our expectation that the students complete a fully functioning AP style game was off the mark. Instead, the game in our project was the vehicle to teach the computational concepts. According to that consideration, our project was successful.

But as Eisen and Tisdell (2002) noted, our interaction with the students and each other created an environment that offered multiple meaningful perspectives that could lead to new knowledge being created. In fact, we have decided to continue to participate in developing interdisciplinary courses. We are also working to develop research opportunities based on our experience in the Cooperative Expertise model. Computer Science and Journalism faculty will continue to develop curriculum to prepare effective programmer-journalists. Imbedded in the computer science and journalism curriculums will be joint class sessions, projects, and competition submissions. In the future, in addition to improving the student collaboration process, we will seek to develop improved assessment tools to foster collaboration among reluctant students.

Skill Building

Although News Game's syllabus was modeled on an existing gaming course, adjustments had to be made for a smaller class size and for journalism students. Faculty also reviewed several Scratch games to demonstrate the attributes of the software to journalism students. It was apparent that previous knowledge of basic programming or an intense Scratch boot camp would have been more helpful for the journalism students. In looking back on the project, the students did deliver a game based on the AP style that was created in Scratch, but the students reverted to their silos with the journalism students producing the creative content and the computer science students building the game incorporating the creative content. In the end, both groups of students were able to deliver on the project, but it was not clear that they benefited as much as they could from the collaborative efforts.

However, it was clear that the students from both groups were reluctant to collaborate inside and outside the classroom environment. Journalism students were encouraged to seek one-on-one Scratch assistance from the computer science students, yet they hesitated to do so. Similarly the computer science students were expected to engage in peer-to-peer Scratch interaction with journalism students. Neither group attempted to collaborate outside class sessions. Male-female differences may have had some impact on collaboration, as the two female journalism students seemed hesitant about working with the all-male cohort of computer science students with programming expertise. In addition, because game development was novel to the journalism students, they may have been unsure what questions they needed answered in order to implement in their game concepts in Scratch.

Team-building Exercises

The two classes convening once per week for joint sessions would have benefited from ice-breaking exercises to get to know one another on a more personal level prior to starting course projects. Such exercises might have resulted in improved communication and collaboration. Cross-disciplinary teamwork was not a component of the Game Engine programming course grade. As such, even though teamwork was promoted and encouraged, it did not a have meaningful impact on the computer science students' games. Computer science students didn't collaborate with the journalism students for any project. The computer science students didn't seek the journalism student's input about their XNA or even producing the video with the journalism students who had documented expertise. The "go it alone" approach resulted in less functionality in their projects.

Conclusion

The Cooperative Expertise model is a valuable tool in helping to infuse computational thinking among college journalism students. The opportunity to work with computer science colleagues who view the communications profession from another perspective has been helpful in understanding the technological changes happening in society. As professors coming from different disciplines, we were able to see new opportunities for collaboration as well as gain another perspective on the range of skills that students need to be successful in today's work environment. Some potential limitations included difficulties in scheduling classes that met at the same time and having them cross-listed in the school catalog.

We, however, made some assumptions about collaboration by the students that did not bear out. A key concern was the balancing individual responsibility with group collaboration that required the computer science students to tutor the journalism students to learn Scratch and the journalism students to deliver the content and other assets to build the game with the computer science students. We did not foresee the cultural differences between the journalism and computer science students. Also, while we assumed students were receiving an immersive experience by dint of their working together in the same room, that may not have been true in practice. Student efforts did not meet our pedagogical goals of student cross-discipline collaboration nor sharing of subject-matter expertise. In the end, the two teams reinforced typical undergraduate tendency toward individualistic behavior.

References

Anderson, C.W. (October 26, 2011). *Notes Towards an Analysis of Computational Journalism.* HIIG Discussion Paper Series No. 2012-1. Available at SSRN:http://ssrn.com/abstract=2009292 or http://dx.doi.org/10.2139/ssrn.2009292

Buskirk, E. V. (2010, April 7). Will Columbia-trained, code-savvy journalists bridge the media/tech divide? Wired.com. Retrieved from http://www.wired.com/business/2010/04/will-columbia-trained-code-savvy-journalists-bridge-the-mediatech-divide

Cohen, S., Hamilton, J. T., & Turner, F. (2011). Computational journalism *Communications of the ACM*, 54(10), 66-71.

Cronk, M. (2012). Using gamification to increase student engagement and participation in class discussion. *World Conference on Educational Multimedia, Hypermedia and Telecommunications*, Vol. 2012 (1), pp. 311-315.

Diakopoulos, N. (2010, January). A functional roadmap for computational journalism. [Online]. Retrieved from http://www.nickdiakopoulos.com/2011/04/22/a-functional-roadmap-for-innovation-in-computational-journalism/

Eisen, M. J., & Tisdell, E. J. (2002). Team teaching: the learning side of the teaching-learning equation. *Essays on Teaching Excellence*, 2002-03, 14. Retrieved from http://cte.udel.edu/sites/cte.udel.edu/files/u7/v14n6.htm

Flew, T., Spurgeon, C., Daniel, A., & Swift, A. (2012). The promise of computational journalism. *Journalism Practice*, 6(2), 157-171.

Francisco-Revilla, L. (2012, June). Digital libraries for computational journalism. In Proceedings of the 12th ACM/IEEE-CS joint conference on Digital Libraries (pp. 365-366). ACM.

Heiberger, G. & Junco, R. (2011). Thriving in academe: Reflections on helping students learn. *NEA Higher Education Advocate.* Retrieved from http://blog.reyjunco.com/pdf/ HeibergerJuncoNEA.pdf

Howard University. (2010). *Presidential Commission on Academic Renewal, Defining the Future: Enriching the Ground on Which We Stand.* Retrieved from http://pcar.howard.edu/PCAR/Reports/PCAR-Executive-Report-6-4-10-final.pdf Washington, D.C.: Thornton, Alvin.

Kirchhoff, S. M. (2009). The US newspaper industry in transition: CRS report for congress. *Congressional Research Service*, report, 7-5700.

Pearson, Kim (2010, January 6). *Distributed Expertise in Enhancing Computing Education With Connections to the Arts.* [blog post]. Retrieved from: http://pearson.net/?p=552

Pulimood, S. M., Shaw, D., & Lounsberry, E. (2011, March). Gumshoe: A model for undergraduate computational journalism education. In Proceedings of the 42nd ACM technical symposium on Computer science education (pp. 529-534). New York, NY: ACM.

Rosenstiel, T., & Kovach, B. (2007). *The Elements of Journalism: What Newspeople Should Know and the Public Should Expect, Completely Updated and Revised.* New York, NY: Three Rivers Press.

Sandford, R., Ulicsak, M., & Facer, K. (2006). Teaching with Games: using computer games in formal education. *Futurelab, Bristol.* Retrieved from http://media.futurelab.org.uk//resources/documents/lit_reviews/Serious-Games_Review.pdf

Way, T., Cassel, L., Pearson, K., Wolz, U., Tatar, D., & Harrison, S. (2010). A Distributed Expertise Model for Teaching Computing Across Disciplines and Institutions. Unpublished paper presented at the International Conference on Frontiers in Education: Computer Science and Computer Engineering, Las Vegas, NV.

Winer, D. (2011, January 24). [blog post]. Retrieved from http://www.niemanlab.org/2011/01/dave-winer-how-can-universities-educate-journo-programmers/

Wolz, U., Ault, C., & Nakra, T. M. (2007). Teaching game design through cross-disciplinary content and individualized student deliverables. *Message from the Program Committee Chair*, 8.

Wolz, U., Cassel, L. B., Way, T., & Pearson, K. (2011). Cooperative expertise for multidisciplinary computing. In proceedings of the 42nd ACM technical symposium on computer science education, Dallas, Texas, 9-12 March, (pp. 329-334). New York, NY: ACM.

Chapter 4
Social Media and Critical Pedagogy
Kehbuma Langmia & Stella-Monica Mpande

The dawn of social media communications has revolutionized inter-human communication in a way that has surpassed the predictions of Marshall McLuhan's dictum that the medium is the message (McLuhan and Fiore, 1967; Stevenson, 2010, Strate, 2010). The Internet revolution may reshape the world in a more radical way than the industrial revolution of 1830. During the industrial revolution, lives were changed. People who were using rudimentary methods of farming certainly resisted new mechanical ways of transforming agriculture and succeeded, but were soon overpowered by the strength of the wave. They soon had to make a choice: either adopt these new technological practices and transform their lifestyles, or resist the changes and incur irreversible costs in a dynamic global economy. The same is happening with the Internet revolution and more especially with social media technology (Trippi, 2008).

Some teachers or professors have expressed resistance and cynicism about the use of social media and its effects on cognitive development and performance in students. However, social media use is not diminishing at any rate; in fact, the use has even been implemented in some curricula. Hence, teachers must embrace opportunities to use social media technology within pedagogical contexts to develop critical thinker-scholars, thus enhancing both teaching and learning practices.

As professors, some of us are yelling at our college students who have embraced social media technology and have transferred its unique, communicative verbal and non-verbal expressions into the classroom and work.

Verbally, these students have almost re-created a new language, as they send and respond to our messages with abbreviations like, "LOL," "BTW- r u in ur office tmrw?", "OMG- gr8 article, Prof!", and more. Students are pushing us to standardize short forms of writing, which they even apply in formal essays, tests, and other assignments. Non-verbally, their attitudes and body language reflect an occasional lack of ease, boredom, and frustration toward teachers who are still stuck in older, more traditional forms of communication and lecturing.

In the 21st century, there is pressure for us, as educators, to keep up with the times. Whether we appreciate social media technology as a blessing, or reject it as a curse, this new technological form does, and will, affect our lives. We should either swim with them or be drowned (Palfrey and Gasser, 2008) in our traditional, conventional forms of reasoning and writing — just as the skeptics of the industrial revolution.

In anticipation that many of us will choose to swim with our students in this new Internet wave, teachers' use of social media must develop students' critical thinking by considering the following variables that affect the process: deconstruction of meaning and language use (epitomized by applications of Jacques Derrida's deconstruction techniques), intercultural dynamics, learning curve differences, identity formation, and perceptions of technology use in classrooms. These factors present challenges that teachers and students must manage effectively when engaging social media in critical pedagogy. Ultimately, college students will become more technologically equipped and empowered to thrive in a highly connected global society as competent, critical leaders.

Critical Thinking and Deconstruction of Meaning

The students we teach need a critical understanding, evaluation, and conscious application of social media communications. When consciously done, meaningful messages meant for the general public are directed accordingly. Critical thinking can only be present when deconstruction is employed: 1) knowing the sender of the message through the photograph attached to the message, and 2) in the absence of the photograph, the self-designed identity encryption will be used to know the sender of the message. If both of these features are not enough for the receiver to guess the so-called author of the message (Person X), he/she is left at the mercy of deducing the content of the message through "proper" language use — with or without abbreviations like "LOL, BTW, OMG, etc." When the abbreviated words outweigh the conventional language use, the reader is left with guesswork and deconstruction fails to manifest itself. Ultimately, critical thinking is lost as the reader is more confused.

Jacques Derrida believed in the 1930s that the only process to fathom meaning through texts was through deconstruction. Deconstruction to him is the key to "uncovering" the multi-facet meanings embedded in a language. Eighty years after Derrida we now swim in the ocean of virtual media communication using different forms of language.

Deconstruction of Meaning and Language Use

In the mid-20th century, Ferdinand de Saussure, French socio-linguist, asserted that meaning can only be discerned through language — not through individual word choice, but through the ensemble of its totality (de Saussure and Perry, 2011). Nothing exists outside of language. It is a locked system. This implies that any information to be learned about a human being is only through the construction of symbols that form the language; nothing else. In other words, the meaning of these symbols, signs, and linguistic terms is derived solely by their existential relationships to other terms. One's being is solely dependent on language and parole. Hence, de Saussure's view limited the understanding of a human being because he or she was "defined" through terms that existed solely in relation, or in opposition, to each other. Without those surrounding terms, a person "existed" as an empty space, a vacuum, and, essentially, an abstract of an entity with no "concrete identity."

However, we are no longer dealing with the medium of communication, but the media; the focus is no longer about the "message," but the "messages." These messages are transmitted through a given language. But whose messages? And for what purposes? The question of coding and decoding messages on this multifarious media has assumed a different meaning beyond the Shannon-Weaver simple model of sender-receiver and feedback, meaning constructions have become complicated because each medium has developed its own unique coding and decoding mechanism.

Consequently, de Saussure's (2011) notion was quickly dismissed by subsequent scholars like Roland Barthes, who introduced the concepts of "signifier" and "signified." He launched the post-structuralist view that was to be closely followed by others, including Michel Foucault and Derrida. Unlike de Saussure (2011) who restricted "meaning" to linguistic terms, signs, and symbols, Barthes introduced the fluidity of the relationship between the signifier and the signified when language use is concerned, in addition to other concepts of communication theory.

Hence, intersecting Barthes' and Derrida's contributions to communication theory further expounds how the level of fluidity in the relationship between the signifier and the signified invariably affects the deconstruction of meaning, resulting in different interpretations of language use. In traditional communication platforms, the fluidity of the relationship between the signifier and the signified may be evident between teacher and student; any resulting miscommunication may also be managed on cue. Managing such fluidity, however, presents a greater challenge between these two parties in social media communication.

Language Use and Social Media

In the context of social media, multiple signifiers and multiple signifieds convolute and blur meaning. The advent of short forms, emoticons, nonverbal character representations on YouTube; "#," "D," and "@" tags for Twitter; and abbreviations like OMG, wall posts, extended hyperlinks on Facebook, Twitter, and other platforms now constitute new forms of communication. These developments now haunt language and meaning through the social media that is akin to Foucaultian's notion of discourse (Foucault, 1982) from the post-structuralist perspective.

Language and symbols use especially in Twitter, Facebook, and YouTube are multifarious. For instance, With Twitter, # tags when used can transmit your messages to multiple consumers, some of whom are not present in your sphere of interaction. For direct messages to the intended parties, @ tags are used. But on most modern keyboards, these symbols are close together above the numbers 2 and 3 strike keys on the American English keyboards. Imagine the damage from a mistake on these keyboards it can do to the receiver (s) of the messages. Who are the recipients of messages on Twitter when the sender uses # tags, as opposed to @ or "D" tags? There are multiple, indirect message recipients for the former and direct message recipients for the latter. But what happens when the @tag message is read by multiple recipients or a mistake is made between "D" (direct message) and @ (direct but not direct)? We can apply Barthes' concept to conclude that in such a scenario, the relationship between the signifier and the signified becomes complicated and, perhaps, would eventually become damaged.

A good example is the mistake caused by a tweet message by Roland Martin about gays and lesbians that led to his job suspension. His FtF apologies to CNN executive and multiple radio and TV appearances to try and retract his statement were fruitless (Stelter, 2012).

Unidentified signifiers and signifieds, including the misappropriation of language and symbol use, have all resulted in complicated relationships and varying degrees of irreparable damage. Social media language transmission cannot be retracted, lives can be lost, and personality damage control can take forever. For example, many users have "un-friended" followers on Twitter and Facebook. Sometimes face-to-face relationships are severely affected (Haslett, 2012) because of that. There have also been multiple cases of bullying and harassment on social media (Cloud, 2010; Alcindor, 2012; O'Keeffe and Clarke, 2011; Yardi and Bruckman, 2011; Agatston, Kowalski, and Limber, 2007).

Social Media and Deconstruction of Meaning

These cases, therefore, reinforce the necessity of teacher's and student's education on how to deconstruct messages from social media platforms, especially Twitter. To echo Marshall McLuhan, Twitter is a medium. That medium is different from the radio, television, or newspaper language use. Language use for these traditional media is almost identical to conventional language use. But Twitter has changed that format and has introduced a new format of writing on that platform that warrants its own dictionary and textbook to be taught across the curriculum. Twitter used does not respect discipline. Ordinary people in the natural sciences and social sciences and the humanities use Twitter and have to conform to the #-tag, @ tag, LOL, and BTW phenomenon. Failure to comply will result in non-transmission or wrong transmission, as already discussed. When properly directed to the right audience or the right recipient, then critical thinking to unravel the hidden meanings can be done through Derrida's deconstruction using the following procedures:

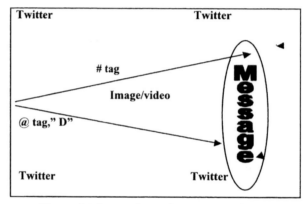

Figure 4.1 Interactive twitter communication

The sender and receiver of tweets act interchangeably. Their roles quickly reverse, as they tweet back and forth. The messages they transmit may be composed of texts/images/video. By the time the receiver is watching the video or gleaning meaning from the images uploaded and the texts that accompany them, tons of other texts have already been transmitted by the same sender or other sender/receiver who are privy to that information.

At this point, critics that oppose social media as a critical educational tool may argue that the feedback of these texts and messages are usually not well thought through because there is no depth of thought. There has been little time for reflection, especially when it is synchronously transmitted. They may further elaborate that language use on Twitter, for instance, has limited characters. Hence, meaning is limited to these few symbols and characters, which would support de Saussure's model of meaning construction.

However, this argument is flawed because information of these 140 characters can be expanded through links and attachments, enabling the student to seek additional information. Language use on Facebook and YouTube can also be expanded to include photographs, links to multiple texts, and attachments of data with more megabytes, which include video and still images.

The critics' argument ensues: given the enormity of such online information and the pace at which content is sent and received, what kind of feedback reflects critical thoughts that show the sender/receiver is well-versed with the issue at hand?

The teacher's challenge, therefore, is to deconstruct massive chunks of social media content into manageable proportions for students to digest more easily, so that they critically understand their various roles, responsibilities, and dynamics within contexts of intercultural, group and mass-related communication.

So when does the process of critical thinking for the social media consumer manifest itself through all these platforms in a diverse classroom setting?

Social Media and Critical Intercultural Thinking

The concept of critical thinking has various interrelated and sometimes divergent interpretations. The debate on critical thinking started from antiquity to Plato, Aristotle, and John Dewey et. al. The debate continues today, especially with respect to pedagogy. Portelli (1994) asks some puzzling questions: "Can critical thinking be taught? Are critical thinking and teaching critically, the same?" (p. 137). To think critically presupposes a rational and objective assessment or evaluation of a given concept or phenomenon. The rationalization can only be achieved if the respondent (teacher) has an overwhelming reservoir of knowledge to challenge an issue at hand. To provide a critical thinking response implies that one (student) can provide a balanced argument from all angles with requisite knowledgeable background to the issue under discussion. Therefore, for such a dynamic process and exchange of critical thinking development to occur between a teacher and student, both teacher and student must connect at a level playing field, where they both have sufficient, requisite content about subject matter in their knowledge banks. The student not only draws from the teacher's bank, but also challenges its content vis-à-vis the issue at hand.

In the era of globalization, teachers must first consider how intercultural dynamics would especially affect this level playing field. The modern classroom setting reflects Marshall McLuhan's "global village," representing a diverse array of cultural backgrounds and learning styles that contribute to a complex teaching and learning experience.

To effectively navigate such diversity in the classroom, teachers should consider potential challenges that may hinder their ability to develop their students as critical thinkers, with respect to new technologies. Some challenges include: the digital divide, preferences of Internet use amongst different nations, ideological differences of learning environments, government censorship, disparities in the learning curve of technology use, as well as the varying perceptions of smartphone use in a classroom setting.

The Digital Divide

Some students may approach the Internet and technological innovations of social media with trepidation if they have been affected by the digital divide in their home countries. While income differentials account for the 53.4 percent gap in personal computer use between the United States and Sub-Saharan Africa, differences of telecommunication infrastructure account for 40.7 percent of the gap (Chin and Fairlie, 2004). Consequently, most developing countries, for instance, rely more on mobile phones than on the Internet (Lallana, n.d.).

However, the limited features on these mobile phones generally do not include Internet capable "smartphones," further restricting the use of these phones to a few basic functionalities. For instance, mobile phones in the Philippines are used primarily for sending and receiving text messages, which are of low cost to the citizens and require less bandwidth and time to transmit (Rafael, 2010, p. 404).

On another note, the digital divide may still present complications for individuals who may have equal access to the Internet, yet access it differently. In a 2003 study that measured the impact of the digital divide amongst college students and high school students, those with more education (college students) were better equipped to navigate and use the Internet for content retrieval to facilitate decision-making and engagement that pertained to political, professional, social, and educational purposes, and less entertainment (Robinson, DiMaggio, and Hargittai, 2003).

International Differences in Internet Use

For international students, or those of the Diaspora, the Internet replaces Habermas' public sphere with a modern-day version of a multinational, virtual public space that fosters political debate and nationalism. Bernal (2006) describes how the Eritrean Diaspora have utilized the Internet to particularly engage in political discourse and actively mobilize resources to address the needs of their country's development. In addition to engaging in political discourse, cyber communities like MyCopticChurch.org and TibetBoard also educate the Diaspora about their cultural and religious traditions and discuss how they negotiate their "authentic" and hybrid identities (Brinkerhoff, 2009). Results of Robinson, DiMaggio, and Hargittai's (2003) study, as mentioned above, may support how the political engagement of these students would impact their performance in the classroom.

In countries like China, the Internet fulfills social needs more for users than it does their commercial needs (Yang, 2008). Hence, e-commerce would not be prioritized as much as in other countries. However, in the United States, the growth of e-commerce, facilitated by high Internet connectivity with tablets, smartphones and other innovative forms of social media account for the 12.6% increase of online retail sales to $176.2 billion in 2010 and an anticipated value of $278.9 in 2015 (Indvik, 2011). Consequently, students who generally use social media for social networking purposes may approach more professional, educational, or commercially related applications of social media differently, especially if courses are of a certain discipline.

Ideological Differences of Learning Environments

Differences of learning styles and environments between China and the United States further epitomize clashes between Western ideologies and with non-Western ones, particularly with issues related to globalization and modern technology. Baruth and Manning (1992) contrast Asian students that are more used to formal, structured, quiet learning environments, from American students, whose academic atmospheres and relationships with teachers are more informal (Feng, 1994, "How Do They Differ," para. 3).

A study by Zhao, Kuh, and Carini (2005) revealed senior international students' higher levels of engagement in academic work, technology use, and diversity-related programs, in contrast to American students, who participated more in active, collaborative learning environments (Zhao et.al., 2005, p. 10).

Government Censorship

Government control of the telecommunications industry varies across different nations, thus influencing the frequency, use, and types of content accessible to different students and their potential to employ social media as a critical learning tool. In some countries, like China, various websites, including those of social networking and other portals must comply with government controls and standards to maintain their business credibility (MacKinnon, 2009). Websites, including blogs, that are hosted both domestically and internationally and contain content that violates national regulations are filtered, blocked, and deleted by government censors and private companies in China (MacKinnon, 2009).

The rise of the Arab Spring has transformed the use of social media amongst users in various Arab countries, with Twitter launching its first Arabic interface in 2012. Increased use of Internet and social media amongst users have also resulted in increased censorship and stringent laws by Arab governments to arrest citizens, whose online content is perceived to be a threat (CIMA, Social Media in the Arab World). Hence, personal experiences with Internet monitoring may account for some students' hesitation to engage in some forms of social media use, particularly for politically sensitive research that may conflict with their home country.

Overall, teachers should be critically aware that social media is used differently for students of different cultures because of various influences that impact how they approach social media.

Learning Curve Disparities

Lastly, another challenge that teachers face in developing critical thinking skills of their students occurs when social media becomes a new mode of communication for the teachers. If the student is technologically savvy, then teachers must also increase their own learning curves on social media and "catch up" to their students. Teachers have to become well versed with the technology before making the students use them critically.

Lam (2000) and Kessler (2010) offer that teachers' hesitations and insecurities with technology reduce their use of social media technology in classrooms. Instead, teachers should regard critically the evolution of technology as having an impact on writing expectations and practices of students (Kessler, 2012, p. 226).

Teachers trained to become proficient with technology could incorporate technology in lessons to represent the dynamics, cadences, and nuances of communication from the real world (Kessler, 2012, p. 218).

Hence, if teachers do not properly navigate and address the differences in technology adaptation and culture between themselves and students, these differences could present clashes that negatively impact the learning experience in various contexts. More specifically, these clashes could amplify the fluid relationship between the signifier and the signified, as described earlier by Barthes. Potential ambiguities in language use could lend to the convolution and blurring of meanings between sender and receiver (signifier and signified), particularly when communicating with social media.

Teachers should respond critically to various needs of the classroom to foster a conducive, rich, learning experience. With increased awareness, teachers would be better prepared to manage the wide range of technological literacy within the classroom, resulting in more effective teaching and learning experiences of critical pedagogy.

Varying Perceptions of Smartphone Use in Classrooms

Various studies have presented the controversies of students' use of cell phones in classroom settings. As many institutions do not present uniform policies regarding cell phone use, teachers' reactions have ranged from strong disapproval (Campbell, 2006; Bowman, 2012) to more moderate (Baker, Lusk, and Neuhauser, 2012). In a more recent study conducted in an Eastern university in the United States by Langmia and Glass (2013) that tested the perception of smartphone use in university classrooms, faculty members perceived students' phone use to be a distraction, especially during instances when teachers found both extreme levels of quietness and ring tones to indicate students' focus on their phone.

Consequently, preconceived biases about social media use amongst students and teachers would need to be effectively managed in order to maintain a level playing field of student-teacher interaction that also includes trust. Furthermore, teachers would also need to address students whose perception of social media use in a classroom environment may clash with their formal regard toward teachers and the educational setting.

Social Media and Socio-Cultural Identity Formation

One other vexing issue that teachers should incorporate in their curriculum, with respect to social media and critical thinking, is that of identity formation. Exploring one's identity from FtF communication dynamics already presents its own headache, given the highly complex mediated world that impacts the deconstruction of meaning. The multiple signifier and multiple signified dimensions of social media communication further exacerbate these complexities, thus rendering it more complicated than traditional media.

Hans Georg Gadamer (1976) insists that for genuine dialogue between two people or a group of people to be fruitful, they have to bracket their prejudices. Bracketing prejudices through online interactions with someone on Facebook or Twitter might present a huge challenge. Individuals have to temporarily shelve their biases of each other when engaging in interpersonal dialogue.

Others like Anthony Giddens in his Structuralization theory (Haslett, 2012) posits that identity formation has a direct correlation with culture. With the advent of the new media communication, socio-cultural context is a precursor to virtual interaction between individuals in cyberspace. Identity, according to Giddens, is a continuum and social media or any other new media communication are only a tool to facilitate the exchange. Hence, social media does not affect identity formation, according to Giddens. So where then lies the truth about self-identity in the age of new media interpersonal communications? Teachers must challenge students to critically seek these truths so that they are not victims of various distortions of identity formations (identity crises) that inadvertently occur with social media use. Also, teachers that understand how such identity crises negatively impact critical thinking development would be able to address these issues in their curricula.

Identity Crisis: Multiple Identities Formations

The reality is that multiple self-identities can, in fact, be created inadvertently during social media interactions, which is a contradiction to Giddens. When this happens the fluidity of truth resurfaces. Multiple identities create chaos and confusion and this can be exacerbated with the endless hyperlinks that are connected and reconnected to a video clip on YouTube with a single click of the mouse. That single click can then be extended to endless other interconnected videos of similar themes. This is what Kavoori (2012) has aptly called "chaining."

Kavoori's (2012) "chaining" is best epitomized through the following scenario: Imagine that I have posted a video of myself playing golf near a beautiful beach. This is a way to introduce myself to people who like golf. But when I publicize this link to people who visit my site to watch my video, they will simultaneously be exposed to a series of semantically related videos on the sidebar of YouTube, for instance, with links they can also click to view. In about 30 minutes, these viewers would be inundated with countless other images of people and places about golf — learning about them, instead of learning the most they can about me. Their inability to learn about me would prevent them from forming an identity of me (my likes and dislikes, hopes and desires, etc.) in their mind.

More specifically, these viewers no longer have an adequate amount of information about me, but have learned of me in insufficient bits and pieces, thus lessening their amount and degree of accuracy of knowledge of me in their knowledge bank. Ultimately, my identity formation in the cyber world has been distorted, reshaped, and counter shaped, and the result is that many people would leave the site with different perceptions of me and golf.

Interestingly, such an identity crisis epitomizes de Saussure's limited view on meaning and language use. By relying on de Saussure's concept of learning about one's "identity," then one would rely solely on signs and symbols (images of golf playing) that relate, oppose, or counteract other people's signs and symbols (images of golf playing). Without these other images, signs, and symbols, one's identity formation remains intact. However, such a view on the construction of meaning and identity formation is restricted and leads to inaccuracies.

Tech-savvy students have a tendency to indulge in a "video-clicking spree," which may limit their exposure to sufficient content and result in identity crises of the subject matter. This reduces their ability to develop sufficient information in their knowledge bank. As reinforced earlier, such insufficient amount of information in the knowledge bank reduces one's ability to tap into a reservoir of information and challenge or critically analyze an issue.

Identity Crisis: The Unknown Messenger- Person X

Whether one is on Linked In, Facebook, Twitter, YouTube, Flickr, or Pinterest, one can be providing another version of his/her identity to the public or to the individual. The dawn of Second Life/Avatars has made it possible for people to assume multiple personalities that have convoluted identity formation or creation through group or interpersonal dialogue.

In these cases, one is able to identify the original messenger and trace messages back to a certain Person X. However, one would not be able to identify the individual's particular name, gender, or background, which Person X may change online at any given time.

On other occasions, one may not even be able to trace the posting to any individual in particular, as his/her message has been re-tweeted, or reposted on numerous occasions on innumerable platforms. All these result in the crisis of one's obscure identity and a heightening distrust of him or her, reducing legitimacy in the sources of information. Through such lack of credibility, one is not in a position to provide strong, critical analyses of information. Students' awareness of these distortions and what it does to the reader or observer can be helpful in the short term, as well as in the long run. The conscious awareness backed by implicit critical insights on the ethics and use of social media is what is needed for the students.

Identity Crisis: When (and) Am I the Real Me?

In addition to Second Life/Avatars that have facilitated the ability for one to mask his or her identity as "Person X," an individual may find it difficult to transition from virtual reality to tangible reality. When am I "me" on the Internet? When am I the real "me" to you and when am I the real "me" to them?

Students that are engaged with social media technology for periods of time, or those seeking to relieve themselves from the stress of academics and the real world, are potential victims of cyber addiction. Avatar addiction, as epitomized in Lee's (2005) study on cyberspace addictive behavior in Korea, reveals that these addictions result in a lack of cognitive development, as well as destructive behavior (Lee, 2005, p. 49). Unhappy, stressed teenagers hide behind the fantasies of avatars to seek emancipation from strict parents, who reinforce rigorous study habits in preparation for a prestigious education at Seoul National University and a successful career (Lee, 2005, p. 50).

Robert Eller, technology consultant, concurs that the fantasies of those who seek to reinvent themselves through avatars will result in real-life manifestations, blurring virtual from reality (Anderson, 2006, "Virtual Reality," para. 3).

Identity Crisis: The "Us-ness" vs "Them-ness"

The "us-ness" and the "them-ness," which often generate the tension originally espoused by Edward Said as "Otherism," can dig a big gulf between people when referring to interaction on social media. I believe that when it comes to the sender/receiver message transactions on the social media, the "we-ness" needs to overcome the "us-ness" and the "them-ness." The "we-ness" presupposes that we are (from all cultural backgrounds) interacting in cyberspace with the same mindset as equals — the same way that we generally aspire to, as thinker-scholars in the FtF world of reality.

The use of cognition should take precedence over any hegemonic supposition, i.e., superiority/inferiority complexes. If we are using Facebook, for instance, to teach distance learning students in foreign universities in India or Africa, we should bear in mind that they too have a cognitive superiority. Hence, we should be cognizant of, and eliminate instances, when one assumes a certain technological arrogance that accompanies a dominant perspective toward various subject matter or those with whom we are communicating. We may have to rely once more on Gadamer's (1976) concept of bracketing prejudices to engage in beneficial human interactions.

We may also have to rely on Stuart Hall's interpretative codes of reading a text, reinforcing the need for one to be critical of the language and text on the social media platform. Teachers would need to challenge themselves and students, to deconstruct meanings of communication on social media and determine if they are operating within dominant-hegemonic, negotiated, or oppositional/ counter-hegemonic codes of messages (Hall, 1973, p. 136-138).

But how do we, as professors, impart this knowledge to the students when we, ourselves, are alien to these new media platforms that are constantly changing, and we have to keep pace with them?

Implementing Critical Thinking in Pedagogy

Blooms Taxonomy: This has been used widely as a template for teaching critical thinking skills in the classroom setting. The concept warrants educators to focus on a six-step process as outlined on figure 4.1 (Remembering, Understanding, Applying, Analyzing, Evaluating, and Creating):

- Remember: Teach our students to remember the different formats of writing/reading materials online;
- Understand: Teach our students to understand writing/uploading formats;
- Apply: Teach them how to apply the formats in their lives/profession;
- Analyze: Teach them to analyze online texts differently from offline texts (Roland Barthe's Semiotics (signifier/signified) Jacque Lacan and Deconstruction);
- Evaluate: Create rubrics for Evaluation, for example,Turnit.com;
- Create: Teach them how to create their own blogs, Shoot-edit-upload-distribute (Ustream), etc.

NB: Most companies only hire students who can be critical thinkers that can create and maintain Twitter, Facebook, YouTube pages for the company.

Practical Examples

Wanda Reyes (2010) teaches a public relations course using YouTube. She states that from the first day of class she makes students watch or read a news story (Remember). When that has been done, they are expected to know the newsworthy issues in their environment (Understand). For Reyes to ascertain that they remembered and are able to understand what is happening, she provides them with a series of questions in the form of a handout that will help them analyze the content of the news (Analysis). When they return to class the next day, she will have them watch a YouTube video on an identifiable problem facing an organization. Then the students browse YouTube.com and look for similar videos (Applying).

These steps are the foundations of developing students' critical thinking process. It will not be surprising to find some of the students will be motivated to shoot and upload their own video clips on issues facing their own communities and sharing them with the class or doing it as an end-of-year project (Creating). The teacher will then come up with a rubric on how to evaluate the video content.

Discussion and Conclusion

The discussion on critical thinking and social media is creating an onslaught of never-ending debate. This is a new phenomenon on the communication landscape, and we are still grappling with it. Our pedagogy is witnessing a drastic shift because of the nature of the discipline. The problem is that the concept of critical thinking was imbibed through the conventional ode of teacher-centered approach to FtF teaching that most of us learned at our various universities decades ago. The emergence of the Internet has taken us unaware because it is engulfing the educational sector and consuming a chunk of our students' meaningful time. We cannot run away from it. It haunts us because the gadgets stare us in the face in the FtF; virtual classrooms and our students are becoming "distracted" by it. As stated earlier, we either have to face this new revolution head on by becoming totally enmeshed with it, or we will face a bipolar educational generation: those who are late or non-conforming adopters and early/state-of-the-art adopters. At the cost of becoming late adopters, we, as professors, miss out on opportunities to provide a dynamic, critical learning atmosphere for our tech-savvy students in the Internet revolution of the 21st century.

References

Agatston, P. W., Kowalski, R., & Limber, S. (2007). Students' perspectives on cyber bullying. *Journal of Adolescent Health*, 41(6), S59-S60.

Alcindor, Y. (2012). States take aim at digital bullying. *USA Today*, p.1a.

Anderson, D. (2006). Elon/Pew Internet project release new study on future of the Internet. Retrieved from Elon University website: http://www.elon.edu/enet/Note.aspx?id=42431

Bernal, V. (2006). Diaspora, cyberspace and political imagination: The Eritrean diaspora online. *Global Networks*, 6(2), 161–179. Retrieved from http://www.socsci.uci.edu/~vbernal/bio/Bernal-diaspora.pdf

Chinn, M.D., & Fairlie, R. W. (2004). The determinants of the global digital divide: A cross-country analysis of computer and Internet penetration (NBER Working Paper No. 10686). Retrieved from National Bureau of Economic Research website: http://www.nber.org/papers/w10686.pdf? new_window=1

Cloud, J. (2010). Bullied to death? *Time*, 176 (16), 60-63.

de Saussure, F. & Perry, M. (2011). *Courses in General Linguistics*. New York: Columbia University Press. Feng, J. (1994). Asian-American children: What teachers should know. *ERIC Digest*. Retrieved from http://www.ericdigests.org/1994/teachers.htm

Foucault, M. (1982). The Archaeology of Knowledge and the Discourse on Language. New York, NY: Vintage Books.

Gadamer, H.G. (1976). On the scope and function of hermeneutical reflection. In D. E. Lange (Ed. and Trans.), *Philosophical hermeneutic*. Berkeley: University of California Press, pp. 18-43.

Ghannam, J. (2011). Social media in the Arab world: Leading up to the uprisings of 2011 (A Report to the Center for International Media Assistance). Retrieved from Center for International Media Assistance website:http://cima.ned.org/sites/default/files/CIMA-Arab_Social_Media-Report%20-%2010-25-11.pdf

Hall, S. (1973). Encoding/ decoding. *Encoding and Decoding in the Television Discourse* (pp. 128-138). Birmingham: Centre for Contemporary Cultural Studies.

Hasslet, B.B. (2012). A structurational interaction approach to investigating culture, identity and mediated communication. In P.H. Cheong, J. N. Martin, & L.P. Macfadyen (Eds.), *New Media and Intercultural Communication*. New York, NY: Peter Lang Publishing.

Indvik, L. (2011). Forrester: E-commerce to reach nearly $300 billion in U.S. by 2015 [STATS]. Retrieved from Mashable website: http://mashable.com/2011/02/28/forrester-e-commerce/

Kessler, G. (2012). Preparing tomorrow's second language writing teachers to use technology. In G. Kessler, A. Oskoz, & I. Elola (Eds.), *Technology Across Writing Contexts and Tasks* (pp. 213-236). Retrieved from http://lrc.cornell.edu/events/papers12/kessler.pdf

Lallana, E. (n.d.). *SMS and Democratic Governance in the Philippines.* Quenzin City: Philippines   Lee, O. (2005). Understanding cyberspace addictive behavior with the critical   social theory. *Communications of the IIMA*, 5(4), 47-52.

MacKinnon, R. (2009). China's censorship 2.0: How companies censor bloggers. *First Monday*, (14)2. Retrieved from http://firstmonday.org.htbin /cgiwrap/bin/ojs/index.php/fm/article/view/2378/2089

Makkonen, P., Siaskas, K., & Vaidya, S. (2011). Teaching knowledge management by combining wikis and screen capture videos. *Campus-Wide Information System*, 28(5), 360-366.

McLuhan, M., & Fiore, Q. (1967). The Medium is the Message: An Inventory of Effects. Boston, MA: Bantam Books.

O'Keeffe, G.S., & Clarke, K. (2011). The impact of social media on children, adolescents, and families. *Pediatrics*, 127(4), 800-804.

Palfrey, J. & Gasser, U. (2008). Opening universities in a digital era: The beginning of the end of the classroom as we know it? *New England Journal of Higher Education*, 33(1), 22-24.

Portelli, J.P. (1994). The challenge of teaching for critical thinking. *McGill Journal of Education*, 29 (2), 137-151.

Rafael, V. (2003). The cell phone and the crowd: Messianic politics in contemporary Philippines. *Public Culture*, 15(3), 399-425.

Reyes, W. (2010). Using social media to develop students' critical thinking skills. *AEJMC Hot Topics in Journalism and Mass Communication*, Retrieved from http://www.aejmc.org/topics/archives/1308

Robinson, J.P., DiMaggio, P., & Hargittai, E. (2003). New social survey perspectives on the digital divide. *IT & Society*, 1(5), 1-22. Retrieved from http://uazuay.edu.ed/bibliotecas/mbaTI/pdf/Digital%20Divide%20Social%20 Surveys.pdf

Stelter, B. (2012). CNN suspends Roland Martin for remarks on Twitter. *New York Times*, Retrieved from http://mediadecoder.blogs.nytimes.com/ 2012/02/08/cnn-suspends-roland-martin-for-remarks-on-twitter/

Stevenson, N. (2010). Marshall McLuhan and media and culture. In P. Grosswiller (Ed.), *Transforming McLuhan: Cultural, Critical and Postmodern Perspective* (pp. 17-36). New York, NY: Peter Lang Publishing.

Strate, L. (2010). Studying media as media: McLuhan and media ecology approach. In P. Grosswiller (Ed.), Transforming McLuhan: Cultural, Critical and Postmodern Perspective (pp. 67-80). New York, NY: Peter Lang Publishing.

Trippi, J. (2008). *The Revolution Will Not Be Televised Ed: Democracy, the Internet and the Overthrow of Everything.* New York, NY: William Morrow Paperbacks.

Troutner, J. (2012). Cool tools, social media, and curriculum. *Teacher Librarian*, 39(4), 48-50.

Wonacott, M.E. (2001). Technological literacy. *ERIC Digest.* Retrieved from http://www.ericdigests.org/2002-3/literacy.htm

Yardi, S., & Bruckman, A. (2011). Social and technical challenges in parenting teens' social media use. Proceedings of the 2011 annual conference on human factors in computing systems (pp. 3237-3246).

Zhao, C., Kuh, G., & Carini, R. (2005). A comparison of international student and American student engagement in effective educational practices. Retrieved from http://www.nsse.iub.edu/pdf/research_papers/international.pdf

Chapter 5
How to Do Communication Research Using Social Media Data
William B. Hart & Erica C. Taylor

This chapter offers advice on how to do communication research on social media data. We specifically cover what should be included in a quantitative research paper on social media and we illustrate our advice with a case study. As we cover each section of a research paper, we highlight aspects of the section that are specifically relevant to social media. For example, in the discussion about the methodology section we address the technical and ethical issues of using social media data. In terms of ethics, the key issue being: is a social media post private data or public? Beyond ethical issues, there are also technical issues when gathering social media data. The general purpose of the chapter is to help researchers address these and other issues and help facilitate more study of social media within communication and media research.

Drawing on the advice given in several sources, what follows is a how-to on writing a quantitative research paper on social media (American Psychological Association, 2010; Frey, L. R., Botan, C. H., Friedman, P. G., and Kreps, G. L., 1992; Galvan, 2009; Girden and Kabacoff, 2011; Keyton, 2006). For a more qualitative perspective on doing social media research see Altheide and Schneider (2013). A quantitative research paper contains a problem statement, a literature review, a methods section, a results section, and a discussion section.

Writing the Introduction or Problem Statement

The beginning of a quantitative research paper contains one or more introductory paragraphs sometimes called the problem statement. Usually there are three main objectives of the problem statement: (1) introduce the reader to the topic, (2) explain the purpose of the research, and (3) explain the significance of the research (Frey et. al., 1992). The general purpose of the research paper is to address the research "problem." The research problem could be an applied problem and revolve around a need to solve some real-world, social problem. The research problem could also be that there are inconsistencies in previous research and there is a need to resolve the inconsistencies (American Psychological Association, 2010). Another common research problem is that there is a "gap" in the research, that is, there is an important area of research that has not yet been studied, or perhaps a whole new area of research recently opened up by technological or societal advances. Lastly, the problem statement should indicate the significance of the research. How would we benefit? Who would benefit from the findings of the research?

In this chapter we use a case study on social TV to illustrate how to conduct communication research on social media data. The introductory paragraph in the social TV case study reads as follows:

> '2012 Is the Year of Must-Tweet TV' proclaimed a recent Reuters article (Shaw, 2012). In the past year, dozens of articles about social media and television viewing have appeared in TV trade publications such as *Broadcasting & Cable* and *MediaWeek*. Also, most prime-time TV dramas now include Twitter hashtags at the bottom of the screen (e.g., #thementalist), encouraging viewers to tweet about the episode. (Hart and Taylor, 2012, p. 32)

The case study paragraph above introduces the reader to the topic and suggests there is a new area of research that exists given the growth of television viewers now using social media while watching TV. To address the significance of the research, earlier in the case study, the authors also indicated that the answers to their research questions "would be of benefit to television scriptwriters and producers as well as advertisers and public relations specialists who seek to understand the viewing behaviors and the mindset of TV viewers" (p. 32).

When writing an introduction or problem statement for a social media paper, it is important to identify and explain the specific social medium under study as part of introducing the reader to the topic. The example case study presented here examines Twitter use. The perspective, tone, rationale, and results of the research may vary depending on which social media are used for data. Each social medium holds an ever-developing specific purpose in the overall arena of social media (i.e., microblogging, photo or video sharing, public commentary, etc.), and such differences need to be explained for readers.

Also, when writing an introduction or problem statement for a social media paper, there is often a need to show that there is continued growth in the use of social media. As more people use social media, there is a stronger need to understand the use. A variety of online sources can be consulted to help show significance via social media statistics. A researcher can consult the media or press pages for the social media sites, such as Facebook (http://newsroom.fb.com/) and Twitter (https://blog.twitter.com/), to find the most recent statistics on social media use. For results from independent parties, it may also be helpful to consult the annual or quarterly social media reports from research firms such as the Pew Research Center (http://pewinternet.org/topics/Social-Networking), GlobalWebIndex (http://www.globalwebindex.net), Forrester (http://www.forrester.com), and Nielsen (http://nielsen.com/us/en/reports.html). Some of the research firms provide extensive reports free of charge and some provide some reports for a fee. Another way of keeping up on the most recent social media metrics is to read and follow secondary sources like Mashable (http://mashable.com/social-media/), TechCrunch (http://techcrunch.com/social/), and Digital Trends (http://www.digitaltrends.com/social-media/).

Writing the Literature Review

After the introduction, which stresses the purpose and significance of the research, there follows the literature review. The literature review summarizes past research and based on this summary states research questions or hypotheses that will be addressed in the research paper. There are three main types of references reviewed: (1) empirical research reports usually found in journals, (2) theoretical paper or books, which evaluate or propose theory, and (3) articles or chapters that are reviews of past literature (Galvan, 2009). The references cited should be those that are "pertinent to the specific issue and not those that are of only tangential or general significance" (American Psychological Association, 2010, p. 28). If there are any gaps in past research, the author should indicate where the knowledge gaps are and how the gaps will be filled. Research questions are also found in the literature review. The research questions can appear at the end of the complete literature review or the questions can be interspersed throughout the literature review as they emerge from coverage of specific, past literature.

The academic study of social media use while watching TV is relatively new and so the social TV case study had only a few relevant empirical reports to draw upon and no relevant theoretical work or literature reviews from the academic literature. As the number of empirical reports increase, theoretical and review work will undoubtedly follow and fill in the gap:

> ... while social media are playing an increasing role in television viewing and social media are adding another layer to our television viewing conversations, there is very little research on the topic. There are two limited studies linking social media and reality television and only one study specifically analyzes what viewers tweeted while watching a TV program. This previous research analyzed about one thousand tweets each from only two programs, a live political event during and a dance competition program (Wohn and Na, 2011). This previous study analyzed about one thousand tweets each from only two programs (a live political event during and a dance competition program). The research shared here is an analysis of thousands of more tweets posted during the showing of several TV dramas. (Hart and Taylor, p. 33-34)

Out of the Wohn and Na (2011) study emerged the first research question: "RQ1: How frequently do viewers tweet while watching a show" (Hart and Taylor, p. 33)? With regards to hashtag use in social TV, the case study covered some relevant literature and a few related research questions emerged:

> Huang et. al. (2010) defined a hashtag as "the specific name for a tag in Twitter. Hashtags derive their name from the fact that they are preceded by the symbol '#', also known as a hash mark, e.g., #nowplaying" (p. 1). They also say that a tagged topic helps to not only filter tweets about a certain topic, but to help users gain awareness of the topic. They discuss individual motivation to participate in such conversations is to see ones tweets in designated stream. "Many of the [hashtags] are constructed in topic-comment format, so people who use Twitter might be interested in skimming a few dozen to a few hundred tweets offering individual (often humorous or insightful) responses." (p. 3)

> In terms of hashtagged tweets,
> RQ7: How many different hashtags used?
> RQ8: What are the most frequent hashtags (Hart and Taylor, p. 34)?

Also, in the literature review of the case study, sources related to social media involvement were covered, concluding with a relevant research question:

> Several studies have examined motivations and practices of conversational tweeting. Diakopoulos and Shamma (2010) stated, "when people tweet live about a media event they are in effect annotating. When mined for their affective content, these annotations can identify parts of the video that gained interest ..." (p. 1195). Such studies indicate another level of tweet analysis which attempts to ascertain emotional and intellectual involvement in the program based on what is said in tweets. As a means of judging the viewers' involvement in the story, this present study looks at the degree to which viewers mention main characters.
> RQ9: How often are the main characters of the drama mentioned (Hart and Taylor, p. 34)?

Advice for what to include in the literature review section includes types of articles to include and how to find relevant literature using social media. As previously mentioned, the types of sources found in a literature review fall into three types: empirical research reports, theoretical works, and literature reviews. As for literature reviews, two social media literature reviews may be helpful to include in a communication-oriented social media research paper. One is the well-cited, "classic" by boyd and Ellison (2007) titled "Social Network Sites: Definition, History, and Scholarship" and the other is a more recent review with a communication and media focus by Pérez-Latre, Blanco, and Sanchez (2011) titled "Social Networks, Media, and Audiences: A Literature Review." Although not strictly a literature review, a third article to include is "Users of the World, Unite! The Challenges and Opportunities of Social Media" that includes an often cited definition of social media (Kaplan and Haenlein, 2010). It may be helpful to define the term *social media* in the literature review section. Social media study is young, but there is a growing theoretical base. As for theoretical works, social media researchers may consider including references to the work of social media theorist like Clay Shirky (e.g., 2008, 2010).

Empirical reports can be found by searching standard databases like *Communication and Mass Media Complete*, but it may also be helpful to actually use social media to find current and relevant social media literature. General research help, including help with literature reviews, may also be found on the variety of social media accounts managed by the American Psychological Association at http://www.apa.org/about/social-media.aspx. Other general advice may be found by using Twitter hashtags like #ecrchat and #PhDchat. For information specifically on social media research, use the #socialmediaresearch hashtag. Also, on Twitter, follow social and new media experts like Clay Shirky (@cshirky), Jay Rosen (@jayrosen_nyu), and Henry Jenkins (@henryjenkins). Social media researchers may also find it helpful to subscribe to the Twitter list called "Social Media Linkers" (https://twitter.com/mashable/social-media). This Twitter list is managed by Mashable and includes the tweets of many noted social media experts.

Writing the Methods Section

The method section of a research paper describes how the research questions are answered or the hypotheses are tested. A methods section contains two parts: one describing the texts or people being studied and one describing the procedures applied to the texts or people to answer the research questions. Surveys and experiments are research methods used to study the responses of people. Textual analysis is a research method used to study texts written or produced by people. Texts can be newspaper articles, diaries, political ads, commercials, conversations, etc.

The case study on social TV used a form of textual analysis to study tweets posted about a set of television dramas. In this context, each tweet is a text.

> To answer the above questions, tweets were gathered from the 2012 season finales of five prime-time police or detective dramas across the top four TV networks (*Bones, Castle, Law & Order: SVU, The Mentalist, and NCIS*). For each drama, a sample of 900-1,000 tweets were gathered 30 minutes before the drama began, 30 minutes after the drama began (on east coast), and 30 minutes after the drama concluded (on east coast). For each of the five dramas 2,700 to 3,000 tweets were gathered for over 13,000 tweets total. A computer-assisted content analysis of the over 13,000 tweets resulted in answers to the above questions. (p. 34)

Before dealing with the technical issues involved in gathering social media data, it is important to first address ethical questions, like, are the data private or public and should the data be used? Ethics can be defined as "the principles of conduct governing an individual or a group" (ethics, 2011). What we are addressing here is the still developing principles of conduct governing what social media researchers should do with social media data. Social media research ethics is broader than just the issue of privacy, but for the sake of brevity it is the key issue highlighted in this chapter. For broader coverage we suggest social media researchers read three key sources that address ethics in the context of social media research: (1) Eckert, Walker, Hemsley, Nahon, and Mason, 2013; (2) Phillis, M. L., n.d.; and (3) Zimmer, 2010.

In 2006 researchers in sociology at Harvard gathered data from 1,700 Facebook profiles of students at an "anonymous" U.S. university. The students being studied did not give consent and did not know they were being studied. When the researchers began making their study public they were accused of breaching the students' privacy. Are social media posts private? If they are private, then consent would be required. And, even if they are "public," as many terms of service agreements legally define them, does that mean they still should be analyzed and reported in research? Do users intend for their posts to be public? As Eckert et. al. (2013) explain:

> you may have picked your nose in a public space at some point in your life. We'd suspect that you'd rather not be photographed picking your nose and then see that photograph on the front page of Reddit. Sometimes public actions aren't intended for public consumption.

If social media data are used, then ethically it is suggested that researchers should make every effort to conceal the identity of individuals and groups being studied. "Do not name the group. Paraphrase [quotes from the posts]. Disguise some information, such as institutional or organizational names. Omit details that might be harmful to individual participants" (Wimmer and Dominick, 2011, p. 82). If efforts are not made to conceal the identity, then searches on a search engine like Google may reveal the identity.

Along with ethical issues, there are also technical issues that must be dealt with. Since Facebook's terms of service does not allow automated data collection, gathering social media data from Facebook usually takes some technical skill or collaboration with those who have the technical skill. Phillis (n.d.) suggests two workarounds, however, one in which the researcher asks the study participants to download their own Facebook data and then share that with researchers or by having participants like a research page and thus giving researchers access to participant information. Unlike Facebook, Twitter does allow automated data collection with some limits. The Twitter APIs (Application Programming Interfaces) allow researchers access to Twitter data (Burgess and Bruns, 2012; Eckhert et. al., 2013). While Twitter does provide access to the data, there are important limitations. Because of upper limits on how much data can be collected and because of some technical quirks with the APIs, it is difficult to say with certainty that the tweets collected are complete or a representative sample (Burgess and Bruns, 2012; Eckhert et. al., 2013).

Another difficulty is that the API instructions are written for website developers and may require assistance from those with some technical skills.

There are some online tools and software that can assist in the collection of social media data. Eckhert et. al. (2013) developed the SoMe Lab Toolkit to help collect Twitter data. Burgess and Bruns (2012) used yourTwapperkeeper to capture and archive the tweets for their study. For specialized network studies of social media data, consult the resources at the Social Media Research Foundation (http://www.smrfoundation.org/) and also an open source application called Gephi. For a more encompassing approach to gathering social media, NVivo, a Windows-based program, can be helpful. NVivo 10 with the optional NCapture feature gathers a variety of social media posts, from Facebook posts to tweets to YouTube content. NVivo also allows researchers to automatically code the social media data and also provides data visualization tools. SAS Social Media Analytics, with a higher cost but richer features, is another option. While these social media tools are helpful, researchers should be aware that social media sites like Facebook may change their software, which may cause the social media data collection tools to stop working for days or longer. Researchers be aware (Phillis, n.d.).

Writing the Results Section

The results section of a typical quantitative research paper simply reports the results of the research, or to put it another way, it provides the answers to the research questions give earlier in the paper. Results are usually reported in the order in which the research questions were identified earlier in the research paper. Since this section is simply the reporting of the results, there is no new advice offered here relevant to social media research. The only relevant issue would be privacy issues in reporting the results, which was covered in the methods section above.

The answers to the research questions in the social TV study were as follows: RQ1: How frequently do viewers tweet while watching a show?

The results show that most viewers (76%) only tweeted once about the episode. Only 1.4% tweeted 11 or more times. These results were consistent across all dramas (see Table 5.1). These results fit the long-tail distributions identified by Anderson (2005) and Shirky (2003).

	# users	1	2	3	4	5	6	7	8	9	10	11+
Total	8345	6375	967	320	188	112	92	38	44	33	21	113
%		76.4%	11.6%	3.8%	2.3%	1.3%	1.1%	0.5%	0.5%	0.4%	0.35%	1.4%

Table 5.1 Number of Tweets Per User

The analysis of the hashtag data lead to the following results:

RQ7: How many different hashtags used?
RQ8: What are the most frequent hashtags?

For each drama a few hundred different hashtags were used (see Table 5.2). The most frequently used hashtags fall into three categories: (1) third-party services hashtags, (2) episode-identifying hashtags, and (3) hashtags for other shows. Viggle is a third-party app or service which allows viewers to check in and let others know on Twitter that the viewer is watching a particular show. The tweets are branded with a Viggle hashtag (#viggle). *The Mentalist* tweets had 506 viggle hashtags (#viggle), whereas the other dramas only had between 47 to 83 Viggle hashtags. Some of the most frequently used hashtags were episode-identifying hashtags. In most cases this was the title of the episode converted to a hashtag (e.g., #tilldeathdouspart for *NCIS* was used 903 times). Other frequent hashtags included hashtags for other television dramas, usually on the same network, a sort of cross-promotional tweet.

	Bones	*Castle*	*L&O:SVU*	*NCIS*	*The Mentalist*
# of different hashtags	425	391	262	375	257

Table 5.2 Hashtags Used

The results section of the case study ended with the research question related to audience involvement:

RQ9: How often are the main characters of the drama mentioned?

The percentage of tweets about main characters ranged from 2.3% for Olivia Benson in *SVU* to 17.4% for Patrick Jane in *The Mentalist* (see Table 5.3). which may suggest a stronger audience involvement with the Jane character.

	Bones	*Castle*	*L&O:SVU*	*NCIS*	*The Mentalist*
Main Character	Bones	Castle	Olivia	Gibbs	Jane
# of mentions	143	156	67	129	477
% of all tweets	4.9%	5.4%	2.3%	4.4%	17.4%

Table 5.3 Tweets about Main Characters

Writing the Discussion Section

The conclusion or discussion section typically contains three parts. The discussion section begins with a brief summary of the research presented in the paper. After the summary there is often discussion of the limitations of the research. The discussion section ends with some discussion of future research given the results of the study and the limitations of the study. The social TV study concluded with the following brief discussion section:

> This is a descriptive study. The above results give a snapshot of how often viewers of TV dramas tweet and what they tweet about when watching a drama. Most viewers (about 75%) only tweet once per episode... Hundreds of different hashtags are used, but the most frequent hashtags are third-party service hashtags, episode-identifying hashtags, and hashtags for other shows. In terms of audience involvement, main characters are mentioned in 2.3% to 17.4% of the tweets in this study. Some main characters get more attention than others. Further exploration into the tweet data is warranted. Those of us who study TV tweets, we are at the surface. We need to dig deeper. The future reports based on the data gathered for this study will, for example, look closer at how the viewer talks about the story in their tweets, what exactly they retweet and what exactly is sent in directed tweets. (p. 37)

Although the above brief discussion section does not address the limitations of the research, there are some common limitations or weaknesses in social media research. As mentioned previously, because of technical issues, it is possible that the data collected are not complete or a representative sample. In addition to the technical issues, there may be another reason that the data collected may not be representative of a larger population. For example, people who use social media may be of a higher socio-economic status. Research should be cautioned not to generalize results beyond the specific group studied.

Conclusion

In this chapter we offered advice on how to write a quantitative research paper on social media. As we covered each section of a research paper, we gave examples from a social media case study and we also highlighted aspects of the section that are specifically relevant to social media. In the problem statement section we identified some resources for current social media statistics which may be helpful in stressing how social media is worthy of further study. In the literature review section we offered advice on key social media literature reviews and key theoretical work in social media. In addition, we offered advice on how to use social media to find current and relevant social media literature by, for example, using the #socialmediaresearch hashtag on Twitter. In the methods section, we addressed important ethical and technical issues related to gathering social media data. In the results section there was no new advice, but in the discussion section we covered common limitations to social media research.

Social media is only about a decade old and social media research is a little less. The literature has exponentially grown from a few journal articles early on to a total of several hundred social media articles in communication and media journals. We hope the advice in this chapter helps researchers address the key issues of social media research and helps facilitate more study of social media within communication and media research.

References

Altheide, D. L., & Schneider, C. J. (2013). *Qualitative Media Analysis*. Los Angeles: Sage Publications.

American Psychological Association. (2010). *Publication Manual of the American Psychological Association*. Washington, DC: American Psychological Association.

Anderson, C. (2005, May 8). The origins of *The Long Tail*. Retrieved from http://longtail.typepad.com/the_long_tail/2005/05/the_origins_of_.html

boyd, d. m., & Ellison, N. B. (2007). Social network sites: Definition, history, and scholarship. *Journal of Computer-Mediated Communication*, *13*(1), article 11. http://jcmc.indiana.edu/vol13/issue1/boyd.ellison.html

Burgess, J., & Bruns, A. (2012). Twitter archives and the challenges of 'Big Social Data' for media and communication research. *M/C Journal,15*(5).

Diakopoulos, N.A. & Shamma, D.A. (2010). Characterizing debate performance via aggregated Twitter sentiment. In Proceedings of the 28th international conference on Human factors in computing systems (CHI '10) (1195-1198). New York, NY.

Eckert, J., Walker, S., Hemsley, J., Nahon, K. & Mason, B. (2013). Opening the black box of social media research methods: SoMe ways forward. Retrieved from http://somelab.net/wpcontent/uploads/2013/01/HICSS_workshops_final29Dec.pdf

Ethics. 2011. In *Merriam-Webster.com*. Retrieved from http://www.merriam-webster.com/dictionary/ethics

Frey, L.R., Botan, C.H., Friendman, P.G., & Kreps, G.L. (1992). *Interpreting Communication Research: A Case Study Approach*. Englewood Cliffs, N.J.: Prentice Hall.

Galvan, J. L. (2009). *Writing Literature Reviews: A Guide for Students of the Social and Behavioral Sciences.* Glendale, CA: Pyrczak Publishing. Girden, E. R., & Kabacoff, R. I. (2011). *Evaluating Research Articles: From Start to Finish.* Los Angeles, C.A.: SAGE.

Hart. W. B. & Taylor, E. C. (2012). Social media use while watching prime-time TV. *Proceedings from Second Annual Social Media Technology Conference & Workshop.* Retrieved from http://socialmediatechnologyconference.com/wp-content/uploads/2013/04/SMTCProceedingsFinal2012-1.pdf

Honeycutt, C. & Herring, S.C. (2009). Beyond microblogging: Conversation and collaboration via Twitter. Proceedings of the Forty-Second Hawai'I International Conference on System Sciences (HICSS-42). Los Alamitos, CA: IEEE Press.

Huang, J., Thornton, K.M. & Efthimiadis, E. (2010). Conversational tagging in Twitter. In Proceedings of the 21st ACM conference on Hypertext and hypermedia (HT'10) (173-178). New York, NY.

Kaplan, A. M. & Haenlein, M. (2010). Users of the world, unite! The challenges and opportunities of social media. *Business Horizons, 53,* 59-68.

Keyton, J. (2006). *Communication research: Asking Questions, Finding Answers.* Boston: McGraw-Hill.

Pérez-Latre, F., Blanco, I., & Sanchez, C. (2011). Social networks, media and audiences: A literature review. *Comunicación Y Sociedad, 24*(1), 63-74.
Phillis, M. L. (n.d.). Using social media in your research. Retrieved from http://www.apa.org/gradpsych/2011/11/social-media.aspx

Shaw, L. (2012, January 17). As social media hits TV, 2012 the year of 'must-tweet TV'. Reuters. Retrieved from http://www.reuters.com/article/2012/01/17/us-socialmedia-television-idUSTRE80G1DA20120117

Shirky, C. (2003, February 8). Power Laws, Weblogs, and Inequality. Retrieved from http://www.shirky.com/writings/powerlaw_weblog.html

Shirky, C. (2008). *Here Comes Everybody: The Power of Organizing Without Organizations.* New York: Penguin Press.

Shirky, C. (2010). *Cognitive Surplus: Creativity and Generosity in a Connected Age.* New York: Penguin Press.

Wimmer, R. D., & Dominick, J. R. (2011). *Mass Media Research: An Introduction*. Boston: Cengage/Wadsworth.

Wohn, D. Y & Na, E. (2011). Tweeting about TV: Sharing television viewing experiences via social media message streams. First Monday, 16, 3. Retrieved from   http://firstmonday.org/htbin/cgiwrap/bin/ojs/index.php/fm/article/viewArticle/3368/2779

Chapter 6
Conducting Research Utilizing Social Media: Best Practices
James Cohen & Paul Mihailidis

A Ubiquitous Digital Media Landscape

In the current digital media environment, differentiating quality content from questionable content is an arduous task. The sheer breadth and scope of content created, aggregated, uploaded, and disseminated to the Internet every day, in real time, with little regard for boundaries or borders is staggering. New events that occur locally, nationally, or globally are now longer stories told by the few in media organizations, but rather told simultaneously by groups of interested onlookers. A savvy citizen is faced with the prospect of locating information focused on a specific topic, yet with few linear pathways for gathering, critiquing, and securing relevant, balanced, and independent information.

To focus research findings, discover authority, explore framing, and navigate source material, the information seeker is now required to have new competencies. Traditionally, the user in search of data would expect "experts to go through information, ideas, and knowledge and put them neatly away" (Weinberger, 2007). In the present, every person who tags, posts, shares, and uploads original content becomes the expert of their data. Identifying authority while researching requires in-depth analysis of information in order to not only satisfy the reader, but also to challenge them to consider a deeper meaning.

This chapter examines a practical approach to researching information using online tools, specifically, the online curation platform Storify. The current digital media environment has allowed access to a multitude of content, but also to information that may be unverified, libelous, or even completely false. To combat this new media landscape, new technologies must be harnessed that reflect and advance the hyper information sphere that digital media culture now exploits. This chapter will examine several methods of research using popular social media tools and platforms, with the hope of creating more effective measures for information gathering, assessment, expression, and dissemination.

Social Media and New Modes of Inquiry

Clay Shirky identified the paradox of authority in *Here Comes Everybody* (2008) when he argued that the definition of journalist was weakened by the fact that "anyone in the developed world can publish anything anytime, and the instant it is published, it is globally available and readily available" (2008:71). From bloggers to Wikipedia editors, those who have access, have authority. In locations with growing access, information from important events gains value when the uploader has the advantage of exclusivity. When terrorists attacked the London subway in 2005, the photo-sharing site Flickr became a source of information for journalists around the world.

"Flickr beat many traditional news outlets by providing these photos, because there were few photojournalists in the affected parts of the transport network (three separate trains on the Underground, and a bus), but many people near the those parts of the transport system had camera-phones that could email the pictures in (Shirky, 2008)." This shift in the sharing and reception of information has led to a new role for social media tools and platforms in how citizens hear about issues, share information and opinions, and gather relevant information. Additionally, social media as a communications technology allows for sharing content instantly from every place a user may be located.

The downed US Airways flight 1549 in the Hudson River sparked a conversation of how Twitter is utilized as value-added information to the news-reporting sphere. Communication through Twitter is limited to 140 characters (a similar count to a text message) and "produces at best eloquently terse responses and at worst heavily truncated speech" (Murthy, 2011). On that fateful day in 2009, Janis Krums, a New York Ferry passenger who happened to be the first to report on the downed airliner, was instantly converted to journalist reporter as his Twitter post and photograph happened to be the first visual of the event.

Having access to Krums' tweets allowed journalists and readers to understand the story in real-time rather than the experience of waiting for printed media or television news trucks to arrive and set up. The chain of events that caused the plane accident throughout the crash aftermath are now in a time documentable format.

The importance of time documentation of event research and storytelling also came about the night of the Osama bin Laden raid in Abbottabad, Pakistan, when Sohaib Athar "liveblogged the Osama raid without knowing it" (ReallyVirtual, 2011), as Athar posted on his Twitter account. When recreating the story for the newspaper or television, these social media posts became part of the narrative. As journalists would have traditionally told the story from a finished informational status, Athar's tweets included a personal narrative that added a valuable addition to the reports. The Twitter posts suggest a more personal attachment to a breaking news story.

Social media posting from citizen journalists are not without their fair amount of criticism. Twitter has been accused of undermining the gatekeeping functions of journalists (Hermida, 2010) and shifting away from the classical paradigm of journalism as a framework to provide reports and analyses of events through narratives (Dahlgren, 1996). According to Bartlett and Miller (2011), young people are not careful, discerning users of the Internet and are vulnerable to pitfalls of falsehoods, ignorance, and scams. Their solution is not greater censorship or tighter control, but to create young people who are careful, skeptical, and savvy judges of Internet content (2011).

Nevertheless, scholars have explored the efficacy of curation as a digital and media literacy tool to build competencies in using social media to facilitate all facets of daily life. In their book *Connected,* Christakis and Fowler (2012) explore the new connective power of social media to build collaborative landscapes for human interaction. They write:

Our interactions, fostered and supported by new technologies, but existing even with them, create new social phenomenon that transcend individual experience by enriching and enlarging it, and this has significant implications for the collective good. Networks help make the whole of humanity much greater than the sum of its parts, and the invention of new ways to connect promises to increase our power to achieve what nature has foreordained. (286)

Recent research by Mihailidis (2013a; 2013b; forthcoming) has found that youth today primarily use aggregated and curated spaces for information consumption, sharing, and production. They start social, exploring and curating information they see from peer news feeds, tweets, video and photo sharing sites, and the like. The maintenance of their social spaces necessarily entails the integration of images, audio, video and print, from top down and bottom up sources, and from a wider array of diverse voices than was ever possible before. This type of information curation is necessitated by the social platforms and abundance of information that young people must navigate with savvy on a daily basis.

The result is a rich and active debate around how these tools will influence social and civic engagement. Scholars have commended the new possibilities that social technologies have provided for increased collaborative production (Benkler, 2005; Benkler and Nissenbaum, 2006; Lessig, 2008), for crowdsourced participative potential in civic activities (Brabham, 2008; Surwowiecki, 2005; Howe, 2008), and for the increased value provided in peer-to-peer participatory models for engagement in daily life (Jenkins 2006, 2009; Shirky, 2010). Some are weary of the impact of social media technologies on the ability for individuals to extend their information and communication needs in real and meaningful ways (Gladwell, 2010; Dean, 2005; Morozov, 2010).

Nevertheless, social media have increasingly become the central facilitators for information and communication in local and global contexts in a digital media culture. With this comes the act of curation as a foundational user tactic to make sense of and sort the steady flow of information that is encountered on a daily basis.

Online Tools

The flow of information previous to the digital environment did not favor the average web users who were at the will of content organizers and suppliers of content. In 2007 this process evolved when Twitter user and consultant Chris Messina discovered a small hack inside Twitter. He noticed that when he added the pound symbol, or hashmark, his work became a hyperlink that created search results organized around that specific keyword which allowed him to create groups inside the site (Gannes, 2010). The keyword became the tag, shorthand for subject category, for that word and the "hashtag" was created. This new organization method allowed the end user to reconfigure the information supply chain and become the researcher of any topic posted on Twitter.

The hashtag, while expanding its location beyond use within Twitter, has become a necessity among users looking to organize and aggregate information. Used widely in Tumblr, Google Plus, and Instagram, among several others, the popularity of the hashtag boomed when utilized as a community organizational tool. At the onset of the Arab Spring in January 2011, the hashtag #Jan25 and #Egypt were used to signify a place for users to contribute to a quickly growing rebellion against the Egyptian government and also a way to gauge support outside of Egypt (Schonfeld, 2011). The hashtag was also in prominent use during the Occupy Wall Street protests that began in New York City and later expanded to the Occupy movement worldwide. The hashtags #OWS, #Occupy, #99percent (and later #OccupyLondon and #OccupySidney) became battle cries for those looking to protest, to help out, to donate, and to spread the word. The information gathered helped protestors figure out meeting places, share and collect new information, and spread awareness worldwide. The hashtag was like a television channel tuned to that specific topic, always feeding the newest information.

Attempting to quantify the data pouring in became an arduous task. Those looking to tell the story of the movements had to manually discover the information across several social media platforms and convert the information into a coherent narrative. In the case of Occupy Wall Street, many of the themes and protests were varied. While the protests began as attacks on income inequality in the United States, the attendees of many of the protests also arrived with protest themes about the environment, student debt, and racism. The varied themes may have diversified the original intent, but the impact was still strong and "created an important national conversation about economic inequality and upward mobility" (Sorkin, 2012).

The news reported and posted during the Occupy Movement and protests, however varied, can be collected and further narrated from multiple points of view and explanations. To create a story based on breaking news or a developing narrative, there are several online tools available to help organize information. To discover a subtext or analyze a story in depth, software like Wordle or IBM's ManyEyes use data sets, especially in the form of text, and analyze it to discover deeper meaning of the written content. If you are to analyze articles regarding Occupy Wall Street, you could accumulate data from dozens of articles and use ManyEyes. The software outputs a word cloud creating a textual display with different sized words based on their amount of usage. For example, if the word "occupy" was used often, the software will output the word larger whereas a word such as "leader" was used fewer times, it would result in a small word (Figure 6.1).

Figure 6.1 – Data visualization by author of Brisbane's (2011) Who is Occupy Wall Street? *The New York Times.*

Curation

The act of curating is rooted in collecting and displaying objects and materials such as paintings, sculptures, and antiques. The goal of a curator is to tell a story, or perhaps to create an environment that communicates a narrative. Curation is a skill that is utilized based on the specific material or media being organized. In the *Journal of the Society of Architectural Historians,* Professor and MOMA Curator Barry Bergdoll (1998) stated that "The art of curating historical exhibitions is young, and if it is to be vital as a medium of scholarship as well as communication, it must remain in a continual state of inventing itself." (1998:257) He argued that curation is kind of authorship because "arguments and insights are made with objects and images rather than primarily with words but also because collaboration is an inherent aspect of the process from conception to installation." (1998:257) Similarly, in the digital environment, curation requires a thoughtful process of aggregating digital material, and in turn, requires the need to address the negotiation between content and display (Bergdoll, 1998).

The digital online curation software Storify does just that: enabling research in the process of aggregating materials and allowing the user to consider the relationship between the content found and the shape the story takes throughout the narrative. Curating antiques is a finite process, the materials exist and can be completely cataloged for future organization. In the digital environment, material and content are infinite, constantly created, remixed, and redesigned (Lessig, 2008). Social media's impact on information is a flow of content that is scattered across more than one billion users who are also inherently creators. Storify recognizes the overwhelming amount of content in its motto: "Storify helps making sense of what people post on social media. Our users curate the most important voices and turn them into stories" (Storify.com/about).

Curation has been a boon to journalists and storytellers who can curate social media messages while allowing for editorial judgment on material, such as links and sources of news and information, based on the needs and interests of a particular audience (Briggs, 2013). Over the last several years, many news outlets have taken to curation as a way of organizing information for their audience. Sites like *The Drudge Report, The Huffington Post*, and *The Daily Beast* offer original content as well as organized articles from contributing authors and from around the web. Other sites, like *Buzzfeed*, work specifically on the model of curating information in nearly every posted article. When a news source uses curation as a service, it caters to their audience thereby bringing views to their site and encouraging audience interaction in the form of comments within the material. The act of curating creates not only the narrative, but also the conversation.

To make sense of the avalanche of data provided by users blogging, tweeting, and commenting, a strong narrative is necessary to communicate and organize a story. A well-researched story requires discovering material from multiple media outlets, as well as the increased diversity in breadth and scope that social media provide. Social media has not only provided an additional outlet for news reporters and commentators, but has also been an additional source of information for traditional media. Researching using social media becomes an act of responsible news literacy. As Renee Hobbs explained in her *Digital and Media Literacy* Knight Foundation Report (2010), "people need to have a good understanding of how knowledge is constructed and how it represents reality and articulates a point of view" (2010:viii).

In a breaking news environment, a curator can be just as responsible for information gathering as a traditional media outlet. When sources such as Reddit rapidly aggregate available material, many online users find their data to be of a higher value than the slower-paced verified news outlet. The online curator should understand that online user-based information is unfiltered and potentially heavily biased. This possibility offers the information curator the ability to curate multiple points of view to offer a well-rounded narrative to an ongoing event or theme.

To return to a strong example, as in the case of the large theme of "income inequality," the curator has to decide what approach to take his or her narrative. The issue is a hotly debated, very partisan topic. To truly inform an audience, approaching the topic from one point of view will not complete the story. The act of curating must be approached from an inherently balanced point of view and data has to be aggregated using specific search terms. Using terms as vague as "income inequality" or "Occupy Wall Street" may yield thousands of results ranging from supporters of the Occupy Movement to information claiming to debunk the movement altogether. The method of research should be focused on a point of view and time should be taken to fully understand a point of view.

Curation and Civic Engagement

The 2008 election between Barack Obama and John McCain marked the first election in United States history that was arguably directly influenced by many-to-many collaborative social media technologies. The major social media sites, which are Facebook, Twitter, Flickr, and YouTube, were not available before the election of 2004; the audience relied on traditional media to supply the narrative of the contest. In 2008, there was an incredible turnout of younger people and minorities, many who voted for the first time (Hesseldahl et. al., 2008).

Facebook turned out to be the most valuable tool of the 2008 election season. Many users posted that they had voted by checking off a box on the site. The social atmosphere of Facebook caused users to encourage their peers to go out and do the same. Meanwhile, Twitter acted as the virtual watercooler for conversations both nationally and internationally on the topic of the election (Hesseldahl et. al., 2008). Social media across several sites provided information updates and a place to discuss the election process. According to the Pew Internet and American Life Project, almost one in five online users used social media during the 2008 election season to post their opinions or provide additional information (Smith, 2009). Furthermore, two-thirds of younger voters who used social media during the campaign season took part in some sort of political activity (Smith, 2009). In the years leading up to Barack Obama's second term, social media has grown exponentially. Social media users made up only one-third of Internet users in 2008; this number has grown larger than two-thirds the online population in 2012 (Smith, 2013).

The Pew Internet and American Life Project's study on Civic Engagement in the Digital Age found that while a large part of the population takes part in civic groups or activities offline, almost an equal number participated in a civic action using online methods, specifically social media like Facebook or Twitter (Smith, 2013). Engaging in civic matters and finding information on a given political topic starts with the exploration of online content. In the digital landscape, educators of all levels and fields have to responsibly negotiate the online lives and digital environments of their students and aid them in critical inquiry, analysis, and evaluation (Jenkins et. al., 2009).

As social media sites grow in their prominence as information outlets, the task of organizing information is paramount to learning. Just as a writer gathers information for research purposes, the online user gathers information to create an informed opinion. As well as the previously mentioned aggregation sites like *Buzzfeed* or *The Huffington Post*, many traditional media have integrated social media into their reporting technique. Reporters now routinely focus some research on how the online audience is reacting to a breaking news event. The downside is the possibility of weak sources, unverified information, or completely false information.

In a study titled *Truth, Lies, and the Internet: A report into young people's digital fluency,* Jamie Bartlett and Carl Miller (2011) found that while there are now a more abundant sources of journalism and experts, there is also a possibility of discovering and collecting mistakes, mistruths, and misinformation. This trap is possible even to those with trained experience in media organization and discovery, as seen in the news reports following the Boston Marathon bombings on April 15, 2013. In the days following the bombings, many Internet users who access Reddit and 4Chan participated in their own form of information gathering, using only available information online. The users focused on several people they believed to be responsible for the bombings, using only the clues available from publicly posted information. Unfortunately, much of the information aggregated resulted in false leads because it lacked official source information from the FBI or police data. While the information was short of official documentation, however, the online tools provided amazing organizational capabilities without the need of one central organizing unit.

Scholars have pointed to users having a shorter attention span and lack of devotion to linear text (Carr, 2010). While the Internet user may focus differently, the act of engaging civically is more possible. Social media is in constant evolution as the user base grows and information structures change. Hobbs (2011), explains that students and users of the digital era need to have human curiosity, the ability to listen, seek diverse knowledge, and constantly share information. To become an informed user of the sea of digital information, the user is responsible for continually learning by seeking.

Participating in information sharing creates a new media environment that is constantly being reshaped by the act of participation itself (Thomas and Brown, 2011). As users grow more accustomed to seeking information online in order to learn more about a given subject, the act of the user as data expert is growing. Almost half of all social media users decided to learn more about political or social issues as result of something they had found on a social media site (Smith, 2013). The value of dispersed information that is found on a social media feed leads to the inevitable possibility that another user may have the most valuable information available on any given topic (Thomas and Brown, 2011).

Becoming an information expert takes guidance and understanding of the new digital environment. To become a trusted source of information, the digital tools available online offer an opportunity to enhance the top-down information model that traditional media supply and reorganize the information into valuable stories. A social media researcher performs the tasks of gathering the data as well as narrating it for the intended audience that may be seeking alternative information to what is available. The Storify software, with its ability to annotate traditional news media and include the social media conversation from several social media sites, offers the possibility of advanced civic awareness and engagement.

Storify

Storify, a free, open-source social curation platform, uses advanced algorithms to explore information from traditional media to any public social media post with the intention the curator should share their story for viewership (Figure 6.2). The term "storify" is traditional newsroom slang for adding color and detail to a fact-based story. The software allows the user to do this through its built-in guidelines.

Figure 6.2 From Storify.com

Many traditional news outlets have hired social media coordinators and reporters to their team in the past several years. Their job is to report on social media stories for their respective outlets. On the front page of Storify, a graphic of featured users shows ABC News, CNN, and The Guardian to encourage users to treat this platform professionally.

To use Storify, users can sign in with their Facebook account, Twitter account, or the standard online method of email logins. The user is encouraged to first collect the data for the narrative and then construct the story. As this chapter is about the methods of curating material, we suggest a slightly different approach.

First and foremost, the software opens with a screen that resembles a newspaper setup. The Storify editor asks the user to input a headline and a subtitle in order to begin. On the right side of the Storify editor, the search system is located (Figure 6.3).

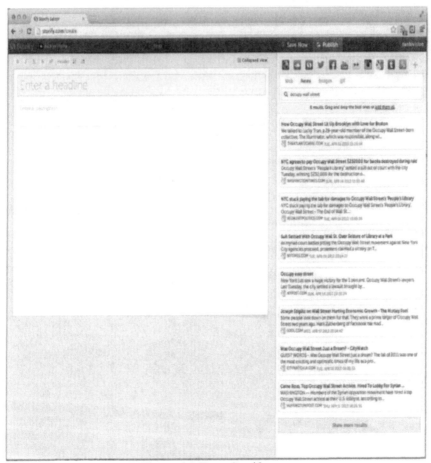

Figure 6.3 From Storify.com

The Storify search system is a built-in search tool that works on keyword searches. It provides search capabilities for its own breaking news, as well as searches on Google and Google News and images. Considering the fact that many breaking news stories are supplemented by user-generated content and actual news reporters using services like Twitter, Storify also provides access to the major social media outlets like Twitter, Facebook, YouTube, Flickr, Tumblr, Soundcloud, and Instagram. In many cases, the user has to sign into their account through Storify in order to access the social media database that some of these sources provide. The following is a method of using Storify as a practical research tool rather than simply collecting data and narrating the results.

Practical Use of Storify

In the process of creating a Storify, the researcher should consider their specific story as a thesis before the onset of curating. A headline should be created as a title and the subtitle should offer a specific thesis statement that allows the reader to understand the point of view of the author/narrator. With that in mind, the curator can properly approach the story and frame their approach. Using Storify's breadth of access, we recommend that the researcher focus specifically on keywords that support the framing of their story. For example, a quality story on "income inequality" may focus on Occupy Wall Street or on the problems with government entitlement systems. With either of these approaches, curators should remain as objective as possible in their research.

The curator should begin by adding supporting information in their aggregation as well as background narrative in order to properly inform the reader of the topic at hand. Using the built in Google News search, the user should locate articles and information that offer the most verified and supportive information to any given subject. Careful attention and reading of the resulting articles are necessary as the author may discover new points of focus for their aggregation in the process of inquiry. It is important to note that the algorithm that Storify employs in the search will result in sources with the most amount of verified information, therefore newspapers of record such as the *New York Times* or *The Guardian* often appear near the top of the results.

In the process of aggregating and organizing, the researcher should narrow their results through the keywords discovered in their initial research with the focus on their thesis in mind. If the story is focused on entitlement loopholes, the first search should focus on a wide-based search result like "Occupy Wall Street" and continue with a Boolean search approach to focus the topic. (i.e., "Occupy Wall Street" + Welfare).

The many voices of social media also play an integral role to online curation. While the multiple voices of the online audience are the experts of their own opinion, the researcher should understand that a Storify story is not complete without the crowd participation into a narrative arc. The opinions, in the form of text and visuals, make up the authenticity of the story.

The researcher is responsible for creating a narrative that includes the voices of the online crowd while also maintaining context for vibrant opinions versus nuanced reporting, dialog, or debate. For partisan issues like income inequality, gun control, or abortion, the researcher is susceptible to a range of highly animated voices. In order to support a point a view, the researcher should focus on multiple search terms that focus their point but support it with actual evidence regardless of personal opinion.

A high-quality Storify displays a multitude of voices that develop the narrative with substantial and knowledgeable points of view. The narrative the researcher is creating gains value by increasing the conversation with posts by users who seem to have firsthand knowledge of the story, are on location, or may be experts who utilize social media to spread their information. The researcher should consider the Storify they are creating to be as important as a national media outlet.

The Social Media Research Narrative

Based on recent Facebook and Weibo statistics (Tam, 2013; Montlake, 2013), social media users make up more than 15% of the world's population. While many more people have access to the World Wide Web, those who have access to social media share in a democracy of participation that allows them to add digital value to offline events. Creating a research paper on any topic before the advent of social media was limited to the extant information that had been published in accessible documents such as newspapers, periodicals, books, journals, and possibly dissertations. The researchers task of creating a narrative from the available information was a process of curating and culling pertinent to their topic. The narrative created was mostly the curated and paraphrased information in a linear fashion. Paraphrasing existing documents is the most valuable process of creating a narrative because the ability to successfully paraphrase means to have a comprehension of the material (Kennedy, Kennedy, and Smith, 2004).

In the social media research environment, extant online information is in overabundance. Storify took this into consideration with a tool they call the "Collection Bookmarklet" that permits the curator to "clip" web-based information and data into Storify's collection in the user's account. These articles, photos, tweets, or anything else that has been clipped can be kept for future use in a story, or just as a bookmark.

A Storify is not just a collection of found articles and social media posts; it is a well-articulated, thought-provoking construct that is both readable and educational. The goal of a fulfilling Storify is to inform the reader by narrating a set of curated articles on the topic, displaying photographs from Twitter, Flickr, and Instagram, and showing social media input from users at large from Facebook posts to tweets to audio files from SoundCloud.

Storify has additional tools to help create the narrative of the story. If the curator were to add material to the timeline while searching through various outlets, the sort feature lines up all of the content in the story either from the oldest source to the newest or vice versa. After the order is established, the text can be added in between each source material to add depth, paraphrasing, and transitions to the findings.

The Storify curation software eschews plagiarism. The curator is encouraged to consider each article or social media post a primary source. As the researcher is accountable for transparency and accountability, the reader may find all the original locations of the material by simply clicking on the link or photograph. The writer is encouraged to pull quotes from the article as an annotation to the information, but the possibility of a direct quote is redundant as the material is readily available and visible on the timeline.

"Exploding" News Information

Breaking news information can lead to an influx of information available instantaneously. The twenty-four-hour news cycle allows for mainstream media to continually stay on air and develop the story. On the night of May 1, 2011, news channels turned their attention toward a podium in the White House awaiting an "Urgent Announcement" from President Barack Obama. While yet to be confirmed by the president, the Internet and news media were already talking about the killing of Osama bin Laden. Information from verified media, amateur accounts, and first-hand accounts of the story were "exploding" online. Researcher Alex Leavitt posted on Twitter the night of the breaking news: "What do we call this news phenomenon? It's not 'saw it on the news late last night.' It's more like 'saw the news explode online" (AlexLeavitt, 2011).

Storify's aggregating software allows for a copy to be made of the Twitter posts dragged into the timeline, which allows the software to act as an archiving device. Therefore, posts made by Twitter users that may be later deleted are backed up on the curator's Storify. In a breaking news event, the curator can be tasked with organizing varying information that is released during a breaking news event. While there was little confusion about the actual story that was being released during the night of the bin Laden announcement, this may not be the case for other such breaking news events.

In the aftermath of the Sandy Hook shooting on December 14, 2012, news reporters utilized Storify to aggregate social media posts from citizens responding to the horrible events, as well as the posts made by those involved. *Canoe News,* Canadian Online Explorer, utilized Storify to aggregate the Twitter posts from Sandy Hook Elementary's principal Dawn Hochsprung. The Storify titled "Scenes from Sandy Hook in happier times" states:

> A shooter opened fire at Sandy Hook School in Newtown, Connecticut, leaving several dead, according to reports. The woman listed as principal on the school's staff directory, Dawn Hochsprung, appears to be an active Twitter user. Here are a few of her posts this school year (http://storify.com/CanoeNews/scenes-from-sandy-hook-school-newtown-ct).

The Storify platform in this case goes beyond traditional news reporting to add supplemental value to a tragic news report. The user can curate social media to add civic value to an ongoing and developing story.

Large-scale stories, especially those where social media users are direct witnesses, offer the curators dozens of different angles to research a story. For example, when Hurricane Sandy swept along the entire East Coast of the United States during the last week of October 2012, stories relating to mass flooding, wind destruction, and the large-scale damage to the New Jersey and Long Island shoreline were created. People in the respective locations were first-hand witnesses to the ongoing disaster, posting updates as they were developing. Social media storytellers were able to aggregate the news articles from reporters on the scene and add depth with social media evidence in both pictures and posts from people in the vicinity.

For stories that do not happen to develop at a very rapid pace, the researcher can become the investigative journalist, piecing together evidence of a story's outcome. When Notre Dame linebacker Manti Te'o's alleged girlfriend passed away, there became significant evidence that she may have never existed. The storytellers can approach the subject of this story as how the audience reacted to the possibility of Te'o as an unfortunate victim of a prank or they may approach the story as a sleuth to discover whether the college football player may have been in on the joke.

Reinforcing Academic Sourcing

Storify can be used to teach the value of source material by focusing on how messages are spread about certain topics. The approach in a source assignment would be to approach a hot-button issue or topic that is highly partisan in politics and beliefs, such as gun control, pro-life/pro-choice, or climate change, and task the curator with telling a story with a point of view from one side or the other. The advanced task would be to assign two separate curations of the story with the same thesis point, but one story would only be allowed to find source material from legitimate sources and verified information while the other curation would only be from amateur and user-generated source material.

The goal of this assignment is to focus on the importance of source material. The curator may find completely different results from mainstream media than the results of amateur voices and opinions. This curation experiment can lead to discussions on the importance of source information (Mihailidis and Cohen, 2013):

- How does authority affect storytelling?
- How are mainstream media reports different than user-generated reports?
- Does social media information have value in a reporting atmosphere?
- When is a story complete?
- What is the process of vetting credible information?

In the changing environment of media information, the value of social media voices may have more substantial value than mainstream media reporting. This approach to curation could lead to an ongoing conversation regarding how storytellers navigate the immense amount of information available online.

Conclusion

In conclusion, narrative storytelling in the digital present requires a researcher with a handle on curating information to benefit readers. The researcher needs to be able to aggregate information on a given topic, understand, analyze, and evaluate a subject, and narrate the information gathered. Several online tools offer the researcher possibilities of creating a narrative for the reader. While many tools analyze data, they leave much out for narrative storytelling. The value of information is greatly enhanced by the aspect of the story. Therefore, the authors believe that Storify offers the most robust search, aggregation, organization, and narrative properties in the social media environment.

Journalists, educators, and students alike can benefit from Storify by using it to search various social media like Twitter or Instagram to creating a narrative by stringing together traditional news stories from various media outlets. Storify empowers the user to "make the web tell stories" and potentially become a information source online. Storify helps the researcher focus on curating information and telling stories to create a more informed audience.

References

AlexLeavitt. (2011, May 2). What do we call this news phenomenon? It's not "saw it on the news late last night." It's more like "saw the news explode online."   [Twitter   post].   Retrieved   from https://twitter.com/alexleavitt/status/64902588604223488

Bartlett, J. & Miller, C. (2011). Truth, Lies and the Internet: A report into young people's digital fluency. *Demos*. Retrieved from http://www.demos.co.uk/files/Truth_-_web.pdf

Benkler, Y. (2007). The Wealth of Networks: How Social Production Transforms Markets and Freedom. CT: Yale University Press.

Benkler, Y. & Nissenbaum, H. (2006), Commons-based Peer Production and Virtue. *Journal of Political Philosophy*, 14: 394–419. doi: 10.1111/j.1467-9760.2006.00235.x

Bergdoll, B. (Sept. 1998). *Journal of the Society of Architectural Historians*, Vol. 57, No. 3, pp. 257+366. Published by: University of California Press on behalf of the Society of Architectural Historians Stable. Retrieved from http://www.jstor.org/stable/991345 . Accessed: 30/03/2013 10:12

Brabham, D. C. (2008). Crowdsourcing as a model for problem solving an introduction and cases. Convergence: *The International Journal of Research into New Media Technologies*, 14(1), 75-90.

Briggs, M. (2013). Journalism Next: A Practical Guide to Digital Reporting and *Publishing (2nd ed.)*. Thousand Oaks, CA: CQ Press.

Carr, N. (2010). The Shallows: What the Internet is Doing to Our Brains. NY: W. W. Norton & Company.

Christakis, N. & Fowler, J. (2011). Connected: How Your Friends' Friends' Friends Affect Everything You Feel, Think, and Do. MA: Boston, Back Bay Books.

Civic engagement in the digital age. (April 25, 2013). Pew Internet and American Life Project. http://www.pewinternet.org/Reports/2013/Civic-Engagement/Summary-of-Findings.aspx

Dean, J. (2005). Communicative capitalism: Circulation and the foreclosure of politics. *Cultural Politics* 1(1): 101-137.

Gannes, L. (2010). The Short and Illustrious History of Twitter #Hashtags. http://gigaom.com/2010/04/30/the-short-and-illustrious-history-of-twitter-hashtags/

Gladwell, Malcolm. (2010, October 4). Small change: Why the revolution will not be tweeted. *The New Yorker*, 42–49.

Hermida, A. (2010). Twittering the News. *Journalism Practice*, 4: 3,297-308.

Hesseldahl, A., MacMillan, D., Kharif, O. (2008). The Vote: A victory for social media, too. *Bloomberg Business Week*. Retrieved from http://www.businessweek.com/stories/2008-11-05/the-vote-a-victory-for-social-media-toobusinessweek-business-news-stock-market-and-financial-advice

Howe, J. (2008). *Crowdsourcing: Why the Power of the Crowd is Driving the Future of Business.* NY: Three Rivers Press.

Jenkins, H. (2006). Convergence Culture: Where Old and New Media *Collide.* New York: NYU Press.

Jenkins, H., Purushotma, R., Weigel, M., Clinton, K., & Robinson, A. J. (2009). "Confronting the challenges of participatory culture: Media education for the 21st century" *A Report for the MacArthur Foundation* (Boston: MIT Press).

Kennedy, M., and Kennedy, W., & Smith, H. (2004). *Writing in the* Disciplines: A Reader for Writers (5th Ed.). Saddle River, NJ: Pearson. Lessig, L. (2008). *Remix: Making Art and Commerce Thrive in the Hybrid Economy.* New York: Penguin Books.

Mihailidis, P., Fincham, K. & Cohen, J. (2014). Towards a media literate model for civic identity on social networks: Exploring notions of community, participation, and identity of university students on Facebook. *Atlantic Journal of Communication*, Forthcoming.

Mihailidis, P. & Cohen, J. (2013). Exploring curation as a core digital and media literacy competency, *Journal of Interactive Media in Education* (forthcoming).

Mihailidis, P. (2013). Exploring global perspectives on identity, community, and media literacy in a networked age. *The Journal of Digital and Media Literacy*. The Knight Foundation, 1/1, January. Retrieved from http://jodml.wpengine.com/2013/01/21/perspectives-identity-media-literacy/

Montlake, S. (2013). Putting a price on Sina Weibo, China's answer to Twitter. Retrieved from http://www.forbes.com/sites/simonmontlake/2013/04/10/putting-a-price-on-sina-weibo-chinas-answer-to-twitter/

Morozov, Eyvgeny. (2010). *The Net Delusion: The Dark Side of Internet Freedom.* NY: Penguin Books.

Murthy, D. (2011). Twitter: Microphone for the masses? *Media, Culture and Society*, 33(5): 779-789.

ReallyVirtual. (2011, May 2). Uh oh, now I'm the guy who liveblogged the Osama raid without knowing it. [Twitter post]. Retrieved from https://twitter.com/ReallyVirtual/status/64912440353234944

Schonfeld, E. (2011). The Egyptian Behind #Jan25: Twitter is a very important tool for protesters. Retrieved from http://techcrunch.com/2011/02/16/jan25-twitter-egypt/

Shirky, C. (2008). Here Comes Everybody: The Power of Organizing Without *Organizations.* New York, NY: Penguin Books.

Shirky, C. (2010). Cognitive Surplus: Creativity and Generosity in a Connected *Age.* New York, NY: Penguin.

Smith, A. (2009). The Internet's role in campaign 2008. *Pew Internet and American Life Project.* Retrieved from http://www.pewinternet.org/Reports/2009/6--The-Internets-Role-in-Campaign-2008.aspx

Sorkin, A. (Sept. 18, 2012). Occupy Wall Street: A frenzy that fizzled. *New York Times*, B1.

Suroweicki, J. (2005). *The Wisdom of Crowds*. New York, NY: Anchor Books.

Tam, D. (2013). Facebook by the numbers: 1.06 billion monthly active users. Retrieved from http://news.cnet.com/8301-1023_3-57566550-93/facebook-by the-numbers-1.06-billion-monthly-active-users/

Weinberger, D. (2007). Everything is Miscellaneous: The Power of the New *Digital Disorder*. Chicago, IL: Holt.

Section II: Social Media Practice
Chapter 7
African Americans and Social Media
Jayne Cubbage

The dawn of the Internet age in the United States has brought about a bounty of opportunities for those who use it to advance and enrich their lives in so many ways. The magnitude of this one technical advancement and the advent of the personal computer and even smaller devices such as cell phones and tablets have given portability to information gathering in ways that a library and a stack of books could never do. Simply put, computer and Internet technology have broadened the ways in which we access and process information.

Regarding technology, those who have it use it a lot, and those who don't have the privilege of unrestricted access to it recognize their need for it. It may be tempting to assume that African Americans are the largest of underserved Internet and new media technology users, but this is not the case. In fact, African Americans are among the highest users of new media and Internet technology, particularly in urban environments. Their usage of portable media devices, such as cell phones and tablets, outranks that of all other ethnicities in the United States (Nielsen Wire Services, 2011). Additionally, African Americans are found to spend more hours each day using Internet and new media technology, and they consume more media across all genres than all other races in the United States (The Nielsen Group Services, 2012; Pew Research, 2013).

While African Americans are consuming more media than all other groups, including social media, they are also consistently ranked at the bottom of all social economic indicators of health and well-being that measure quality of life, economic stability, political influence, access to health and wellness, educational attainment, stable and intact families, exposure to environmental hazards, employment stability, and rates of incarceration, as well as obesity (National Urban League, 2013).

Despite the gains of the previous generations, which include the ascent of a person of color to the nation's highest office, the historic and legal gains from social justice movements, and the current political campaigns, which continue to assert the rights of the oppressed and downtrodden, African Americans appear stuck in a perpetual state of inertia lacking a roadmap on how to improve the current condition for themselves individually and the black community today. There are those, such as Shapiro (2010, 2004), who state that despite the best of efforts, African Americans remain locked within poverty's grip, which points to generations of economic disenfranchisement and wage disparity.

Given the ongoing work of civil rights organizations the need for continued progress in social indicators is still quite apparent (National Urban League, 2013). The largest and most widely recognized civil rights organization in the United States has only 500,000 members (http://www.naacp.org/pages/naacp-history). Can social media make a difference in civic participation? Byrne (2008) points to the propensity of African Americans to use social media for more personal uses rather than political uses. On the other hand Harp, Bachman, Cantrell Rosas-Moreno, and Loke (2010) offer encouraging data stating that African American youth are actually more politically and civically involved and social media may play a large role in this process.

However, if African Americans are using social media in such large numbers that a person's grandmother has a Facebook profile and children as young as five are using email and blogging (Pew Research, 2013), then what do these phenomena say about the potential for social media to work in targeted ways to mobilize the community to take steps to improve the overall condition of African Americans, or, at the very least, make smaller inroads to progress?

If improving one's life via social media is too much to ask for too soon, despite the obvious examples of social media's benefit in the Arab Spring of 2012, the U.S. presidential elections in 2012, relief campaigns for Hurricane Katrina, the Haiti earthquake, Super Storm Sandy, and the Boston Marathon Bombings in 2013, then under what circumstances will the power of social improvement become apparent for African Americans? Is it reasonable to expect to use media, particularly social networking, as a method of entertainment while overlooking its potential to empower socially? Are African Americans wasting precious time being entertained and hooked into the agenda of the dominant culture by failing to seize upon the untapped potential of social media?

Regardless of race, the concept of displacement is very real when it comes to online and Internet technology. In fact, many scholars point to the potential negative impact of a society that engages in mediated communication rather than in sustained interpersonal communication. Social media scholars have long found that Facebook friends are not the same as real friends, although some of your real friends may be your friends on Facebook (Bazrova, 2012; Tong, et. al., 2008). There is also the issue of time spent online among frequent users. Is this medium being used in the most effective way, or is it simply a waste and a drain on a finite resource of time?

Social Media Overview and Terminology

Social Networking Site or SNS will often be referenced in this work. It refers to all online forms of mediated communication, which allows users and subscribers to contribute content and network with others.

Also, for the purposes of this study, Facebook is the world's most popular and heavily used social networking site, launched in 2004 by Mark Zuckerberg and his college dorm mates. In 2012, the company began trading its shares publicly. Today, the site has more than 800 million users worldwide.

YouTube is the video sharing service founded as an "alternative to watching television" (van Dijck, 2013). At its founding, its primary goal was to foster more interactivity between content producers and creators, whereby consumers became the producers. According to Yeo (2012), YouTube "offers opportunity for large audiences with low barriers to entry —appeals that have attracted professional and ordinary consumers alike to create and upload videos. User-generated videos on YouTube produced with little to no budget have attracted millions of other users, overshadowing even the audience of larger television networks," (p. 299). Yeo added that as of January 2012, YouTube is the second most visited website on the Web and has thus far parceled more than four billion video streams on a daily basis (p. 298).

Twitter is the world's largest microblog service and was designed for users to express concise thoughts, ideas or updates using 140 characters or less. These thoughts or ideas can then be shared with the general public or a select group of followers. Trends and thoughts are communicated by following or trending. Jack Dorsey, Noah Glass, and others launched the site in 2006. Today, the site boasts of 88 million active users per month and 500 million registered users (van Dijck, 2013).

Displacement is a term coined by media scholars to denote the loss of valuable time by users of mediated communication (Potter, 2008). It suggests that while consuming large amounts of media, users could possibly be engaging in more socially constructive and meaningful activities. Those activities include talking with family members, participating in civic activities, being physically active, resting, creating a plan for the future, and living in the moment. This trend is addressed in the decline of well-being (Verger & Pelzer, 2009). Instead, scholars have noted that for many who use Internet and new media technology, large swaths of time and productivity are being lost to the addictive lure of the screen and mediated technology (Cai, 2005; Lee and Leung, 2008).

Displacement and new media technology are also used in tandem with the prevailing concern that Internet communication could possibly eclipse traditional forms of media such as newspapers, television, and radio despite the predominance of converged media; which combines new and old technologies.

New media scholars are watchful of how Internet technology divides the media audience into tiny fragments of individual segments of consumers who are no longer bound by the constraints of legacy media and singular points of information dispersal (Eastin and Cooper, 2003; Newell, et. al., 2008).

Statement of the Problem

While African Americans are large users of online and new media technologies research has shown that as a community their online usage is largely limited to social activities rather than political and economic activities. Those social activities prevent the community as a whole from benefitting from new media technologies that would lead to improvement in political and economic ways. This work examines the ways in which this technology is being used and how such usage can either benefit the African American community or prove to be detrimental. Additionally, this research will serve as a comparative analysis of social-political websites of organizations targeted to African Americans and will detail how these groups are using social media sites to garner more members and broadcast news about their political agenda. This work will also examine how sites geared toward African Americans either use the power of social networking to further galvanize groups of people to engage in self-empowerment and employ methods, which encourage or foster agency in the larger community.

Research Questions

Accordingly, this work seeks to answer the following questions:

RQ 1: How are political and civil rights organizations using new media technologies to foster greater membership and social and political awareness in the African American community?

RQ 2: What other positive examples exist to display culturally relevant techniques that may be applied on a community-wide basis to foster greater avenues to political, economic, and social empowerment in the African American community?)

RQ 3: Beyond the social, political, and economic advantages of more directed and targeted online and new media usage among African Americans, in what ways can these new ideas be imparted to the community at large to ensure wide scale implementation?

Theoretical Framework

The theory associated with this research is innovation diffusion theory. This theory asserts media are an elite resource and its adoption and implementation into society or a community is a one-way process whereby dominate members of society are imposing their perspective via technological advances onto other members of society (Baran and Davis, 2009, pp. 271-272). This theory is appropriate for the study of how African Americans use social media to advance their own social, political, and economic needs, because it directly addresses the ways in which new technology and information, or in this case information about how new technology is spread or diffused and ultimately utilized into the community at large once it has been introduced.

Currently, there are a select group of individuals in the African American community who know the full power of social media and its ability to mobilize citizens to become full participants and advance the common political and economic agenda. A recent example of this is the mobilization of the NAACP to garner signatures from African Americans and other concerned U.S. citizens after the acquittal of George Zimmerman in the murder of 17-year-old Trayvon Martin in Sanford, Florida (UPI.com, 2013). Seizing upon the outrage of the community, the NAACP used social media sites such as Facebook and Twitter, as well as their own website, to start an online petition requesting further investigation into the case. As of August 2013, the petition has garnered 1.5 million signatures and was delivered to the United States Department of Justice (NAACP, 2013 http://www.naacp.org/news/entry/naacp-petition-to-doj-reaches-1.5-million-signatures). A federal investigation into the shooting death of the unarmed Florida teen and the subsequent murder trial has begun.

Citing the work of Paul Lazarsfeld, Baran and Davis (2009) provide an overview of the process of information/innovation diffusion theory and how these early adopters who, either individually or via their community or civil rights organizations, are users of social media beyond the typical entertainment and social purpose and are the virtual agenda setters who impart the importance of social media to the community. Opinion leaders, who learn from early adopters can be viewed as members of existing groups who may be aware of the power of social media through their own involvement with such groups in their own experience. Opinion leaders are those who then impart the importance of use of a new medium or media technology to their friends who are considered opinion followers. Ultimately, late adopters join the process and begin using the new technology or medium (Baran and Davis, 2009, p. 271).

Literature Review

The existing literature on this social phenomenology is vast. First, Mesch (2011) explores the ways in which African Americans use the Internet. Byrne (2008) discussed how use of social media sites has increased a sense of community and social gatherings and examined ways in which the trend can be directed toward social engagement. Racial differences in usage of social media sites like Facebook revealed the ways in which African Americans use the site differently than whites (Appiah, 2003; Grasmuck, Martin, and Zhao, 2009).

Regarding possible solutions to the quandary, Harp, Bachman, Rosas-Moreno, and Loke (2010) discussed ways in which new media technology can foster a sense of civic engagement among African American youth. Farrow and Yuan (2011) and Means and Coleman (2003) also discussed the necessity of educating the African American community about media meaning and creating media education or media literacy programs to broker that result. Additional solutions from other communities that directly addressed the sociopolitical component of online sites and how they can be applied in the African American community are discussed in work of Mesch (2011) and Paradise (2011).

In speaking about the Civil Rights Movement of the 1960s, instigated by the initial sit-in by North Carolina A&T students at a Woolworth lunch counter in Greensboro, North Carolina, and ultimately spread via word of mouth throughout the South and as far away as Texas, Gladwell (2010) illustrates the power of word of mouth. Word of the protests spread as far away as Texas and soon other students were eager to join their fellow students in protests of their own. Of these protests, which served as a critical point in the Civil Rights Movement, Gladwell writes "fifty years after one of the most extraordinary episodes of social upheaval in American History, we seem to have forgotten what activism is" (p. 3).

Gladwell wrote of the groundswell of enthusiasm and determination of the college students to participate in the growing movement. He further noted:

> Some seventy thousand students eventually took part. Thousands were arrested and untold thousands more were radicalized. These events in the early sixties became a civil rights war that engulfed the South for the rest of the decade — and it happened without email, texting, Facebook or Twitter. (p. 2)

His work also addressed the limitations of social media (p. 5), stating that "the platforms of social media are built around weak ties." Twitter is a way of following (or being followed by) people you may have never met. Facebook is a tool for efficiently managing your acquaintances, for keeping up with the people you would otherwise not stay in touch with. That's why you can have a thousand "friends" on Facebook, as you never could in real life.

Gladwell also expressed the notion that despite these limitations, social networks do have some redeeming qualities. He explored some of those circumstances, which he illustrates in his article, such as a young Silicon Valley computer engineer who needed a bone marrow transplant and rallied friends and supporters via social networks to join a registry and ultimately donate if they were a match, and the case of a Wall Street investment banker who misplaced his phone only to learn that an African American high school student in Queens had found the phone and was posting photos of herself and her boyfriend online.

The investment banker was able to establish through a campaign of social media exertion that his Sidekick phone had been stolen and publicly shamed the high school student and the NYPD, who ultimately labeled the phone as stolen after initially stating it was lost in original police reports (pp. 9-10).

Regarding youth and political engagement, Zukin, Keeter, Andolina, Jenkins, and Delli Carpini (2006) highlighted through a series of surveys of parents and teens the variations in civic engagement between youth and older citizens. The authors found that while mature adults were more interested in the electoral process to make their voices heard among officials and lawmakers, young people preferred to engage in volunteer and community activities to highlight their political stance via projects and causes they believe in.

Community organizing was the primary focus in Shirky (2008), who examined the power of SNS to mobilize large groups of individuals who shared common interests and create opportunities for interaction in ways previously deemed impossible through the advent of new media technologies. This work not only addressed myriad ways in which technology is changing and evolving, it also detailed the ways in which humans are changing and becoming more efficient in their approach to ideas, adaptations of technology, and scientific innovation as a result. Shirky also pointed out that unlike other social media sites, which have a financial underpinning, social networking without concern for profit is the most effective measure of sustainability. He pointed to sites like Wikipedia with its file sharing and wiki format to entice would-be contributors to participate in the process of sharing what they know about a particular subject (pp. 188-212). Though this work provided detail for the merit of other methods of social networking and community organizing, its most important component was the focus on how community groups may use SNS to rally concerned citizens. He urged for an understanding of the social media process and touted the application of successful sites: a plausible promise, an effective tool, and an "acceptable bargain" with users. In this "promise, tool, bargain" formula, Shirky described theses items as the why--as in why would anyone join or contribute to this group? The how addressed the ways in which the actual tool itself will be used and ultimately coordinated among users. Ultimately, he wrote that the rules of engagement are part of the bargain and agreement between the user and the SNS and ultimately detailed the shared expectations of the relationship.

van Dijck (2013) discussed the benefits and demerits of social media. In his work, he examined the rise of SNS and how they have changed the way the world communicates and gains access to information. Using Facebook and other social networking sites, he analyzed their history, viability, and usefulness and merits for the end user and the business community via marketing and advertising campaigns. He also examined the social-political context that has allowed some sites to rise to prominence and near monopoly status while others have been left in the dust. He also raised important points on the notion that while these sites are often touted for their benefit for the end user, there are typical financial underpinnings interwoven into each site, which make for unspecified profitability of user information and marketability.

He also wrote that Facebook has some 835 million users as of March 2013. He added that the site is the world's largest social networking system and is most favored in Western cultures such as the U.S. and Europe and globally is most popular among Internet users. New users to social media are likely to choose Facebook over other lesser-known sites because of market saturation and brand recognition of the company. He added: "Looking at Facebook's powerful position in the ecosystem, one can hardly underrate its impact on networked manifestations of sociality" (p. 46).

Additionally, he wrote, "The steadily growing masses of users signing up for the service are proof of the site's becoming a centripetal force in organizing people's social lives. The principal benefits for users are, first, to get and stay connected and, second, to become (well) connected," (p. 51). Even though human contact through Internet sites has never replaced offline sociality, SNSs have arguably replaced email and the phone as the preferred media of interaction for the younger generation (Raynes-Goldie, 2010). Getting and staying in touch are now activities completely centered on SNSs; the services facilitate the bridging of space and time and help people to keep updated on their friends' lives. Facebook's design makes subscribing feel like hooking up to a utility. Once a member, the social push to stay connected is insidious, especially for young people, because *not* being on Facebook means not being invited to parties, not getting updated on important events, in short, being disconnected from a presumably appealing dynamic of public life. SNSs, as researchers confirm, have become a leading space for accumulating social capital (Valenzuela, Park, and Kee, 2009). Of Twitter, van Dijck wrote:

> Touted as the "SMS of the Internet," the technology allowing users to send and receive text-based messages of up to 140 characters known as tweets was characterized as something between a short message service, a phone call, an email, and a blog; less cumbersome than keeping a blog, less exclusive than talking to one person on the phone, less formal than email exchange and less elaborate than most social networking sites. (p. 70)

He added that initially, Twitter started out as a "tool for connecting individuals and communities of users" (pp. 73-74). The initial user for the site was older than 35 and was a government or media professional. Unlike other social media sites that were started with a largely young audience of college students, Twitter's core demographic only began trending younger once the site became more established and younger people, businesses, and entertainers began to realize its usability and effectiveness and replaced the older users. Of YouTube, he wrote (p. 111): "YouTube was originally conceived in 2005 as an alternative to television viewing. It was alternative on all levels: a different technology, a shift in user routines, a new type of content, and a radical overhaul of the traditional broadcast industry, including its business models."

Researchers, such as Rheingold (2008), Silberman and Purser (2012), and Simon, (2012), found social media can be an effective tool for community organizations to preserve heritage and increase the sense of community and civic engagement. Using the framework, authors detailed the importance of SMS to impart or preserve components of individual cultures. Silberman and Purser (2012) examined the use of SNS for community-based heritage activities, such as in the participatory culture in communities including Ecuador, Fiji, South Africa, and in Europe that allow for a continuous view of past and traditional cultural practices along with current traditions, which through the use of technology ultimately shape future practices.

Simon (2012) in his chapter "Remembering Together" discussed ways in which social media can be used to recall and further discussed through collective memory events commonly shared. To illustrate his points, he discussed the Union Carbide gas leak and explosion in Bhopal India, which killed 3,787 people and injured hundreds. In this chapter, he also addressed corporate obfuscation of events and their ultimate financial liability to the ongoing medical expenses of the injured and the remaining community. More pointedly, he addressed SNS as a method of connecting the affected community and their ability to share their memory of occurrences, not for a fanciful trip down memory lane, but more for a coordinated and strategic accounting of the events that occurred more than 25 years ago. He outlined the formation of a group called the International Campaign for Justice in Bhopal, or ICJB, and the offshoot, Students for Bhopal or SFB, and their Facebook page. Originally, the group only had modest postings, while today there are some 1,851 members (p. 95). Simon also pointed out that while the formation of both ICJB and SFB were ideal as was the group's foray into social media, when examining some of the posts he noted that as they were not moderated, they were fairly vain in nature and requests to mobilize and engage in social protests went largely unanswered, essentially failing to take advantage of SNS as a way to bolster the effectiveness of both the group and ultimately the Bhopal justice campaign.

Rheingold (2008) also wrote of the value of "digital media" to encourage and foster greater civic engagement among the world's youth. He spoke to the apparent innateness of the propensity of many young people to use and engage in social or digital media platforms, but he also addressed the natural benefit of new media technology and its offshoot SNS to engage a community of political activists. He also noted that youth in the United States not only wanted to engage socially via SNS, they also wanted to connect and engage civically (p. 97). Citing an MTV survey of youth, some 70% of youth polled revealed that they were interested in civic engagement through social networks (p. 98). While Rheingold also detailed areas of contention regarding how encouragement of youth civic participation should actually occur, he noted that educational settings are the most logical spaces to encourage this sort of youth participation. He states that using all forms of digital media, including wikis, blogs, digital storytelling, podcasts, and video, and introducing them into school curricula and after-school programs would be highly beneficial to students. This implementation can be achieved in the classroom as well as in after-school programs and on an informal basis through community groups and activities.

He continued by offering a step-by-step outline of how young people can use their voice through social media to begin a campaign of citizen action to foster civic action and progress. He noted that youth can use a blog, wiki, comment on other social media sites, and use podcasts to tell their story using social media as it relates to the civic undertaking. He also advised young people to practice their interviewing skills by practicing with their friends discussing in Q&A format on topics on which they are passionate about. They were advised to practice being both the subject and the interviewer. Finally, he urged young people to take their practice and social media presence to "the next level" by going out in public and actually interviewing other youth about topics, which are of interest to young people today. In doing so, he advised young people working on such topics to create a series of podcasts, which detail some of the most pressing issues relating to this age group. Additionally, Rheinhold suggested creating journalistic interviews for the podcast and sharing them with local news outlets and bloggers on the local and national level to generate further interest and support.

Similarly, Charmaraman (2011) provided insight into the activities of high school students who participated in media production activities designed for the students to determine through exploration of media themes how they would ultimately become more involved in their communities and what kinds of social support systems would need to be outlaid to affect that result. The author found that by encouraging participation in alternative media that maneuvered around the dominant themes of mainstream media, which may actually oppress the desire in youths to engage civically, youths could empower themselves through re-imagined civic engagement realities.

While treated elsewhere in this volume, no work on SNS would be complete without some discussion of the Arab Spring. Hamdy and Gomaa (2012) discussed the ways in which the media framed The Arab Spring by examining social media posts to determine how central new media and SNS were in precipitating the uprising throughout the Arab world. The study, an analysis of media in Egypt, examined government-run newspapers and compared coverage of political uprisings to social media posts on the same subject in order to evaluate the nature of positive or negative coverage of the political revolution. In general, the author found that social media sites framed the protests in a positive manner, urging followers and readers to engage in the rapidly spreading campaign for social justice and political democracy. On the other hand, the study found that government-sponsored newspapers were especially harsh and provided inflammatory coverage of the uprisings often referring to them as "a harmful catastrophe" and overwhelmingly failed to get official word from the ground as to the cause and nature of the protests. Essentially the government-sponsored or quasi-government publications acted as a mere agent or mouthpiece for the former government of Egypt that ultimately sought to stamp out the protests. The authors of this study suggested that social media is much better equipped to relay the truths of political movements at the grassroots level.

Sayeed (2011) continued with this theme in his work, taking the analysis from the viewpoint of the coverage of the uprisings to bringing the voice and rationale of the primary actors of the movement into focus. In his work he outlined the ways in which social media can act as an agent of empowerment. Sayeed conducted an historical overview of the chain of events that sparked the revolution in Egypt and the initial seeds that were sown courtesy of the successful uprising in neighboring Tunisia. More specifically, the author seeks to uncover the motivations of why SNSs were used to spark protests that ultimately overthrew the oppressive Egyptian regime. He examined the ways in which social media fostered participation along with the motivation to participate in political protests despite living in a non-democratic society in where dissidents would face severe punishment. Ultimately, the study found that use of social media provided the necessary level of anonymity, which in turn bolstered the courage of the participants to engage in political dissent despite the heavy social mandate for conformity.

Similarly, Atkinson (2008) examined the ways that social media can foster greater participation in alternative media by encouraging consumers to take part in the selection of content and affording the opportunity to shape the context of media programming to reflect the needs of the local community. This can be a useful tool not only for the creation of programming, but also to foster community-organizing campaigns.

Yeo (2012) discussed the nature of social media users on YouTube to determine their motivations for use of the SNS. He divided the users into two groups: individualist or rational. The study found that relational users were more reachable targets for activists seeking to bolster the number of supporters of a political campaign. He found the latter group was more pliable in spreading the word about campaigns and receptive to messages.

Zuniga and Valenzuela (2010) in their work established how a link between strong social ties both online and offline has the tendency to engage in civic duties. The study found that those who had strong social ties offline also benefitted from strong online ties. These individuals were found to be more likely to be involved in civic activities in their community. Alternatively the study found that those with fewer ties socially also had fewer ties online and were also less likely to be involved with civic activities. This study essentially minimized the ability of social media to engage those who are not typically engaged. However, it made the strong assertion that the best and most effective use of social media is with those who are also civically active with strong social ties. In a later study, Zuniga (2012) confirmed these findings and further suggested that those who seek information via social networking sites have levels of social capital and are also more inclined to engage in civic activities both on and offline.

In the same vein, Cohen (2012) made the bold assertion that social media should be renamed to social energy in an effort to downplay the concept of social media's ability to foster increased social interaction. He further wrote that the very popularity of social media and its captivating stories of empowerment are nothing more than a series of "happenstances" whereby social media appeared to be of great benefit to it users. Beyond that the author posited that the very nature of online or new media technologies, the reference to the concept of what is typically considered social, is off base and simply not applicable.

Similarly, Sacks and Graves (2012) used the setting of a business communications course to impart the difference to their students between online and offline friends and power and effectiveness of both communities. The authors explained using the concepts of network size and quality to differentiate between a person's ability to gather and learn new information and also to network and expand the social and professional circle (p. 81). Ultimately, they directed their students to use social networks to their advantage in a way that will lead to personal empowerment rather than disgrace.

Most central to this work is the research of Appiah (2003), which highlighted the variances in the way African Americans and those of other races consume online media and evaluate "race-targeted" websites. Among the author's findings is the notion that African Americans are more receptive and retain more information from black-targeted websites, even though they evaluate race neutral and race-targeted sites in the same vein. The positive reception of targeted websites toward African Americans extended into receptiveness and retention of banner ads on sites, as well as memorization of key information points. This spoke to the high effectiveness of targeted and race-directed online media content for maximum effectiveness.

Byrne (2008) detailed the online social networking habits of African Americans who use the social media site BlackPlanet.com. Byrne surveyed the nature of the discussions on the site's forums and determined that for the most part the topics were focused on socializing rather than on topics related to community service. Ultimately, the study found that while many of the threads on the discussion board addressed some topics related to social activism as indicated in the titles of some threads, such as AIDS, Grassroots, Police Brutality, Slavery, Justice, Leadership, Education, and Economic Empowerment, among others (p. 332), the discussions did not ultimately lead to any productive or tangible action among site members. The author ultimately asserted that use of social media sites can be viewed as a possible avenue of growth to foster increased civic involvement in the African American community.

In a further debate on race and civic engagement, authors Harp, Bachmann, Cantrell Rosas-Moreno, and Loke (2010) asserted that while race does have a small impact on civic engagement, African American youth were more likely than their white counterparts to engage in civic and political activities in both online and offline settings. The study also established an important link between civic and political engagement and determined also that African American youth, like their older counterparts, also consume more news than other racial groups in addition to a greater likelihood of engaging in political discussions.

As noted earlier, this work is a content analysis of political and civil rights organizations that serve the interests of the African American community and their use of social media sites. According to Berger (2011), a content analysis is used most often to examine sets of data on a particular topic. The method is often used to examine specific themes and details of communication content. In this case, the social media usage of civil rights and community organizations is the focus of the content analysis. Accordingly, the social networking presence of five civil rights organizations was examined. The organizations examined were: the Congressional Black Caucus, the NAACP, the National Urban League, the National Action Network, and RainbowPUSH Coalition.

- The Congressional Black Caucus (CBC) was founded by a group of U.S. congressmen and congresswomen during the 92nd Congress, which was seated from 1971 to 1973. The primary mission of the CBC is to support and promote legislation that pushes social and economic equality among neglected communities, particularly African American communities, through the protection of major civil rights legislation.
- The NAACP (National Association for the Advancement of Colored People) was founded in 1909 by a group of civil and political activists in Springfield, Illinois. Historically, the NAACP has challenged the legal and social practices, which have contributed to the continued oppression of people of color, such as voting injustices, education, and racial diversity in media. The group is the oldest and most widely known civil rights organization in the United States and has more than half a million members.
- The National Urban League is a grassroots civil rights organization founded in New York City in 1920 by the Committee on the Condition of Urban Negroes. Its primary mission is to ensure employment, educational, economic, and political opportunities for African Americans in the urban centers of the United States. The National Urban League also authors several publications, including the annual *State of Black America.*
- The National Action Network was founded by the Reverend Al Sharpton in 1991 in New York City in order to "promote a modern-day civil rights agenda." Some of the group's main initiatives include criminal justice, education, voter rights, corporate responsibility, and employment.
- RainbowPUSH Coalition is the civil rights and social activism organization founded in 1996 by the Reverend Jesse L. Jackson Sr. The organization is a combination of two former organizations PUSH (People United to Serve Humanity) and the Rainbow Coalition. The primary mission of the group is to improve the lives of the powerless and to make the American Dream a reality for all.

The SNSs that were examined for all groups were Facebook, Twitter, and YouTube. To provide further comparison about alternative sites, a search was conducted using *The Network Journal's* online site, which provides a comprehensive list of African American service organizations titled "Black Organizations and Organizations Serving Black Communities" (http://www.tnj.com/lists-resources/black-organizations-and-organizations-serving-black-communities).

In comparison, a total of five lesser-known organizations were chosen to analyze the social media imprint of grassroots efforts that receive less media attention to determine how these groups are using SNS to reach their constituents. Those organizations are as follows:

- A Better Chance is an educational organization with the mission to support higher college admission rates for young people of color. The program helps high-achieving students from economically disadvantaged backgrounds realize academic success in elite educational institutions.
- National Association of Neighborhoods is a nationally based grassroots organization designed to foster social, economic, health, and environmental improvement and advocacy at the community level. The group achieves its mission through coordinated strategies with local leadership and targeted campaigns.
- National Black Child Development Institute is an organization dedicated to improving outcomes for socially vulnerable black children. The group's mission is accomplished through education, training, and advocacy programs for parents and children.
- 100 Black Men is a national organization that supports the educational and economic upliftment of black communities nationwide through local chapters. Many chapters sponsor mentoring programs for young African American males, college preparation and scholarship opportunities, as well as health and empowerment programs.
- 21st Century Foundation is a philanthropic organization with the mission to eradicate social inequities that have historically plagued African American men and boys. The group also encourages community empowerment initiatives through their work with grassroots organizations.

Data sets were gathered from each site in May 2013. It should be noted that the numbers provided in the tables below are non-static and change rapidly.

Findings and Discussion

While African Americans are large consumers of online media, they predominately use new media technology for social networking and entertainment. Although the African American community engaged in an historic and expertly organized social movement to obtain civil rights from the 1950s to the 1970s, there is little reminder of that social and political infrastructure in place today that would serve as an impetus for continued organization and further advancement of social equality in the United States. Accordingly, while young people in Middle East nations adeptly used social media to overthrow the oppressive regimes in Egypt, Tunisia, Yemen, and Libya, and engaged in countless protests in other countries, African American community organizers have yet to fully realize the galvanizing power of social media to see their own political and economic needs met in the United States.

Accordingly, social-political organizations in the United States, which historically have served African Americans and continue to do so today, are using social media to connect with members and to continue to advance the cause of equal rights. Despite the widespread use of social media by civil rights organizations, African Americans are still more likely to follow their favorite celebrity online than seek social justice or promote economic independence using new media technology.

Each of the civil rights and political organizations shown has a strong SNS presence. Icons posted on each website facilitated access to each organization's accounts. Of all the organizations, the NAACP was by far the most followed and discussed organization of the grouping, followed by the National Urban League. RainbowPUSH Coalition was the least followed on social media. However, there were dual opportunities to follow the coalition and its founder, Rev. Jesse Jackson Sr., on Facebook and Twitter, which may explain the low numbers for the organization. See Table 7.1.

Entity	Facebook	Twitter	YouTube
CBC	Likes: 50,153 Talking About: 1,022	Tweets: 3,568 Following: 333 Followers: 9,195	Subscribers: 12 Views: 2,642
NAACP	Likes: 177,572 Talking About: 9,816	Tweets: 6,428 Following: 11,520 Followers: 40,374	Subscribers: 1,306 Views: 936,287
National Action Network	Likes: 12,612 Talking About: 245	Tweets: 2,334 Following: 262 Followers: 7,403	Subscribers: 105 Views: 3,506
National Urban League	Likes: 15,605 Talking About: 172	Tweets: 5,661 Following: 212 Followers: 17,907	Subscribers: 129 Views: 41,748
Rainbow PUSH Coalition	Likes: 969 Talking About: 62	Tweets: 4,653 Following: 612 Followers: 1,562	Subscribers: 78 Views: 88,686

Table 7.1 Social Networking Presence of Civil Rights Organizations

As the awareness and national exposure decline with community organizations, so does the SNS imprint. Of the smaller groups surveyed, only 100 Black Men of America, Inc. showed a following on Facebook, Twitter, and YouTube. The other organizations did not have accounts with the major SNSs; their followers were very small in number. A Better Chance is an educational organization designed to give urban youth ample opportunities to pursue their educational goals. While this organization did not have an official link to a YouTube account, one or more of the group's affiliates posted videos about activities online.

RQ 1: How are political and civil rights organizations using new media technologies to foster greater membership and social and political awareness in the African American community?

Social media is widely used among the most-known civil rights organizations. Groups such as the NAACP and National Urban League enjoy substantial followings on Facebook and produced video links on YouTube. As noted, each of the well-known civil rights organizations uses SNS to promote their causes and to broadcast major events, press coverage, and public service campaigns. Members and non-members alike can gain access to these materials and keep abreast of the activities of each group. Groups were more likely to have more usage of Facebook than the other SNS sites. The NAACP used social media widely across all platforms analyzed (Facebook, Twitter, and YouTube). The group's YouTube videos were the biggest draw of all the SNSs, with nearly one million video views, compared with more than 177,000 Facebook followers. RainbowPUSH Coalition showed the biggest disparity in use of social media with just fewer than 1,000 Facebook likes corresponding with more than 88,000 video views on YouTube. The National Urban League showed similar numbers with slightly more than 15,000 likes on Facebook compared with more than 41,000 video views. The National Action Network used social media in an average manner across all platforms.

Twitter is more commonly used by these groups to generate conversation about ongoing events and community protests. While these efforts appear to be somewhat effective, the numbers of followers for these groups belie the actual numbers of African Americans who are using SNSs in general. If one were only examining social media use by looking at the imprint on social media sites for civil rights groups, it would be falsely concluded that African Americans don't use SNSs as much as other groups. African Americans are known to actually use social media sites, particularly Twitter and Instagram, more than other races, (Pew Research, 2012). Table 7.2 shows the social media usage among lesser known community groups. While larger groups use social media more frequently, community groups shown are only using social media on a sporadic basis.

Entity	Facebook	Twitter	YouTube
A Better Chance	Likes: 1,225 Talking About: 23	Tweets: 597 Following: 318 Followers: 404	Subscribers: N/A Views: N/A
National Association of Neighbor-hoods	Likes: N/A Talking About: N/A	Tweets: N/A Following: N/A Followers: N/A	Subscribers: N/A Views: N/A
National Black Child Develop-ment Institute	Likes: 1,507 Talking About: 71	Tweets: 1,286 Following: 578 Followers: 753	Subscribers: N/A Views: N/A
100 Black Men of America, Inc.	Likes: 10,941 Talking About: 61	Tweets: 1,384 Following: 3,553 Followers: 10,405	Subscribers: 81 Views: 17,656
21st Century Foundation	Likes: N/A Talking About: N/A	Tweets: N/A Following: N/A Followers: N/A	Subscribers: N/A Views: N/A

Table 7.2 Social Networking Presence among Lesser-Known Black Civic and Community Organizations

Further, while the community and civil rights organizations do use social media, the potential for even greater use appears to be lost. While the sites of top-rated TV shows watched by African Americans and celebrities most likely to be known to African Americans enjoy substantial followings on SNSs, in comparison the numbers of civil rights and community groups are substantially lower. Several examples abound in the body of research that detail how social media can lead to greater social and political advances as they have in the Arab Spring, or in the examples provided of how African American youth used social media to engage in community activism. The participation numbers for community groups suggest only a minimal interest among African Americans in political activism and a greater interest in TV programs and celebrities. As mentioned previously in the work of Coleman (2003) and Harp et. al. (2010), there are a vast number of social ills that continue to plague the African American community. A greater sense of urgency with regard to combating these ills can be implemented through the use of social media as noted in previous examples. Lacking a greater sense of urgency in the use of social media to increase social activism, the medium may continue to see underutilization by civil rights and community groups. Further, lacking the necessary training, leaders of such organizations may not realize the full potential of SNSs to increase their membership and promote more involvement with primary issues of great importance today (National Urban League, 2013).

RQ 2: What other positive examples exist to display culturally relevant techniques that may be applied on a community-wide basis to foster greater avenues to political, economic and social empowerment in the African American community?

Based on the review of literature, there a number of solid examples, such as those cited in the work of Zukin et. al., (2006) and Rheingold (2008), who each discussed the success community organizations have had with imparting the example of civic involvement in youth. Additionally, the work of Simon (2012) provides an historical construct for African Americans who may want to employ the use of SNS to relive the successes of prior campaigns for civil rights and other movements to serve as the blueprint for campaigns for today.

While each of the major civil rights organizations in this research had a respectable showing on social media, the NAACP outpaced all of its nearest challengers in every category, with nearly 180,000 followers on Facebook, more than 936,000 number view of their YouTube content, and more than 40,000 Twitter followers. The most eminent civil rights group led the way in social networking usage when compared to other civil rights and community activist organizations. The nearest competitor was The Congressional Black Caucus, with a little more than 50,000 followers on Facebook and more than 9,000 Twitter followers. RainbowPUSH Coalition has a high number of YouTube views at well more than 88,000 compared to the NAACP's strong showing. The NAACP's video content on YouTube provided first-hand accounts and reviews of major events such as press conferences and the announcement of the State of Maryland's historic decision to the repeal the death penalty. Other videos shown were PSAs about voter ID laws, AIDS and the black church, and the widely covered Silent March NYC campaign designed to bring awareness to and end the Stop and Frisk laws, which allow police to stop without question or cause anyone under suspicion in New York City. Civil rights advocates say the law unfairly targets persons of color, particularly black and Latino males. Interested parties are able to not only keep abreast of current events by the organization, but also receive a review of all of its previous activities. Because the organization has shown a large volume of videos on YouTube, this may add to an increased following on Twitter and Facebook. To encourage participation in its social media imprint, the NAACP prominently display all participating logos for Facebook, Twitter, YouTube, Flickr, and a mobile icon that allows users to receive updates from the organization via mobile device. Beyond the current efforts outlaid by the NAACP, it is not known if there are plans to heighten their social media imprint to possibly grow membership to one million.

As the only group among the lesser-known civil rights or community organizations surveyed to employ the use of discussed social media sites, 100 Black Men had the most solid social media usage with imprints in Facebook with nearly 11,000 likes, more than 10,000 Twitter followers, and more than 17,000 video views on YouTube with 81 subscribers. The videos shown on YouTube featured highlights of the 26th and 27th annual conventions, messages from the organization's leadership, and a promotional video, which promoted the mission and accomplishments of 100 Black Men in the United States and around the world. The displayed videos also showcased the works of local chapters of 100 Black Men, including community involvement in Phoenix; a backpack give-away in Madison, Wisconsin; and the establishment of the first international chapter in London, England. These video clips can not only be used to highlight the good works of the organization, but may also serve as an invitation to uninvolved members of the community to engage with some of the established major initiatives.

RQ 3: Beyond the social, political and economic advantages of more directed and targeted online and new media usage among African Americans, in what ways can these new ideas be imparted to the community at large to ensure wide-scale implementation?

The data suggests that while African Americans were using social media for entertainment and social purposes, there is a greater opportunity to use online technology for social and political advancement. Community groups, organizations, political leaders, and individuals may well benefit from the increased use of this technology to bolster their campaigns and actively engage the citizenry. For example, while 100 Black Men and the NAACP have used social media to their advantage, the other groups surveyed may do more to increase awareness about their central mission and to encourage community involvement through participation in the many sponsored activities. The National Urban League publishes an annual report, *The State of Black America*. How does the organization use social media to promote the findings and publication of a report, which outlines ways in which African Americans must improve the condition of their communities nationwide? It is also possible that an organization like A Better Chance, which provides educational funding and support to children of color attending elite schools throughout the nation, could also do more to not only broadcast their central mission, but to also encourage strengthening of intellectual prowess and academic achievement in the Black community. Similarly, the study revealed that the National Black Child Development Institute had an extensive website that displays a wealth of information for parents of color. This site also detailed the organization's initiatives, including early-child education, family engagement, health, and child welfare. Beyond the use of Facebook and the 1,500 likes on the group's page, perhaps a more aggressive campaign to reach members of the community to deliver crucial information about child rearing, legislation, and upcoming events would prove effective. While NBCDI is a national organization, there are currently some 21 affiliates in most major cities, including New York; Los Angeles; Chicago; Philadelphia; Atlanta; Greensboro, North Carolina; Houston; Jackson, Mississippi; and Seattle. Of the 21 affiliates, only Ft. Lauderdale, Florida, has a Facebook page of its own with 111 followers. The page also serves as a source of information about the local chapter and features a call for membership and a banner ad about the upcoming annual convention in New Orleans, as well as scores of photos with inspirational sayings about parenting, child achievement, and physical fitness.   For NBCDI and the other community organizations, one could only imagine the possibilities for membership and increased involvement at the grassroots level if there were more encouragement for participation on social media sites. One possible solution, since it is known that African Americans are using social media largely for entertainment and social purposes according to Byrne (2008), perhaps community groups might post on the sites of celebrities or popular television programs to encourage traffic on sites of their own.

Conclusion, Limitations, and Implications for Future Research

In conclusion, while African Americans are heavy users of social media sites, those sites are largely entertainment and social in nature. While the top civil rights groups, such as the National Urban League and the National Action Network, enjoy substantial followings on Facebook, Twitter, and YouTube, social network sites for lesser-known organizations are used sparingly. Only one group, 100 Black Men, employed a SNS footprint across all three sites surveyed. While these organizations engage in necessary work, their numbers might be greater and community involvement may be bolstered with more use of social media (Byrne, 2008; Harp et. al., 2010; Zuniga and Valenzuela, 2010).

While African Americans continue to suffer from a host of social injustices and disparities (National Urban League, 2013), there is no real social impetus to foster change on a national level, as in the days of the Civil Rights Movement of the 1950s and 1960s. Researchers do, however, point to an overall drop in civic engagement across all racial groups (Howard and Parks, 2012; Zukin et. al., 2006). Despite the limited civic engagement for all groups, African Americans are actually considered more socially and civically engaged than other groups and this is particularly so when it comes to youth and their use of social media (Bachmann and Cantrell Rosa-Moreno, 2010).

This is a brief survey of social media use, and this study was by design limited in scope. The study does not detail the various trends in usage among African Americans, nor does it explore the various implications of each medium such as why Facebook might be considered more impactful than Twitter. In the nature of brevity, how the number of YouTube hits might speak to a celebrity or civil rights organization's compelling nature was not explored. These avenues of additional research can propel the topic further and advance and broaden both the nature of why individuals use social media and the power of such sites. Further, only three SNS sites were featured in this research; Facebook, Twitter, and YouTube. These sites are the top three SNS sites and that positioning alone opens up even further avenues of research as some scholars have pointed to the heavy commercialism of these sites and the notion of social is lost on many users (van Dijck, 2013).

While there are a host of other social networking sites, each has a unique design and appeal for individual users and organizations. Future studies may consider the overarching impact of social media in aggregate as well as individual sites and their meaning for individual users, particularly African Americans. African Americans, in turn may do themselves more good by using SNS for the ultimate good, civic, and political advancement, as the NAACP did in the wake of the verdict in the George Zimmerman trial.

References

Appiah, O. (2003). Americans online: Differences in surfing and evaluating race target websites by Black and White users. *Journal of Broadcasting, 47*(4), pp. 537-555.

Atkinson, J.D. (2008). Towards a model of interactivity in alternative media: A multilevel analysis of audiences and producers in a new social movement network. *Mass Communication & Society, 11*(3), pp. 227-247.

Baran, S.J., & Davis, D.K. (2009). Mass Communication Theory: Foundations, *Ferment, and Future.* Boston: Wadsworth Cengage Learning. pp. 271-273.

Berger, A.A. (2011). Media and Communication Research Methods, An Introduction to Qualitative and Quantitative Approaches (2nd Ed). Thousand Oaks, CA: Sage.

Byrne, D. (2008). Public discourse, community concerns, and civic engagement: Exploring Black social networking traditions on BlackPlanet.com. Journal of Computer-Mediated Communication, *13*(1), pp. 319-340.

Cai, X. (2005). An experimental examination of the computer's time displacement effects. *New Media & Society, 7*(8), pp. 8-21. Charmaraman, L. (2011). Congregating to create for social change: Urban youth   media production and sense of community. *Learning, Media and Technology, 38*(1), pp. 102-115.

Cohen, H. (2012). From social media to social energy: The idea of the 'social' in 'social media.' Global Media Journal Australian Edition, *6*(1).

Gil de Zuniga, H. & Valenzuela S. (2011). The mediating path to a stronger citizenship: Online and offline network, weak ties, and civic engagement. Communication Research, *38*(3), pp. 397-421.

Hamdy, N., & Gomaa, E.H. (2012). Framing the Egyptian Uprising in Arabic language newspapers and social media. *Journal of Communication, 62*(2), pp. 195-211.

Harp, D., I. Bachman, T. Cantrell Rosa-Moreno, & J. Loke, (2010). Wave of Hope: African-American youth use media and engage more civically, politically than Whites. *The Howard Journal of Communications, 21*(3), 224-246.

Howard, P.N., & Parks, M.R. (2012). Social media and political change: Capacity, constraint, and consequence. *Journal of Communication, 62*(2), pp. 359-362.

Hutton, G., & Fosdick, M. (2011). The globalization of social media consumer relationships with brands evolve in the digital space. *Journal of Advertising Research, 54*(4), pp. 564-570.

Gladwell, M. (2010). Annals of Innovation: Small change, why the revolution will not be tweeted. *The New Yorker* October, 2010. Retrieved from http://www.newyorker.com/reporting/2010/10/04/101004fa_gladwell? printable=true&current/page=all, pp. 1-10

Kestnbaum, M., Robinson, J.P., Neustadtl, A., & Alvarez, A. (2002). Information technology and functional time displacement. *IT & Society, 1*(1), pp. 21-37.

Kunur, P. (2011). What's the most social of all media? *Advertising Age, 82*(33), p. 1.

Lee, P. & Yeung, L. (2006). Assessing the displacement effects of the Internet. Telematics and Informatics, *25*(3) pp. 145-155.

Loader, B.D., & Mercea, D., (Eds.), (2012). *Social Media and Democracy, Innovations for Participatory Politics.* New York: Routledge.

Means Coleman, R. (2003). Bringing diversity and activism to media education through African American-centered pedagogical cases: The mediation of ebonics and the NAACP television networks boycott. *Television New Media,* 4(4), pp. 411-438.

Mesch, G. (2012). Minority Status and the use of computer mediated communication: A test of the social diversification hypothesis. Communication Research, *39*(3), pp. 317-337.

National Urban League (2013). 2013 State of Black America: Redeem The *Dream Jobs Rebuild America.* New York: National Urban League.

NAACP (2013). NAACP Petition to DOJ Reaches 1.5 Million Signatures. Retrieved from http://www.naacp.org/news/entry/naacp-petition-to-doj-reaches-1.5-million-signatures

The Nielsen Company (2012) Report: African Americans Still Vital And Growing. *The U.S. [Report].* Retrieved from: http://www.nielsen.com/us/en/newswire/2012/report-african-americans-still-vital-and-growing-in-the-us.html

Paradise, A.M. (2011). Bridging service-learning with media literacy: Creating contexts for communication students to educated youth on media content, consumption and effects. *Communication Teacher, 25*(4), pp. 234-239.

The Pew Research Center (2013). Report: The Demographics of Social Media Users – 2012. Retrieved from: http://www.pewinternet.org/topics/Social-Networking.aspx?typeFilter=5

Pew Research Points out different (social) strokes for different folks (2013). Advertising Age, *84*(7).

Potter, W.J. (2008). *Media Literacy, 4th Edition.* Thousand Oaks, CA: Sage.

Pozner, J.L. (2010). *Reality Bites Back: The Troubling Truth About Guilty Pleasure TV.* Berkeley, CA: Seal Press.

Rainie, L., Smith, A., Lehman Scholzman, K., Brady, H., & Verba, S. (2012). Social media and political engagement. *A Report of the Pew Internet &*

American   Life   Project.   Retrieved   on   11/1/12   from:
http://pewinternet.org/Reports/2012/Political-Engagement.aspx

Rheingold, H. (2008). Using participatory media and public voice to encourage civic engagement in L. Bennett (Ed.). *Civic Life Online.* Cambridge, MA: MIT Press. pp. 97-118.

Sayed, N. (2011). Towards the Egyptian Revolution: Activists' perceptions of social media for mobilization. Journal of Arab & Muslim Media Research *4*(3 & 4), pp. 273-298.

Sacks, M.A., & Graves, N. (2012). How many "friends" do you need? Teaching students how to network using social media. *Business* Communication Quarterly, *75*(1), pp. 80-88.

Schmeltzer, J.C. (2011). Developing a social media plan for the community press. *Grassroots Editor*, Winter, 2011 *54*(4), pp. 6-9.

Shapiro, T.M. (2010). The hidden cost of being African American. In M.L. Anderson & P. Hill Collins (Eds.), *Race, Class & Gender, An Anthology (7th Ed.).* Belmont, CA: Wadsworth. pp. 129-137.

Silberman, N., & Purser, M. (2012). Collectible memory as affirmation: People-centered cultural heritage in a digital age. In E. Giaccardi, (Ed.), *Heritage* and Social Media, Understanding Heritage in a Participatory Culture. London: Routledge. pp. 13-29.

Simon, R.I. (2012). Remembering together: Social media and the formation of the historical present. In E. Giaccardi, (Ed.), *Heritage and Social Media,* Understanding Heritage in a Participatory Culture. London: Routledge. pp. 89-106.

Target Market News (2013). Black TV Ratings for Week of April 29 - May 5. Target Market News, The Black Consumer Market Authority, retrieved from http://targetmarketnews.com/storyid05101301.htm

UPI.com (July 13, 2013). Jury Finds George Zimmerman Not Guilty in Trayvon Martin's   Death,   Retrieved   from http://www.upi.com/Top_News/US/2013/07/13/Jury-finds-George-Zimmerman-not-guilty-in-Trayvon-Martins-death/UPI-77661373726360/

van Dijck, J. (2013). *The Culture of Connectivity A Critical History of Social Media.* New York: Oxford University Press.

Vergeer, M., & Pelzer, B. (2011). Consequences of media and Internet use for offline and online network capital and for well-being. A causal model approach. Journal of Computer Mediated Communication, *15*(1), pp. 189-210.

Yeo, T.E. (2012). Social-media early adopters don't count: How to seed participation in interactive campaigns by psychological profiling of digital consumers. *Journal of Advertising Research, 52*(3), pp. 297-308.

Zukin, C., Keeter, S., Andolina, M., Jenkins, K., & Delli Carpini, M.X. (2006). *A New Engagement? Political Participation, Civic Life, and the Changing American Citizen.* New York: Oxford University Press.

Zuniga, H.G. (2012). Social media use for news and individuals' social capital, civic engagement and political participation. *Journal of Computer-Mediated Communication, 17*(3), pp. 319-336.

Chapter 8
The Seven Sisters and Their Siblings Go Digital: An Analysis of
Women's Magazine Content on Websites, iPads, and Cell Phones
Yanick Rice Lamb & Kendra Desrosiers

For more than a century, the "Seven Sisters" have dominated the women's magazines category (Johnson and Prijatel, 2007). They have also been leaders in magazine publishing overall, with some titles ranking in the top 10 for circulation and advertising revenue. The eldest sister, *McCall's*, was born as *The Queen: Illustrating McCall's Bazaar Glove-Fitting Patterns* in 1870 (Endres and Luech, 1995). Her siblings appeared from the 1880s to 1930s: *Ladies Home Journal, Good Housekeeping, Redbook, Better Homes and Gardens, Woman's Day,* and finally *Family Circle.*

Over the years, the magazines have undergone periodic makeovers, as feminists and others questioned their relevance and historical focus on homemaking, especially during the women's movement of the 1960s and 1970s. One of the most severe makeovers led to the death of *McCall's*, which morphed into *Rosie the Magazine* in 2001 to compete with upscale women's magazines such as *O the Oprah Magazine* and *Martha Stewart Living*. In November 2000, comedian and talk-show host Rosie O'Donnell signed an agreement with Gruner & Jahr to be a partner in what was originally conceived as *Rosie's McCall's* (Kuczynski, 2001). By the end of 2002, *Rosie* had ceased publication amid a flurry of counter-suits (McCafferty, 2003).

In light of one of the most radical eras of media transition, this study will analyze whether the survivors are keeping up with technological advances to serve readers and remain competitive with younger women's magazines. It will seek to determine if the magazines are effectively using websites, cell phones, and iPads, which are the primary tools at the center of this digital transformation. Effective use of these tools can impact a media company's success, and the success of the major publications examined in this study has implications for magazine publishing in general.

"If you don't read the signs that tell of a changing field, a successful title can become a disaster" (p. 87), warned magazine consultant James B. Kobak in a March 1990 article in *Folio: the Magazine for Magazine Management*, "25 Years of Change; What's Been Happening in the Consumer Magazine Industry? Emerging Trends May Come as a Surprise." When Kobak (1990) sounded his alarm, combined circulation for the Seven Sisters had fallen to about 37 million, down from 45 million in 1979 near the end of the first wave of the Women's Liberation Movement (Carmody, 1990). Twenty years later in 1999, it stood at 32.6 million, according to the Association for Magazine Media. By 2009, combined circulation had fallen to 20.7 million for the surviving six sisters. Even with *O the Oprah Magazine* as a replacement for *McCall's* or *Rosie,* the number hit just 23 million (Association for Magazine Media [MPA], 2009).

Nevertheless, at least five sisters held onto spots in MPA's top ten for paid and verified circulation. *Better Homes and Gardens* led the pack at No. 4 with 7.6 million in circulation, followed by *Good Housekeeping* (No. 5), *Woman's Day* (No. 7), *Family Circle* (No. 8), and *Ladies Home Journal* (No. 9). *Redbook* held the 30th spot at 2.2 million.

In the mid-nineties, many consumer magazines, including *Woman's Day*, launched online versions of their publications (Daly, Henry, and Ryder, 1997). "The Internet is now the third most popular news platform, behind local television news and national television news" (p. 2), according to a March 2010 report by Pew Internet & American Life Project, *Understanding the Participatory News Consumer: How Internet and Cell Phone Users Have Turned News Into a Social Experience* (Purcell, Rainie, Mitchell, Rosenstiel, and Olmstead, 2010).

The social experience also included tablets or e-readers, which took off with the introduction of Apple's iPad (Stone and Vance, 2009). "As of September 2010, 4% of American adults own a tablet computer such as an iPad," up from 3% four months earlier in May, according to a 2011 Pew report, Generations and Their Gadgets (Zickuhr, 2011, p. 13). Apple Inc. (2011) sold 15 million iPads between April 2010, when it was released, and March 2011. On a typical day, Pew reported, 92% of Americans obtained news from multiple platforms and only 7% used one platform. The question arises then as to what extent are the remaining Seven Sisters keeping up with technological advances to serve readers and remain competitive with other women's magazines? Are the magazines using technology effectively? These questions will be addressed in this chapter.

Literature Review

Scholarly research is limited on magazine use of platforms such as tablets or e-readers. This study seeks to add to the body of knowledge during this era of rapid media transformation. A major characteristic of this media revolution is the focus on "personal media" with greater consumer interaction (Moggridge, 2010, p. 14), notes trend forecaster Paul Saffo, a consulting associate professor at Stanford University, where he is also a visiting scholar in the mediaX research network. Traditionally, Saffo noted, mass media has allowed for limited participation or talkback by consumers. In the 20th century, interactivity in media meant consuming advertisements or an editor printing a handful of letters submitted by readers.

"The personal media world, in contrast, is a world where answering back is not an option — it's required. Otherwise you don't have a personal media experience," Saffo said. "That is a profoundly new territory for people designing systems" (Moggridge, 2010, p. 14-15). This two-way conversation is increasingly important as more people use iPads, smartphones, and other mobile devices to view magazines.

Saffo described the following as the core differentiators between mass media and personal media revolutions: the nature of the experience, the location, and the nature of the dominant players. Mass media was delivered to consumers' living rooms, and the industry was dominated by "the few and large" major television networks, publishers, and producers. Personal media, conversely, became dominated by "the many and small," allowing consumers to participate. Consumers could always "carry personal media" with them (Moggridge, 2010, p. 16).

With the digital, or personal media, revolution came a large demand from consumers for new media options. In 2010, for example, 49 digital and online magazines were launched and 53 publications ceased printing on paper and moved exclusively online (State of the Media Report, 2011). Additionally, the number of consumer magazines with websites increased by 50% since 2006 (MPA, 2010). With the rise of web and mobile, it was clear that as consumers adopted emerging platforms they expected media to evolve with their consumption behavior, an expectation magazine publishers were slow to realize.

Consumers are interested in reading magazine content across platforms. Of print subscribers, the majority are also interested in digital content and of non-subscribers, 61% are interested in digital-only magazine options, according to MPA (2010).

About 31% of readers used a computer or a mobile device to visit a magazine's website during a six-month period as reported in 2011, and the majority of U.S. consumers planned to purchase an e-reader or tablet within the next three years. Of the prospective e-reader consumers, 80% wanted to read magazines on their e-reader/tablet devices (MPA, 2010). Researchers predicted that this trend toward web, mobile, and e-reader content and applications would continue to increase (State of the Media Report, 2011).

Early adopters of tablet magazine technology were able to remain competitive in the changing media consumption landscape. However, this competitive advantage didn't always translate in sales. This only added to the apprehension of latecomers to tablet publishing.

The percentage of newsstand sales captured by early purchases of iPad magazine apps ranged from single to low double digits. With its technology-oriented audience of early adopters, *Wired* was the front-runner and began developing its app even before the iPad had been released. The magazine exceeded its newsstand sales by selling 105,000 copies of its inaugural iPad edition. Sales later leveled off to about 37% of monthly newsstand sales. *Glamour,* one of its sister magazines at Conde-Nast, came out with an iPad edition just months after the iPad's debut. "*Glamour* — one more major newsstand seller — sold 4,099 copies of its first issue on the iPad, the big September issue," Nat Ives (2011, p. 1) wrote in a fall 2010 issue of *Advertising Age.* "That's again equivalent to less than 1% of its newsstand sales (Ives, 2011, p. 1)."

While no one could foresee the high demand for iPads, this knowledge might not have made a difference for magazines that took a wait-and-see approach. Many companies are afraid of making the wrong decision and unwilling to take a chance in investing blindly on emerging technologies, according to studies by George S. Day and Paul J.H. Schoemaker (2000) cited in "A Different Game" in *Wharton on Managing Emerging Technologies.* A preeminent challenge facing magazines when embracing new platforms is tailoring content for each particular platform — developing a cross-media publishing strategy (Paxhia and Rosenblatt, 2008).

Philosopher Alasdair MacIntyre's theory of a practice can be useful in balancing out the challenges of cost versus comprehensiveness in achieving such an online strategy across platforms, suggested David A. Craig, Ph.D., professor and associate dean for academic affairs in the Gaylord College of Journalism and Mass Communication at the University of Oklahoma. Craig examined the pressure of profits and the difficulty in dealing with so many multimedia platforms and devices in his book *Excellence in Online Journalism: Exploring Current Practices in an Evolving Environment.* "Online journalism has the potential to be more thorough than journalism in any other medium," he noted. "By pursuing a standard of excellence of comprehensiveness, which shows up online in distinctive ways, journalists can help realize internal goods such as knowledge and inquiry and reshape what excellent journalism looks like" (Craig, 2010, p. 56).

Jakob Nielsen, Ph.D., who has conducted extensive research on website, mobile, and app usability, noted that media companies should not only tailor content to each platform, but that they must also design for the specific platform to improve the user experience. Nielsen defined a mobile site as "one designed specifically for use on mobile devices, whereas a 'full' site is a regular website designed mainly for use on a full-screen desktop computer." The key, he said, was to design for small screens to minimize "the fat-finger syndrome" and to include only the features that matter most. "While a mobile site is good, a mobile app is even better," added Nielsen (2011, p. 1), especially if there is more interactivity. Given recent improvements, the usability success rate increased to 76% for mobile apps versus 64% for mobile sites.

Nielsen's research supports other findings that reproducing print content in digital with little to no added value, a practice often referred to as "shovelware," is disadvantageous. According to National Museum of Design chief Bill Moggridge, magazines were shoveling print content down digital channels:

> They had content that they could send down different pipelines — the print pipe, the Internet pipe, the mobile phone pipe — and they thought that the more pipes they sent it down, the more value they would gain. They were wrong. This dangerously simplistic view didn't take into account how people consumed each medium and what mode they were in. The art of creating content that is tuned for consumption in each medium tends to separate the versions, so that the material prepared for a glossy magazine — rich with images and elegant typography — will not fit well on a pixilated screen of limited size, be it personal computer or a PDA (Moggridge, 2010, p. 73).

According to Neil Stevenson, leader of design firm IDEO's Kid+Play domain, magazines that use the same content on all of their platforms have bleak prospects of success. "The magazines that have done well have optimized their content over a long period of time to deliver exactly the right magazine experience, which means that it is exactly wrong for these other media" (Moggridge, 2010, p. 73).

Merely adopting iPad, mobile, and web technology is not enough to be competitive for magazine publishers. Efficacy across those platforms is imperative to their success, but the costs of the resources required often outweigh the benefit of optimization. This is exacerbated by the growing competition from amateur blogs and websites with low cost and quick time-to-market advantages.

Leaders in the digital publishing realm such as *Wired*, whose magazine is optimized for web, mobile, and e-reader, have been able to adapt their content successfully to various platforms. According to *Wired* editor Chris Anderson, magazine websites should take advantage of the unlimited space on the web and not serve as lower-quality versions of the print editions, but in doing so there are challenges in production cost and competition (Moggridge, 2010).

"The cost structure is not right," Anderson said, "because we're competing with amateurs who are creating an infinite amount of content on very narrow subjects for free" (Moggridge, 2010, p. 57). The "many and small" dominant players described earlier by Saffo in personal media also included a number of outlets producing content for free consumption (Moggridge, 2010, p. 16).

To combat this, Anderson recommended that media companies embrace user-generated content. "Our challenge really is how to bring amateur energy into our domain — how to use our brand, our kind if catalytic power, our leadership, and our technology to incentivize people to create valuable content within our confines" (Moggridge, 2010, p. 57).

Methodology

This study incorporated Nielsen's widely cited usability research as a theoretical framework to analyze 10 magazines along with their websites, mobile sites, and any iPad apps to address the following research questions:

RQ1: Are the Seven Sisters keeping up with technological advances to serve readers and remain competitive with other women's magazines?
RQ2: Are the magazines using technology effectively?

The steps included determining the sample size, identifying a coding instrument, adapting it for this study, selecting an observation period, conducting the content analysis, and finally answering the research questions. The research was primarily quantitative, with some qualitative analysis in examining best practices, drawing conclusions, and making recommendations.

The sample included six of the surviving Seven Sisters: *Ladies Home Journal, Good Housekeeping, Redbook, Better Homes and Gardens, Woman's Day,* and *Family Circle.* The newer magazines were selected, because of their association with the Seven Sisters, audited circulations, comparable content, and ability to develop digital versions based on their resources and success. *Essence* has been called the "eighth sister" in terms of diversity, and *Glamour* has been described as a younger sister with *Marie Claire* as its sibling. *O the Oprah Magazine* is considered one of the most successful women's magazines of modern times. Along with the six survivors, all are on the Association of Magazine Media's list of the top 100 magazines in paid circulation as verified by the Audit Bureau of Circulations (ABC), whose name has recently changed with the times to the Alliance for Audited Media (AAM). The younger siblings are also properties of major media corporations: Time Inc., Conde-Nast, and Hearst.

After examining several coding instruments, the researchers selected one used by Xiaopeng Wang (2006) to analyze *The New York Times* website, nytimes.com, in "Exploring Sample Sizes for Content Analysis of Online News Sites" for AEJMC's Communication Theory & Methodology Division. Wang's methodology was best suited for this research, because it was among the most current, relevant, and comprehensive models available. (See Appendix A for Wang's model.)

The researchers then adapted and expanded Wang's coding instrument to incorporate Nielsen's theories on mobile, app, and website usability as well as the research of Mark Tremayne (2004), who used network theory to analyze the use of hyperlinks. They expanded the multimedia categories to reflect new developments on the Internet and attributes measured in other digital research. They added variables for social media, reader engagement, and digital representation of cover stories, particularly for iPad apps. The cover of the printed version became the primary unit of analysis, because magazines consider cover stories as the best of the best in each issue. Magazines often devote more resources to make cover stories engaging and reader friendly. Cover stories would also be featured most prominently on other platforms, such as websites, iPads, and cell phones, and therefore, they were the easiest content to find, code, and analyze along with other multimedia features.

When coding the cover stories, researchers evaluated technological variables based on the presence or lack of interactive tools on the sites, similar to the methodology in widely cited Internet studies by the Bivings Group, an Internet communications firm that also conducts content and technology audits. A pre-test was useful in selecting an observation period. This preliminary analysis of digital and print content helped the researchers determine that the March 2011 issue would be sufficient, based on efficiency, redundancies in the pre-test, and the iPad's limited time on the market. The iPad, introduced in April 2010, had been available less than a year during the research period in early 2011, but had quickly captured the attention of magazine companies and consumers.

For the actual study, three coders analyzed the March 2011 issue of the 10 magazines across four platforms, a total of 40 versions. (They also coded March 2012 issues for comparison and updates.) Coding 40 versions multiple times would have proved to be more unwieldy than beneficial, given the "digital snapshot" nature of the content analysis in capturing a moment in time. Coding only March 2011 issues allowed the researchers to meet their goals of determining whether the magazines were effective users of technology and early adopters of mobile devices such as the iPad. (See Appendix B for the coding instrument used for this research.)

Finally, the researchers used the results to compare the surviving Seven Sisters to each other and to their younger siblings. They also used secondary data analysis to examine how the magazines adhered to best practices employed by other media companies, including early adopters of the iPad such as *Wired* magazine. Nielsen's usability theory proved useful in interpreting the findings.

Findings

RQ1: Are the Seven Sisters keeping up with technological advances to serve readers and remain competitive with other women's magazines?

All six survivors had websites that upheld their service-oriented missions and that reflected the focus of their print versions. Their websites were rich with text and photos, but used multimedia features and social media to varying degrees of effectiveness and creativity as described below. All but one optimized their sites for mobile phones such as the iPhone or BlackBerry. *Good Housekeeping, Redbook,* and *Woman's Day* had rudimentary iPad apps. The other three — *Family Circle, Ladies Home Journal,* and *Better Homes and Gardens* — displayed their pages using the Portable Document Format (PDF) through Texterity.

The survivors were competitive with the younger magazines in terms of websites, since all 10 had shortcomings that leveled the playing field. However, the younger magazines did a better job in adapting their content for mobile platforms such as smartphones and especially tablets. In the rush to keep up with mobile technology and other magazines during the current media revolution, the six survivors were only marginally "in the game." They weren't totally on the sidelines with magazines that lacked resources or those that were taking a watchful waiting approach, but they weren't playing with the best equipment. Once a reader has experienced an interactive iPad app, the static nature of a PDF just doesn't cut it. The iPad apps for *Good Housekeeping, Redbook,* and *Woman's Day* weren't much better.

RQ2: Are the magazines using technology effectively?

The six survivors used technology more effectively on their websites than on mobile sites for smartphones and tablets. However, there was still room for improvement as noted below. On mobile sites for cell phones, *Woman's Day* held its own with *Glamour* and *Essence*. The rest had mixed results, especially *Ladies Home Journal*, which lacked mobile optimization, forcing readers to maneuver the standard-sized website around on the tiny screens of their phones. *Good Housekeeping, Redbook,* and *Woman's Day* used the technological features of the iPad much less effectively than *Glamour* and *Marie Claire,* both of which took advantage of the unique capabilities and tactile nature of the device to provide a more engaging experience for users.

Additional findings below answer the research questions in greater detail and explain how the 10 magazines used various multimedia features across platforms.

iPad Applications
Many magazines seemed to have iPad apps for the sake of having iPad apps. Many failed to take better advantage of the features and appeal of the iPad as had been the case with the aforementioned *Wired* and *Martha Stewart Living,* which used stop-action photography, for example, to show flowers bloom.

In fact, some of the magazines in this study were not much more interactive than magazines using basic flip technology, which simulates the effect of a reader turning or flipping pages. This included *Good Housekeeping, Redbook,* and *Woman's Day*. All of their content was shovelware, albeit far more beautiful than on a website because of the iPad's crisp resolution. Readers couldn't tap on the cover lines to go to the stories, except for one of eight cover lines on *Redbook:* "Better Sleep for Life." The table of contents, which is essential in an app, had limited interactivity. Readers could tap on hyperlinked page numbers or headlines to reach stories, but not the pictures. However, they could see the entire issue by tapping the upper right corner of the device for a page viewer of numbered thumbnail layouts or scroll through them along the bottom of the screen. These navigation elements became standard in some form on most apps. In the study "Usability of iPad Apps and Websites," Raluca Badiu and Jakob Nielsen (2011) recommended consistent "padding" to add invisible space around items in a table of contents so that readers could tap anywhere near the words to navigate to an article.

Other features in the survivors' iPad apps were minimal. *Woman's Day* readers could click continued lines to go to the next page of an article, reach a blog on the website through a link at the end of a column, or download certain content. In *Redbook,* the link at the end of a fashion spread went to a shopping page on the app. On the editor's page, readers could click the editor's email to send her a message or another link that took them from the iPad to the website to see a scarf video. *Marie Claire and Glamour* would embed the video link in their iPad apps. *Redbook* missed an opportunity to add interactivity to the arrows and directions shown in the "Vacation or Staycation?" game that appeared on the last page of the magazine.

Family Circle, Ladies Home Journal, and *Better Homes and Gardens* used Texterity to display simple PDFs of the pages, which paled in comparison to more engaging iPad apps. Readers could view links; share a story with others as an email; or send a copy. Unlike some iPad magazines that had thumbnails of the pages along the bottom, Texterity showed them on a separate page.

Marie Claire and *Glamour* had the strongest iPad apps of the 10 magazines analyzed; *Essence* lacked an iPad app for its March issue. *Glamour* also redesigned its app for the April 2011 issue. *Better Homes and Gardens* introduced an iPad app with its April 2011 issue that rivaled those of its younger siblings. Other women's magazines, outside this analysis, introducing apps in spring 2011 included *Shape* and *Self.*

Apple designed the iPad without flash capabilities, so magazines either skipped or compensated for any flash in their website versions by using other visual and audio features along with HTML5. This markup language makes it easier to run multimedia content, especially on low-powered computers and handheld devices. It makes multimedia more secure, allows web pages to perform better, and is less likely to crash or eat up bandwidth, the amount of data transferred during a given time.

Using HTML5, magazines employed some, but not all, of the features below to play up the tactile action of swiping, tapping, scrolling, pinching, and zooming on iPads:

- Videos
- Slide shows
- 360-degree views
- Static and video thumbnail demos
- Pop-ups
- Audio clips
- Panoramic images
- Scrolling type/recipes

- Pinch and zoom images
- Tap-to-buy links
- Excerpts
- Stop-action photography
- Interactive table of contents
- Text features
- Emailable text

Marie Claire made the best use of the attributes of the iPad. Readers couldn't tap a cover line and go immediately to a story, but the cover rotated to feature four versions of singer-actress Miley Cyrus. This was a good way to display mockups and give readers an inside look at cover selection. Other elements included a behind-the-scenes video of the cover shoot, and a video interview of hair stylist Chris McMillan.

"Joanna's Journal" featured a light-hearted video of the editor saying the fashion issue is biggest of the year and wearing a different outfit in each scene. The fashion videos were engaging, such as the moody and scenic "One for the Road" or the one with "Cuba Libre." The printed magazine showed a shot of Alber Elbaz at a spring 2011 Lanvin rehearsal. On the iPad, a video automatically started of models in flowing garments on a runway.

On the interactive table of contents, readers could swipe a vertical slider to review videos and other content or tap to reach a specific page. In "Spring Fashion A to Z," readers could tap certain items for 360-degree views, highlighted by opaque spinning circles with red edges. Tapping "A-Z Mashup" revealed a combination of lettered accessories, i.e., T is for tribal or K is for khaki.

"Braving New World" had a bonus interactive map. Readers could tap on countries to see a photo of Americans abroad with statistics in the caption.

In "What's Best Babies at 20? 30? 40?" readers could click a red dot on the main photo for bonus content: "Tap here to take our interactive baby quiz." Clicking takes readers to "How Much Do You Know About Being a Mom?" The blurb says: "Whether you're preparing for motherhood or have a bun in the oven, test your mom wisdom with this quiz." The components included:

- A video showing a baby sitting on white against blue drapes
- Another red dot: "Pregnant? Tap Here" (a multiple-choice quiz on foods to avoid, and whether sex, running, coloring hair are safe while pregnant).
  -Tap black to switch to conceiving quiz.
- A black dot: "Want to be a Mom Soon? Tap Here"
  -"Take This Conceiving Quiz (six multiple-choice questions about fertility and conception)
  -Tap red dot to go to other quiz on pregnancy

Typography was animated on several pages. Letters shifted when a reader landed on the "Nude Swings" page. Pink dots flew into place to dot the i's in the title "Wild Things." The second word of "Minor Threat" split diagonally. Polish, eye shadow, and other makeup cascaded onto the page for "It's Electric: Get the Look."

Glamour quickly replaced its March 2011 app with the updated version at the beginning of the month to the joy and chagrin of some readers. One commented that she preferred the old version for viewing blog posts and planned to keep it, but liked the features on the new one, especially the speed. *Glamour* also had a preview app and an app called Glamour Girls that was billed as "an original iPad series" presented by Gap. The new app also made use of the iPad's capabilities more than most magazines in this study. The app is user-friendly with a "How to Use This Thing" introduction and an interactive cover and table of contents.

A reader could toggle between before and after photos to see clothing on different body types or blush for various face shapes; slide text and photos; tap on an astrological sign for her horoscope or icons to read more about items in sidebars; follow the editor on Twitter; get details on a model's clothing; or hear fashion director Anne Christensen's take on outfits.

One headline had a fill-in-the-blank feature that used script to complete the statement "I Wish My Sex Life Were More _____!" with subheads from sections of the story. Some stories contained sliders with sidebars or pictures, including wide-angle shots. The letters page had a slideshow with readers who had traveled around the world with issues of *Glamour*. Behind-the-scenes videos and YouTube videos could be shared or saved.

The downside was that readers couldn't enlarge pages, and it would have been ideal to turn quizzes set up as board games in the magazine into interactive content. This was similar to the shortcoming of "Vacation or Staycation?" on *Redbook's* iPad app.

The iPad app for O is not as interactive as those for *Glamour* and *Marie Claire*, but some O readers still praised it in reviews. The app included book excerpts and tap-to-buy links. An ad for the iPad mentioned exclusive videos of Oprah, but there were none to be found. Editors missed numerous opportunities to add interactivity to the special March issue on clutter, a topic that resonates with readers. In the O List, readers could click on shopping information to go to a purchase site, but nowhere else in the issue. There was a feature to provide plain text of an article, which could also be emailed.

Better Homes and Gardens had an iPad app on Zinio for its India edition in March 2011. It launched an iPad app for the U.S. edition in late March for the April issue. In an article for Mashable.com, Laura Indvik said that *Better Homes and Gardens'* app "reflected much of the best of iPad magazine design, with crisp, colorful layouts packed with scrolling galleries and text, and discreet buttons that can be tapped to furnish additional information, such as recipes, about photographed subjects" (2011, p. 1). On the iPad, recipes could be saved to a box, which would be useful for other women's magazine. *Better Homes and Gardens* used transcripts for recipes that had flash on its website.

However, Indvik criticized the inability of readers to share content and the promotional tone of one of the videos of chef Jaime Oliver:

> I was disappointed by the complete lack of sharing options, especially given how comparatively late the magazine has arrived on the device compared to others in the category, such as *Martha Stewart Living*, which remains one of the most beautiful and user-friendly magazines on the iPad to date. A video of Jaime Oliver, which appears to be more of an ad for *Better Homes and Gardens'* website than an interview, could have been left out as well (2011, p. 1).

While the video cited by Indvik was too promotional, the other one demonstrating a recipe for fresh peas was more service-oriented and reader friendly.

Other Mobile Applications
Glamour, Essence, and *Woman's Day* had the most impressive smartphone apps. *Essence's* app resembled the website. It did not sacrifice graphics and fonts, but lacked in content, social media, multimedia, and search. Where *Essence* lacked, *Glamour* and *Woman's Day* picked up and vice versa. *Woman's Day's* application lacked an interactive menu and strong branding, but did a good job of including diverse content. *Glamour* included all the social media buttons and lots of content, but could use a better menu and aesthetics as well as a search option. Of all the magazines, *Glamour* was the only one to include the option of viewing recent content or most popular content, and the navigation between the two tabs was seamless. Slideshows allowed a user to use the swipe motion to navigate.

It was difficult to find cover stories on most of the mobile apps. Videos are popular and work well on smartphones. On *Family Circle's* mobile app, it was difficult to locate content with video on both mobile and web; this is likely due to the lack of multimedia integration in the content. One post that included a YouTube video played fine on the mobile device. Once the page orientation was changed to horizontal for the video, however, the app would not revert to vertical.

Better Homes and Gardens invited users to join its mobile club to receive alerts about new content and special offers. *Good Housekeeping* listed a dedicated mobile email address, and the footer had a link to a reader contribution page to submit tips. In a similar footer on *Redbook's* mobile app, readers could answer the question of the week, but the question was unclear. Some of *Redbook's* feature stories were truncated. "I Went Undercover on America's Cheating Website" displayed an excerpt. To read more, the user was redirected to the full website.

Oprah had a general mobile site for all media properties. The stories in mobile were not shareable. Once the user left the main page, a drop-down menu was available, but it navigated only between major departments of Oprah media and not magazine-specific sections. There was no search bar to find cover stories or multimedia.

Ladies Home Journal was the only magazine among the 10 that did not optimize its site for cell phones.

Website Design

Few of the 10 websites were aesthetically pleasing, and navigation was for the most part confusing. All of the websites made it difficult to distinguish between magazine content, original articles, slideshows, and blogs. *Good Magazine* and Google's new magazine, *Think Quarterly*, are examples of well-designed sites, but they both have some room for improvement.

Enhancing Print Content

The magazines needed to do a better job at balancing print content and timely content. Some magazines seemed reluctant to put content from current issues on the web or to make it easy to find. It was difficult to locate stories from print on the web and mobile. This was true for *Family Circle*. It was also difficult to find some of *Better Homes and Gardens'* cover stories, such as those on spring containers, laundry tips, and "30 Try-It-Now Decorating Ideas."

The search engines were not always effective. The print and online headlines did not always match when an article from the magazine was shoveled onto the web. Search Engine Optimization (SEO) should be used to include the appropriate tags on content and the headline listed on the magazine cover, as reader might use the print headline as a search term. For example, the main cover story for *Better Homes and Gardens*, "Make It Easy," would show up with a search on the headline from the inside pages of the magazine, "Smart Eating Made Simple," which mirrored the online headline. However, photos of the five experts featured in this package did not appear on the website, which would have provided a more engaging presentation.

All of the magazines shoveled content onto mobile and web. The use of interactive elements and/or bonus content to augment a print story was inconsistent. At most, some included a video to enhance a story. The stories could be more dynamic if they also featured tweets, Facebook comments, real-time streams, videos, and interactive informational graphics. Storify is a tool that allows for the creation of multimedia stories though it may be too chunky for feature stories.

A *Ladies Home Journal* reader interested in the cover line "Prettiest New Clothes for Spring" would find that as "Weekend Update" inside the magazine and as "Weekend Style Update" online with the three spreads as a seven-frame slideshow. The cover line "Smarter Ways to Organize Your Kitchen" appeared inside and online as "Conquer Kitchen Clutter." The quick hits worked well as an 11-frame slideshow with such subheads as Counter Intelligence, Mixed Doubles, and Hang Time.

Although Rachael Ray was on the cover, she received equal play with other TV chefs inside. The presentation and typography could have been enhanced online. More importantly, a previous Q&A with Ray could have been "repurposed" to complement and highlight the March package. This was a missed opportunity.

"The Heart-Health Danger That Threatens Women" had a better presentation in the magazine than online. Some sections were text heavy and could have been enhanced with photos, hyperlinks, and pull quotes. There was no jpeg of the current cover on the website for *Ladies Home Journal* or *Better Homes and Gardens.*

With the exception of actress Diane Kruger, most stories on *Glamour's* cover were not prominently featured on the homepage. Kruger's fashion sense, love life, and magazine Q&A were featured, but there was no video of her. Some of Kruger's content appeared in blogs, which received top billing and were changed regularly.

For "29 Things He's Thinking When You're Naked" on the March cover, the closest match on the homepage was "36 Things He's Thinking in Bed." On the department page, "10 Things He's Thinking When You're Naked" was listed, but it was a slideshow with one sentence per image. Two women were bylined for the slideshow, but in print the story was lengthy and featured many contributors, including 300-word sections from men, a small anecdotal male poll, and a checklist. The online version paled in comparison. The slideshow seemed more humorous than helpful and an attempt to garner page views.

One example of how an *Oprah* story appeared across platforms started with the cover line "Paul Walsh on What to Keep, What to Toss." The magazine headline inside read "Make Over My Garage." For the web, it was "Paul Walsh's Life-Changing Garage Makeover." Step 1 included "Purge the Junk" subheads online; blue boxes with subheads in print. Before and after photos appeared in both versions. "Peter's pointers for cleaning out your garage" appeared as a seven-screen slide show online; it was bulleted in print. "The Science of Stuff" appeared as pink sidebars along the edge of two pages in the magazine, but couldn't be found online.

Marie Claire's cover story on Miley Cyrus was online, but was not linked on the home page. A behind-the-scenes video on the photo shoot was included, but without added features.

The magazines, except for *Essence* and *Marie Claire*, avoided news content; little content on the sites had any urgency. Magazines unable to keep up with breaking news could opt for news analysis and commentary like *Essence.* Unfortunately in *Essence's* case, the news commentary lacked in reporting and links. It read more like the piece of an untrained blogger as opposed to a journalist. It also focused disproportionately on the Obamas and entertainment. Magazines can get an edge on their blog competitors by having better quality blogs with more credibility.

Dating and Linking Content
Some magazines did not include dates on content. Because many magazines report on the same topic but with a new angle in each issue, it is important to include dates so that readers don't stumble onto something they have already read. The magazines failed to include adequate hyperlinks in slideshows and stories. They often made references to brands and events, but did not link to additional or background information, nor did they adequately link to similar stories already published in the magazine.

Engagement
The magazines attempted to lure and keep readers with polls, quizzes, games, freebies, and assorted tools. *Family Circle, Good Housekeeping, Ladies Home Journal,* and *Glamour* had BMI and other health and fitness calculators. *Good Housekeeping* also had makeovers and recipe finders. *LHJ* had a lunch planner and bra sizer; *Glamour* and *Essence* had virtual makeovers. The magazines also generally had e-newsletters, forums, and other opportunities for community. *Family Circle* linked readers to the "Momster" site of its parent company, Meredith; *BHG* had a Motherboard. *O* had forums, chats, and Skype.

The contact information and Twitter account should be included for each contributor so the conversation can continue in other social media sites. Some sites received a great deal of spam and others, like *Essence*, that receive many comments from readers aren't moderated.

More community management would prevent some readers from bullying others and encourage lurkers to join the conversation. Threaded comments and the ability to vote up and moderate comments have been successful on websites like The Huffington Post. Magazines should consider incorporating this option. If a magazine fears it receives much too many comments to be able to moderate offensive and inappropriate comments, then a system should be put in place by which readers who consistently comment can become moderators and police the others within reason. Contributors, if possible, should also join in on the comments. In addition, posts could end with a question such as "Do you think … ?"

User-generated Content
Websites like Thisis50.com have thrived off user-generated content and user moderators. A system that allows readers to have a profile (via Twitter or Facebook Connect) and contribute photos, tips, etc. for other readers to vote on and comment can help with overall content generation for a magazine. Some magazines allowed for forums or Q&As, but they need to be developed further into a community. *BHG* allowed readers to submit photos of children and answers to questions from fellow readers.

Social Media
Most of the magazines appeared unfamiliar with networks outside of Twitter and Facebook at the time. Integration of social bookmarking websites like Reddit could result in the spread of viral content from the magazine. Additionally, websites like Formspring allow for a great deal of reader engagement, and more magazines should embrace Tumblr, a microblog that encourages the sharing of content from other blogs. *Newsweek* has seen success there. Also, the culture of Tumblr encourages more behind-the-scenes content and smaller (read: more manageable) posts from magazines and brands.

YouTube
All of the magazines could do a better job to promote their YouTube channels on their main websites as well as include it in the mobile application. YouTube works well on mobile devices and is a great way to include multimedia.

Location-based Apps/Features
If a magazine is not already on Foursquare, then it should join and prominently display a badge on the magazine homepage and in the mobile application. GetGlue is an entertainment check-in tool that is growing in popularity. It would behoove magazines to create a profile and "check in" when certain shows or movies air.

Twitter and Facebook
It is important that magazines do not simply shovel content onto Facebook and Twitter. Magazines should go the distance and not only produce updates asking questions of their readers, but also respond to readers and affiliated blogs. They will gain a stronger following of readers who are willing to spread content on the magazine's behalf. It was not clear whether any of the magazines hosted Twitter chats, but this would help further the conversation on different magazine content. Ustream/webcasting would also help facilitate this. The goal of the magazines should be to engage with the readers in order to strengthen their readership.

On Facebook, brands can manage Fan Pages populated with content from both the brand and Facebook users. Facebook users who "like" a page are then subscribed to the page's posts (i.e., content updates), which users receive in their home content feed. Users on Facebook are able to "like" and share particular posts as well as comment.

On Twitter, brands can create profiles, which they can populate with tweets (i.e., content) from both the brand and Twitter users. Twitter users who "follow" a profile are then subscribed to the profile's content updates, which they receive in their home content feed. Users on Twitter can "retweet" (i.e., share) particular posts as well as reply in reference to a particular tweet (i.e., content post) or @mention (i.e., reference) the profile generally in a post of their own.

Here is a look at social media engagement, including Facebook and Twitter traffic, as of March 16, 2011, along with the number of tweets that the magazines send to their followers:

Facebook Engagement

	Likes
1. Glamour	202,393
2. Better Homes and Gardens	117,371
3. Essence	67,560
4. O the Oprah Magazine	57,708
5. Woman's Day	55,822
6. Marie Claire	41,940
7. Family Circle	24,126
8. Good Housekeeping	13,233
9. Ladies Home Journal	11,936
10. Redbook	11,767

Twitter Engagement

	Followers	Tweets
1, Marie Claire	361,517	5,730
2. Oprah	140,530	2,344
3. Family Circle	92,136	1,554
4. Glamour	57,729	9,895
5. Essence	30,576	2,907
6. Ladies Home Journal	10,852	6,099
7. Woman's Day	9,580	2,471
8. Better Homes and Gardens	9,004	1,607
9. Redbook	8,231	2,554
10. Good Housekeeping	6,775	2,242

Conclusion

This study provides a digital snapshot of a segment of the magazine industry. It offers insight on how some of the leading women's magazines — and leading magazines, period — are trying to remain solvent and relevant to their readers. While it offers examples of how magazines are trying to maintain a competitive edge, it is still too early to determine the success of these efforts. What constitutes best practices today could very well change tomorrow. No one *really* knows what works on the iPad, which was barely a year old during the initial phase of this study; cell phones; or even the Internet with social media thrown into the mix. More research is needed to track the delivery of content on these platforms over time.

The same is true for consumer behavior across various demographics and psychographics. Even then, these findings could vary from one magazine audience to another and even within an audience. A magazine could have statistically twin readers with one who is content to savor each word of narrative journalism without bells and whistles versus her counterpart who craves behind-the-scenes videos of a cover shoot, spots a pair of Christian Louboutin shoes that she wants to rotate on her iPad for a 360 view, and then tap the screen to purchase them.

It is clear, however, that usage of mobile and tablet technology is growing and fast. In 2013 for the first time, a third of Americans older than 18 (34%) owns a tablet or e-reader device, up from 18% in 2012. The most prevalent demographics are adults aged 35-44 (49%), college graduates (49%), and those living in households earning at least $75,000 per year (56%) (Zickuhr, 2013). Similarly, 91% of Americans own a cell phone; 56% of them are believed to be smartphone adopters (Smith, 2013). Smartphone adoption among Americans in 2013 is up 10% from 2012. The highest smartphone adoption is found among adults aged 25-34 (81%), with adults aged 18-24 (79%) and 35-44 (69%) also reporting considerable adoption. At least 78% of smartphone adopters have household incomes starting at $75,000 per year, and 70% are college educated.

As consumers with considerable buying power continue to demonstrate their willingness to consume content on tablet and other mobile devices, the magazine publishers who innovate on these platforms are poised to win the digital revolution race. To put it another way, he or she who has the consumers has the power.

So far, the surviving Seven Sisters still have both. They are clearly doing something right, based on the consistent ranking of five of them among the top 10 in the magazine industry. Despite their head start, size, and resources, they can't afford to rest on their laurels. It's too easy to become the giant that falls victim to disruptive innovation, which forces slow-moving companies to keep up with their competitors or die.

Therefore, the conventional wisdom is to attempt to reach readers wherever they are and to hold onto them at whatever cost one can afford. This strategy fueled the rush to adopt the iPad, especially given the media corpses that withered from watchful web waiting. With the surges in social media and mobile from smartphones to iPads, few can afford to remain idle. Nielsen and others recommend focusing more on apps than on mobile sites. Indeed, many magazines are doing that, or both, with customized apps for beauty, gardening, or specific events. "I do believe mobile sites will win over mobile apps in the long term," Nielsen said. "But when that will happen is less certain" (2012, p. 1).

While half of the surviving sisters lacked apps during the iPad's debut year, they came on board during its second year, beginning with *Better Homes and Gardens* in time for the iPad's first anniversary in April 2011. *Family Circle* and *Ladies Home Journal* had February and March 2012 issues on Zinio. The Meredith Corp., which owns *BHG* and *Family Circle*, had been focusing on mobile sites until it saw iPad usage expand beyond early adopters and techies to an increase among its mass audience of women. It initially avoided Apple, which had been criticized for taking 30% of subscription revenue and holding onto demographic information and other metrics. *BHG* joined Apple's popular digital newsstand. With a circulation of 7.6 million, *BHG* became the print sales leader of magazines selling on iPads (Ives, 2010).

"Our consumer is coming in as more of a mass market play," said Liz Schimel, executive vice president for consumer relationship management and digital media at Meredith's National Media Group. "But I think that's the tipping point I think we're at here" (Ives, 2010, p. 1).

Lauren Wiener, senior vice president at the Meredith Women's Network, added, "We felt the foundation was mobilizing our websites because we were increasingly seeing data that showed people accessing our sites from their mobile phones, and they weren't having an optimal experience" (Ives, 2010, p. 1).

Consumers won't have an optimal experience when they can't find a truly digital magazine on a website or mobile site. "The fact that a print magazine has an online presence does not mean that its 'online version' is a digital 'magazine," said Dora Santos Silva (2011, p. 301) in a journal article on "The Future of Digital Magazine Publishing." Silva explained that a true digital magazine must be "created from scratch" (p. 302), which is why PDFs are unsatisfying on iPads.

In order to provide an optimal experience for readers, according to Nielsen, media companies must design for the small screen, whether it's on a cell phone or tablet, and focus on only the most essential features. He recommends "clear, explicit links from the full site to the mobile site and from the mobile site to the full site" (2011, p. 1). Here continues with recommendations for the iPad:

- Design for repeat users.
- Deliver extra value. Add a "secret weapon" not found on the website, such as "superb usability, or just enough usability as to make a repeated task bearable." Nielsen cites as an example being able to read a recipe without having to touch the screen a great deal during food preparation.
- Add "affordances" so that users can clearly see that buttons, icons, labels, and other items are touchable and relevant in accomplishing tasks.
- Maximize read-tap asymmetry by making touchable areas larger with enough space around them to prevent readers from touching the wrong one. Targets (such as home buttons and arrows) should be at least 1 centimeter by 1 centimeter, Nielsen advises.
- Add a back button to minimize accidental navigation.
- Provide visible cues (i.e., tips, arrows) if it isn't obvious that readers must swipe or use other gestures.
- Don't overload design features that interfere with swiping, such as a carousel containing photos and captions.
- Use the same navigation scheme whether a layout is shown with a landscape or portrait orientation. Explain that content will change if the viewer turns the iPad.

- Make sure that small modal views (a screen within a screen) are large enough to allow readers to interact with sidebars or graphics. Consider a separate page if necessary.
- Keep downloads to 20 seconds or less, and use a progress bar.
- Design launch screens to mirror the first functional screen as much as possible without noise, animation, or video when the app starts.
- Clue the reader on a story's focus in the opening layout if the app contains dual navigation, allowing users to swipe vertically to read the article and horizontally to move through the magazine.
- Minimize the need for typing (Badiu and Nielsen, 2011).

For the cell phone, "one of the basic rules in web interface is to maximize the use of the limited space by putting important content in the most prominent area, where users can see it without scrolling down" (Jeong and Han, 2012, p. 182). An optimal experience might include the following, based on the findings of this and other studies:

- Interactive menu with a drop-down feature to prevent scrolling
- Twitter and Facebook feeds with tweet and "like" buttons
- Comments (mobile contributions)
- Blogs
- Location-based and other tools to help readers find stores or other venues mentioned by the magazine
- User-generated content, such as photo submissions
- A share button that stands out; not a white one that blends in
- Photos included in all or most stories
- HTML 5 video/multimedia
- More content that reflects the web and print versions
- Search bar
- Slideshows

In addition to keeping up with technology, other indicators of viability and excellence among magazines are awards and industry acclaim. In 2007, *Advertising Age* named *Better Homes and Gardens* as Magazine of the Year. In addition to circulation and advertising success, *Ad Age* chooses magazines for The A List that are "truly operating as brands" and "building smart cross-media content." It said that "*Better Homes and Gardens* rode a February redesign to a huge spike in newsstand sales ... The brand team also fixed Better Homes' website" and added a video channel, Better.tv (Advertising Age, 2007, p. 1). In 2009, *BHG* was No. 2 on The A List, followed by *Family Circle* (No. 3) and *Essence* (No. 6).

The American Society of Magazine Editors (2011) named *Glamour* as Magazine of the Year at the National Magazine Awards, the leading honor for the industry. The award "honors publications that successfully use both print and digital media in fulfilling the editorial mission of the magazine." *Glamour* also won for personal service in 2007 and general excellence for magazines with more than two million in circulation in 2005. It was a finalist for essays in 2009.

Marie Claire was a finalist for the National Magazine Awards for Digital Media 2011 in the Interactive Tool category for its "Fall Fashion A to Z" iPad App. *O the Oprah Magazine* won for Leisure Interests in 2007 and was a finalist for Magazine Section in 2009 and Personal Service in 2011. *Family Circle* was a finalist for Personal Service in 2009 while *Good Housekeeping* was a Personal Service finalist in 2008 and 2011.

The media landscape has already experienced seismic shifts. No one knows what the future holds, especially with the speed of some of these shifts. What's clear, however, is that media organizations need to invest more in research and development. Change is the cost of doing business. Those who move too slowly might pay more than the perceived savings from doing nothing or moving cautiously, as evidenced by the legions of fallen or ailing media giants.

Taking the iPad as an example, it will probably be worth the investment in the long run for magazines and advertisers that took an early chance on the new technology. And early is even earlier these days. Industry analysts and consumers considered the second year of the iPad's existence as late entry into the market. Nevertheless, Meredith probably had the right strategy of introducing an iPad for *Better Homes and Gardens* just before the one-year mark. It was early enough to not be too late, but late enough to come out with an engaging app, unlike the apps of three of the earlier Seven Sisters: *Good Housekeeping, Redbook,* and *Woman's Day.* Should the trio have waited? Not necessarily. The three magazines serve a more mainstream audience that might not care as much for bells and whistles as readers of *Marie Claire* or *Glamour.* It's good that they entered the game early, but they have to play harder as more readers see and experience the possibilities of the iPad along with other tablets and mobile devices that have since gained more market share.

Consumers can be unpredictable, but they value innovation and what's new. With more speed than ever before, they change cars, sneakers, phones, and other mobile devices. Some of them are addicted to new media, social media, and the tools that present them. Their habits rub off on others. Traditional media organizations are fretting as numbers continue to dip for their core businesses. Their best bet for survival, it seems, is to foster a climate of innovation internally from top to bottom and remain open to extending their brands by any means necessary while delivering excellence to their readers.

References

Advertising Age (2007). The A list. Retrieved from http://gaia.adage.com/images/random/1007/TheAList.pdf

American Society of Magazine Editors (2011). *National Magazine Awards winners & finalists*. Retrieved from *http://www.magazine.org/asme/national-* magazine-awards/winners-finalists

Apple Inc. (2011, March 2). Apple launches iPad 2: All new design is thinner, lighter & faster with FaceTime, smart covers & 10-hour battery [Press release].   Retrieved   from http://www.apple.com/pr/library/2011/03/02ipad.html

Association of Magazine Media. (2009). Circulation trends & data. Retrieved from   http://www.magazine.org/insights-resources/research- publications/trends-data/magazine-industry-facts-data/circulation-trends

Badiu, R., & Nielsen, J. (2011). iPad app and website usability. Nielsen Norman Group: UX   Training,   Consulting,   &   Research.   Retrieved   from http://www.nngroup.com/reports/mobile/ipad/ipad-usability_2nd-edition.pdf

Carmody, D. (1990, April 6). Identity crisis for Seven Sisters. *New York Times.* Retrieved from http://www.nytimes.com/1990/08/06/business/identity-crisis- for-seven-sisters.html

Craig, D. A. (2011). Excellence in Online Journalism: Exploring Current Practices in an Evolving Environment. Thousand Oaks, CA: Sage Publications.

Daly, C. P., Henry, P., & Ryder, E. (1997). *The Magazine Publishing Industry*. Boston, MA: Allyn and Bacon.

Day, G. S., Schoemaker, P. J., & Gunther, R. E. (2000). *A Different Game: Wharton on Managing Emerging Technologies*. New York, NY: Wiley.

Endres, K. L. (1995). Women's Periodicals in the United States Consumer Magazines. Westport, CT: Greenwood Press.

Indvik, L. (2011, March 15). Better Homes and Gardens comes to the iPad [PICS]. *Mashable*. Retrieved from http://mashable.com/2011/03/15/better- homes-and-gardens-ipad/#11605-5

Ives, N. (2010, October 22). Meredith finally adds first iPad editions for its magazines. Advertising Agency & Marketing Industry News. Retrieved from http://adage.com/article/mediaworks/meredith-finally-adds-ipad-editions- magazines/149400/

Ives, N. (2011, March 15). Making sense of early sales for magazines' iPad editions. *Advertising Agency & Marketing Industry News*. Retrieved from http://adage.com/article/mediaworks/making-sense-early-sales-magazines-ipad-editions/146640/

Jeong, W. & Han, H. J. (2012) Usability study on newspaper mobile websites. *OCLC Systems & Services*. 28(4), 182.

Johnson, S., & Prijatel, P. (2007). *The Magazine from Cover to Cover* (2nd Ed.). New York: Oxford University Press.

Kobak, J. B. (1990, March). 25 years of change; What's been happening in the consumer magazine industry? Emerging trends may come as a surprise. *Folio: the Magazine for Magazine Management, (19)3*, 87.

Kuczynski, A. (2001, January 15). Media talk; New magazine to be Rosie's, not McCall's. *New York Times*. Retrieved from http://www.nytimes.com/2001/01/15/business/media-talk-new-magazine-to-be-rosie-s-not-mccall-s.html

Magazine Handbook: *Engagement to Action*. (2010). New York: Magazine v Publishers of America.

McCafferty, J. (2003, December). Rosie from accounting. *CFO Magazine*. Retrieved from http://www.cfo.com/article.cfm/3011135/c_3046603?f=insidecfo

Moggridge, B. (2010). *Designing Media*. Cambridge, MA: MIT Press.

Nielsen, J. (2012, February 13). *Mobile sites vs. apps: The coming strategy shift*. Fremont, CA: Nielsen Norman Group: UX Training, Consulting, &   Research. Retrieved from http://www.useit.com/alertbox/mobile-sites-apps.html

Nielsen, J. (2011, September 26). *Mobile usability update*. Fremont, CA: Nielsen Norman Group: UX Training, Consulting, & Research. Retrieved from http://www.useit.com/alertbox/mobile-usability.html

Paxhia, S., & Rosenblatt, B. (2008, May 5). *Digital Magazine and Newspaper Editions: Growth, Trends, and Best Practices*. Cambridge, MA: Gilbane Group Inc. Retrieved from http://gilbane.com/Research-Reports/Gilbane-Digital-Editions-Report-May-2008.pdf

Santos Silva, D. (2011). The future of digital magazine publishing. *Information Services & Use.* 31(3), 301-302.

Smith, A. (2013, June 5). *Smartphone Ownership 2013.* Pew Research Center's Internet & American Life Project. Retrieved from http://pewinternet.org/Reports/2013/Smartphone-Ownership-2013/Findings.aspx

State of the Media Report. (2011). Beltsville, MD: Vocus Marketing Software. Retrieved from http://www.vocus.com/resources/the-guides/

Stone, B., & Vance, A. (2009, October 4). Just a touch away, the elusive tablet PC. *New York Times.* Retrieved from http://www.nytimes.com/2009/10/05/technology/05tablet.html

Tremayne, M. (2004). The web of context: Applying network theory to the use of hyperlinks in journalism on the web. *Journalism & Mass Communication Quarterly, 81,* 237-253.

Purcell, K., Rainie, L., Mitchell, A., Rosenstiel, T., & Olmstead, K. (2010, March 1). Understanding the participatory news consumer: How Internet and cell phone users have turned news into a social experience. *Pew Internet & American Life Project.* Washington, DC: Pew Research Center, 3-5.

Wang, X. (2006, August). Exploring sample sizes for content analysis of online news sites. Paper presented at the meeting of the Association for Education in Journalism and Mass Communication, San Francisco.

Zickuhr, K. (2011, February 3). Generations and their gadgets. *Pew Research Center's Internet & American Life Project.* Retrieved from http://www.pewinternet.org/Reports/2011/Generations-and gadgets/Report/eBook-Readers-and-Tablet-Computers.aspx

Zickuhr, K. (2013, June 10). Tablet ownership 2013. *Pew Research Center's Internet & American Life Project.* Retrieved from http://pewinternet.org/Reports/2013/Tablet-Ownership-2013/Findings.aspx

Appendix A

This is the coding instrument used by Xiaopeng Wang (2006) to analyze The New York Times website, nytimes.com, in "Exploring Sample Sizes for Content Analysis of Online News Sites" for AEJMC's Communication Theory & Methodology Division.

Online Sampling Coding Sheet

1. Web site: NYTimes.com
2. DATE_MM/DD/2005
3. TIME:____
4. Story topic
____1) Politics and government acts
____2) War and defense
____3) Diplomacy & foreign relations
____4) Economic activity
____5) Agriculture
____6) Transportation and travel
____7) Crime
____8) Public moral problems
____9) Accidents and disasters
____10) Science and invention
____11) Public health and welfare
____12) Education and classic arts
____13) Popular amusements
____14) General human interest
____15) Others_____(SPECIFY)
5. Geographic bias
____1) U. S.
____2) U.S. neighbors
____3) Central/South America
____4) Western Europe
____5) Eastern Europe
____6) Middle East and North Africa
____7) Africa (Sub-Sahara)
____8) South Asia
____9) Japan
____10) Other East Asia
____11) Oceania
____12) Others_____(SPECIFY)
6. Number of links _____
7. Uses of Multimedia
____1) Images (including slideshows)
____2) Video clips
____3) Audio clips
____4) Interactive media (e.g. Flash)
____5) Others_____(SPECIFY)

Appendix B

This is the coding instrument that was adapted for analyzing content in this study:

Coding Sheet for Mobile Magazine (Cell Phones, Tablets, etc.)
1. Date:

2. Magazine:
  Issue Date:

3. Specify Platform (Use separate sheet for each):

____a) Tablet
        ____iPad
        ____Other:_____
____b) Cell Phone
        ____iPhone
        ____Droid
        ____BlackBerry
        ____Other:_____

4. Is the website optimized specifically for cell phones?
____a) Yes
____b) No
If you answered yes, which phones?
        ____iPhone
        ____Droid
        ____BlackBerry
        ____Other:_____

5. How are the cover stories represented on this cell phone/tablet? Please specify whether stories with cover lines are "shoveled" onto the mobile platform without changes (shovelware) or whether they were varied to feature additional content and interactivity. Please explain, add specific details, and discuss whether the features work. Are user-friendly? Engaging? Why or why not?
____Presentation of main cover story
        Shovelware? ____Added/varied features? ____ (Specify)

____Story No. 2
        Shovelware? ____Added/varied features? ____ (Specify)

____Story No. 3
        Shovelware? ____Added/varied features? ____ (Specify)

____Story No. 4
       Shovelware? ____Added/varied features? ____ (Specify)

____Story No. 5
       Shovelware? ____Added/varied features? ____ (Specify)

____Story No. 6
       Shovelware? ____Added/varied features? ____ (Specify)

____Story No. 7
       Shovelware? ____Added/varied features? ____ (Specify)

____Story No. 8
       Shovelware? ____Added/varied features? ____ (Specify)

6. Describe interactivity elsewhere on this device. Please add comments
below or on another sheet.
____a) Interactive table of contents
____b) Slideshows
____c) Audio slideshows (i.e., Sound Slides)
____d) Videos
____e) Audio clips/podcasts
____f) Animated type
____g) Rotating photos
____h) Polls and quizzes
____i) Tools (i.e., virtual makeovers)
____j) Interactive graphics
____k) Mashups
____l) Other (SPECIFY)_____

Chapter 9
Social Branding of College Students to Seek Employment
Jamila A. Cupid & S. Lenise Wallace

> In the electric age, when our central nervous system is technologically extended to involve us in the whole of mankind and to incorporate the whole of mankind in us, we necessarily participate, in depth, in the consequences of our every action.
> – Marshall McLuhan (1964, p. 4)

Social media have become the medium of choice for college students to express themselves since the advent of early social networks such as Facebook. Over the last decade, social media have expanded to include blogs (weblogs), often supported by sites like Wordpress and Blogger, as well as endless social networks such as Twitter, Google Plus, Tumblr, LinkedIn, Instagram, YouTube, Flickr, Friendster, Pinterest, Black Planet, Orkut, Blogster, MySpace, Xing, Zing, and many more. These outlets have fostered a social space that allows a unique form of interactivity, which is continually changing as a growing number of users become increasingly media literate in and dependent on the digital medium.

People of all walks of life, demographics, and cultural backgrounds are currently using social media to best suit their needs and wants, from leisurely activities to work duties to home management. College students, in particular, use social networks to help them stay connected to others despite their busy, multifarious schedules. They use social media to post ideas, share photographs, display activities and accomplishments, promote events, and present a multitude of expressions. Generation Y, or Millenials, which is the age group today's college students fall into, commonly uses social networks for career development purposes, including to seek employment (Kelly Services, 2011). As students engage on these platforms, they build images and establish personal brands that become their online reputation. This reputation can follow them from the Internet to the offline world. Consequently, students of Generation Y have expressed the most concern that their representation on social network pages can have an adverse impact on their careers and, therefore, they are likely to censor content to protect their professional images (Kelly Services, 2011).

The intersection of social media, professional image, and job seeking pertains particularly to college students as a group within society that consistently seeks employment during and upon the conclusion of their college careers.

Social Media as a Branding Tool

Today, social media have given the individual an opportunity to establish and control his or her personal brand. Through social media, Internet users have the ability to channel their own images directly to their publics and the world. Part of the brand and reputation that one presents to the world, whether intentionally or unintentionally, is one's professional character. When engaging in social media, users are giving others insight into their work ethic as well as how they solve problems, handle difficult situations, tackle the creative process, or perform under pressure.

All of the information an individual chooses to divulge over the Internet matters, since once it is in cyberspace it never truly disappears. The common Internet user can access and save information that just about anyone posts. Sites usually offer limited privacy options to protect users (and themselves) from legal repercussion, but many people are unaware of the full terms of agreement and intricacies of account settings for certain social media outlets and end up portraying themselves negatively with inappropriate language, jokes, innuendos, or pictures they later wish to retract. As a result of this behavior, some individuals have been suspended from work, disqualified from certain competitive events, or ultimately terminated from their jobs. Professionals now advise students looking to enter the workforce to filter the material that they share online by asking themselves whether what they are about to post is something they would want their parents or employers to see (Barrett-Poindexter, 2012). Many people have been able to apply this concept and utilize social media to create impressive professional profiles that would pass the parent/boss test, indicating to employers that they are desirable workers.

Social Media for Job Search and Recruitment

Social networks are used by proactive job seekers at growing rates with more than 18 million Americans finding employment using Facebook (Jobvite, 2011; Jobvite, 2012; Kelly Services, 2011). LinkedIn, blogs, and Twitter are also popular social media platforms used for searching job openings. Although LinkedIn offers features specifically for professional networking in a social space, such as career summaries, résumé listing, ease of connecting to other professionals, company searching, access to professional groups, and keyword highlights, it is second to Facebook for job searching, based on a Jobvite (2012) study. LinkedIn subscribers are mostly composed of users ages 18 – 34. In addition, social networks XING, Google Plus, Viadeo, and BranchOut are becoming more popular for job search purposes (LindkedIn Insights, 2013). The research makes it clear that social media are playing a more significant role in the job search process, not only among the general population, but especially among Generation Y Internet users and active job seekers.

Consequently, employers have begun to pay closer attention to the social pages and personal blogs of potential employees to determine viable candidates for coveted internship and entry-level positions. It has even been reported that many employers are now requesting job candidates to supply login information for their Facebook accounts (Valdez and McFarland, 2012). Even if the candidates decline to disclose their passwords or the potential employer does not openly request permission, an Internet data mining company like Social Intelligence Corp. is often retained to scan the social Web instead of performing traditional criminal and credit records checks to uncover negative information about job applicants (Hill, 2011). Job recruiters are curious about how these candidates present themselves in spaces where their frivolous and inner-most thoughts, private and conspicuous photos, work experiences, and personal life experiences are all on display. The question becomes, "How has this person branded his or herself and will it be beneficial to our company?" To demonstrate this point, here are some statistics regarding this issue.

A study conducted by SelectMinds, a company specializing in social talent sourcing and business alumni relations, reveals that the majority of the companies (72%), represented by the study's 216 respondents, are using social media to actively engage in some form of social recruiting (Oracle, 2013). According to the data, recruiting is the number one purpose for social media usage by these organizations. They identify Facebook pages, LinkedIn groups, and Twitter accounts as the most popular social networks for overall corporate usage (Oracle, 2013).

LinkedIn's Communications Manager Richard George said more than 7,400 companies use Linkedin Recruiter service to find passive candidates who are not actively searching for job opportunities on social media (Wright, 2012). According to the Bullhorn Reach Ranking Report (2012), LinkedIn is the most widely used social network for social recruiting in the United States with 77% of jobs posted on the site. Twitter follows with 54% and Facebook trails with a quarter of U.S. jobs posted to the social network.

The online presence of employers and their recruitment efforts on social media sites are prevalent. Thus, it would be an apropos endeavor for college students to wield this dynamic to their advantage. Since employers are already searching for them, students need only to reach out and make themselves visible.

Theory in the Network

As Internet users present their images and messages in the social media realm, they engage with other users in chat rooms, posts, comments, likes, pokes, pins, and so on. Therefore, social media mirror interpersonal communication traits. From another perspective, users have the potential to distribute to and reach mass audiences. In this case, social media resemble the mass communication model. It must also be taken into account that mass producers release the messages to the audience, which moves the interaction beyond that which resembles traditional mass media (Chandler, 1998). So there is a unique communication process in which people engaging on social media feel as though they are experiencing interpersonal interaction. Yet, they simultaneously participate in multi-way communication commonly seen in mass media, as they release information and receive feedback from others. Once this concept is comprehended, the uses of social media to present oneself and communicate become more evident.

Uses and gratifications theory has been used to demonstrate how Internet users navigate social media sites through two-way communication to serve their own purposes. The theory posits that people actively choose which media to use depending on their needs and goals (Katz, Blumler, and Gurevitch, 1974a). Alan M. Rubin explains that the main elements of the theory include, "... our psychological and social environment, our needs and motives to communicate, the media, our attitudes and expectations about the media, functional alternatives to using the media, our communication behavior, and the outcomes or consequences of our behavior" (Rubin, 1994).

In accordance with this assumption, uses and gratifications theory is useful in examining the way college students behave on social media. The theory can be applied to explore whether or not the students have a need for maintaining professionalism over social media in order to obtain jobs. It also helps to determine the consequences or results of their online behavior in terms of attracting or repelling employers.

With the adoption of social media, users have access to more information in one place and can search their interests as well as produce materials that add to the pool of information. The need to seek employment is still prevalent in today's economy and people still turn to media to find employment opportunities. Social media are convenient for fulfilling this societal need that was once achieved through tedious searches in the classified sections of printed newspapers. Students are now able to use social media to accomplish the goals of not only searching for job openings, but also applying for positions. Additionally, users can choose to connect with others online, building a professional network of employers, professionals, and peers in their field and related areas of interest. Once users opt to engage in this manner, they are placing themselves on display in cyberspace. It is conceivable that these same users want to construct a professional image and maintain an optimal online reputation, setting further goals such as attracting employers and obtaining employment.

Now that we know Generation Y is the group identified to contain the largest amount of social media users for seeking employment, college students who aim to obtain internships while they complete their degrees and enter entry-level jobs upon graduation are perfectly situated to use this digital medium for achieving the previously mentioned goals. Students who successfully attract employers, apply for suitable jobs, and obtain jobs through their social media acumen enjoy the gratification that comes with retaining employment immediately upon leaving school.

The Social Identity Model of Deindividuation Effects Theory (SIDE) in computer-mediated communication (CMC) stems from the psychology perspective on media effects. SIDE posits that depersonalization of self, and even others, can cause a sense of visual anonymity within group behavior (Lea, Spears, and de Groot, 2001). The theory is predicated on the idea that within the context of depersonalization and anonymity individuals are likely to relate to and align with those who appear to have similar social identities and distance themselves from those who do not (Carr, Vitak, and McLaughlin, 2013). The perception of anonymity experienced in CMC, impacts social identity and social boundaries. Pulling it all together, SIDE, as it pertains to CMC, asserts that there is a juncture between three key elements: the characteristics of a communication medium, the social context, and the social definition of one's self that will create media effects of sorts (Postmes, Spears, and Lea, 1998).

In the social media sphere where individuals are moving in and out of online communities, chat rooms, forums, blog commentary, and group boards, people are prone to look for others who have similar interests. The intention is for one to feel comfortable among a sea of people who mainly know each other through their online representations. In line with this thinking, college students may connect with other college students, and plausibly with professors with whom they have a good rapport as well as professionals in their field of study, and organizations with which they wish to affiliate or join.

SIDE theory aids in the examination of the connection between the three elements of 1) college students' self-defined images; 2) the job seeking and recruiting arena in which their images are observed by employers; and 3) the social media sites on which it all takes place. In addition, SIDE affords insight into students' perspectives on how anonymous or private they believe their images are on social media sites and how much access they believe employers or potential employers have to their images across social media.

A Study in the Social Branding of College Students to Seek Employment

This current study was conducted to specifically examine how college students use friend-networking, professional networking, photo-sharing, video-sharing, and microblogging sites as well as blogs to brand professional images in order to promote themselves in the job market. Therefore, this research seeks to discover how college students are using social media to build professional images and whether this is an effective medium that allows them to secure internships or full-time employment.

Although some of the results parallel prior research that revealed Generation Y is using social media to search for jobs, for the most part, the survey data show evidence of students not using social media to its full potential to gain employment. Based on the data, most of the college students in this study are engaging in social networks, but more than half are not establishing professional brands or acquiring jobs online. The students in this study who do use social media to find jobs actually fare worse than those who do not. Let us take a closer look.

Methodology

This study was conducted using a quantitative research method, specifically the questionnaire/survey approach. This approach is the most effective and efficient method for this study, which examined college students as the sample. The questionnaire/research method is convenient for the students in several different regions in the United States to access. In addition, this method via online platform is a cost-effective and convenient method for the researchers to access and analyze results electronically. The survey was electronically based and placed on Surveymonkey.com, an online survey portal, where the students were able to log on from a link provided to them. The survey had 20 questions and took approximately 10 minutes to complete. Sample questions from the questionnaire included: a) Do you have a profile of any sort on any social media outlet?; b) If so, please check those that apply: (choices include) Facebook, Twitter, LinkedIn, Instagram, Youtube, Blogs, ePortfolios, etc.; c) Are you aware of terms of agreements of each social media outlet that you have a profile with?; d) Have you ever been invited to interview at an organization or obtained employment due to your profile on a social media outlet?; and so forth.

The survey link was sent to college students in the northern, central, and southern regions of the United States. The link was also emailed to professors to distribute to students. The qualifications to participate in this research study required that participants be enrolled in a college or university and be older than the age of 18. The sample is a convenience sample of the investigators' former students, their colleagues' students, and all college students who chose to participate. Two hundred and sixty-eight students completed the survey.

Sixty-seven percent of the respondents were female and 32% were male. The racial breakdown of the students was: African American/Black (55%), Hispanic/Latino (23%), Caucasian (12%), Asian/Pacific Islander (6%), Asian Indian (.84%). The classification of the college students was Freshman (32%), Sophomore (26%), Junior (21%), and Senior (21%).

Survey Results

The students maintain profiles on Facebook, Tumblr, Twitter, LinkedIn, Instagram, YouTube, Blogs, ePortfolios, and Coursera. Facebook, Twitter, LinkedIn, and Instagram are the leading sites utilized by the college students. Eighty-nine percent of the students had a Facebook account, while 61% had Twitter profiles and 66% had Instragram accounts. Thirty-four percent of the respondents maintained a LinkedIn account. Forty-two percent of the students posted on average of one to five times per week, while 58% of the students posted 6 or more times per week.

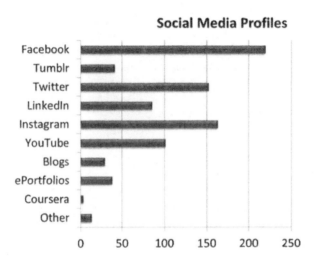

Figure 9.1 Social media sites on which college students maintain profiles.

On the social networking websites, the students shared initial comments (posts on their own pages), responsive comments (on others pages), articles, photos, music, videos, quotes, events, job announcements, and job searches. Seventy-two percent of the students shared initial comments, while 65% responded to comments on others' pages. Only 9% shared job announcements and 6% shared job searches. Seventy-one percent of the respondents categorized the content of their posts as entertainment related. Sixty percent agreed that their posts were life events and personal achievement related, while 47% categorized the posts and statuses as educational and 26% professional based.

In response to the following question, "Are you aware of the terms of agreement of each social media site on which you have a profile?" Sixty-seven percent said "yes," while 32% said "no." Regarding privacy, 76% of the students had implemented the privacy settings on their profiles and 23% had their social networking profiles open to the public.

The following questions were geared directly toward the students' professional image, potential employers, and employment. Fifty-six percent of the college students did not utilize social media sites to build professional images and reputations for themselves, while 43% did. Fifty-three percent of the respondents said that they decided whether to share certain personal information in their profiles based on what they thought potential employers and professionals would think of them. More than half of the students (52%) did not follow any employers (companies or professionals) on social media sites. Six percent of the students did follow employers and 10% followed professionals. In addition, 30% followed both employers and professionals.

Thirty-nine percent of the students agreed that no employers (companies or professionals) followed them on social network sites. Some students were followed by employers (5%), and others professionals (8%), or followed by both (15%). However, 31% of the students did not know whether they were being followed or if their profiles were being viewed by employers (companies or professionals). In response to the question, "How many times per month do you interact (talk, message, chat, comment, tweet, etc.) with professionals or potential employers on social media sites?" Nearly 87% of the students agreed that they interact with professionals or potential employers between one to five times per month on social media sites.

The majority of the students (59%) said that they received no feedback — positive or negative on their posts, comments, or photos from professionals or potential employers. Twenty-six percent of the respondents received positive feedback, while less than 1% received negative feedback from professionals or potential employers. Seventy-six percent of the students have had internships or jobs prior to the survey and 46% were actively seeking an internship and 22% seeking a full-time job.

Lastly, 63% of the students did not use social media sites to seek job employment, while 36% took advantage of the medium and sought employment opportunities. In response to the question, "Have you ever been invited for an interview or obtained employment due to your profile on a social media outlet?" Seven percent of the respondents said "yes" for an interview; 4% said "yes" for an internship; less than 1% for a full-time job and 3% said for an interview, internship, and full-time job. Eighty-three percent of the students agreed that they had never been invited for an interview, internship, or obtained employment as a result of their profiles on a social media outlet.

Professional Image

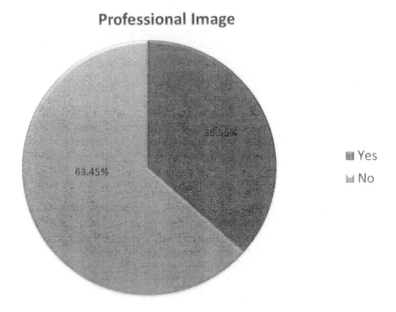

Figure 9.2 College students' use of social media to seek job employment.

Obtained Interview or Employment

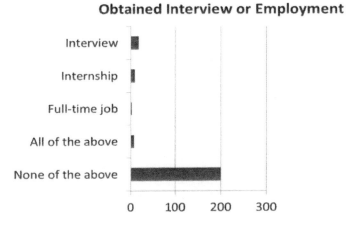

Figure 9.3 College students who have been invited for an interview or obtained employment due to their social media profiles.

	N	Minimum	Maximum	M	SD
Students maintaining a Facebook profile	219	1.00	1.00	1.0000	.00000
Students maintaining a Tumblr profile	41	1.00	1.00	1.0000	.00000
Students maintaining a Twitter profile	152	1.00	1.00	1.0000	.00000
Students maintaining a LinkedIn profile	85	1.00	1.00	1.0000	.00000
Students maintaining an Instagram profile	163	1.00	1.00	1.0000	.00000
Information shared on social media sites (initial comments posted on student's own page	178	1.00	1.00	1.0000	.00000
Information shared on social media sites (responsive comments on others' pages)	162	1.00	1.00	1.0000	.00000
Information shared on social media sites (articles)	98	1.00	1.00	1.0000	.00000
Information shared on social media sites (photos)	210	1.00	1.00	1.0000	.00000
Information shared on social media sites (job announcements)	23	1.00	1.00	1.0000	.00000

Information shared on social media sites (job searches)	17	1.00	1.00	1.0000	.00000
Social media profile posts categorized as entertainment	176	1.00	1.00	1.0000	.00000
Social media posts categorized as professional	64	1.00	1.00	1.0000	.00000
Social media profile posts categorized as life events/personal achievements	149	1.00	1.00	1.0000	.00000
Times per week students posted on social media sites	245	1.00	11.00	3.2245	3.1144
Use social media sites to build a professional image and reputation	240	1.00	2.00	1.5625	.49712
Decide whether to share content based on what potential employers might think	240	1.00	4.00	3.3500	.62914
Follow employers on social media sites	240	1.00	4.00	3.2917	.89998
Following or subscribed to employers on social media sites	239	1.00	12.00	2.0628	1.7199
Actively looking for an internship or full-time	236	1.00	3.00	1.8475	.87156

job at this time					
Use social media to seek employment	238	1.00	2.00	1.6345	.48260
Invited for an interview or obtained employment due to social media profile	238	1.00	5.00	4.5042	1.2178

Table 9.4 Descriptive Statistics of College Students' Use of Social Media

Conclusion

As the results revealed, the majority of the college students (56%) did not utilize the social media sites to build a professional image and reputation for themselves. Therefore, there is no correlation between college students who use social media to build a professional image being more invested in their careers than those who did not. The data collected did not indicate that the students who built their professional images on social media sites were necessarily more invested in their careers than their counterparts who did not build their professional images utilizing social media. However, more than half the students (53%) did make a conscious effort to refrain from posting anything that may be deemed inappropriate by a potential employer or professional. The results from the survey data addressed the hypotheses:

Hypothesis I: College students who build professional images to establish their personal brands via social media are more invested in their careers than college students who do not.

Hypothesis II: College students who utilize social media to seek job employment are more successful at obtaining employment than college students who do not.

With so few students sharing job searches (6%) and job announcements (9%) via the social media sites, it is not surprising that 83% of the students had never been invited for an interview, internship, or obtained employment as a result of their social media profiles.

Sixty-three percent of the students surveyed did not use social media sites to seek employment. However, prior to this research 76% of the students did have internships or jobs. Although 46% of the respondents are seeking an internship and 22% seeking a full-time job, it is evident that a clear majority are not utilizing social media sites for job search. Interestingly enough, even though 76% of the students state that their profiles were private and 23% open to the public; 31% of the students did not know whether their profiles were being viewed by potential employers or professionals.

Lastly, of the 36% of college students who use social media sites to seek employment, it is evident that they are not as successful obtaining employment as are college students who do not use social media sites to seek employment. Eighty-three percent of the students had never been invited for an interview, internship or actually obtaining employment.

Given the data on Generation Y social media usage, this is the group that is most prepared to figure out how to use social media to best meet their needs, specifically when seeking employment. The 2012 survey by Jobvite reported that one in every six job seekers claimed to have found his or her current job through some form of social media. Job boards are shown to be the number one social resource for landing those jobs. According to the Kelly Global Workforce Index (2011), nearly one-third of Generation Y job seekers used social media to get their current position. So what is off kilter with the students in this study?

The theoretical framework of this chapter brings it into scope. Through the lens of uses and gratifications we see that the students utilized the social media sites primarily for personal reasons, i.e., a large percentage posting personal statuses and more than 70% categorizing their posts as entertainment related. However, a majority of the students do not use social media to seek jobs and 87% interact with professionals or potential employers a mere 1-5 times per month on social media sites.

SIDE theory helps to demonstrate that as these students get online, they aim to blend in and be accepted socially, rather than to stand out professionally. There is evidence that the students are disassociating from professionals and employers that resemble their career aspirations. Based on the concepts of SIDE, the students desire to associate with their peers instead of professionals. Since most of these college students are not creating professional brands or alliances for the sake of seeking employment, here lies a weak convergence of the communication medium (social media), the social context (online job market), and the social definition of one's self (professional image). Hence, the media effects are not potent enough to achieve the desired result: job attainment.

A perceived issue in The Social Branding of College Students via Social Media to Seek Employment study, as admitted by the respondents, is many are not consciously branding themselves as professionals ready to enter the workforce. Although they possess a heightened sense of caution about sharing inappropriate materials; that alone is not enough to assert themselves as an all-around reliable and desirable budding professional. Moreover, the Bullhorn Reach Ranking Report (2012) shows that employers' in the northeast are most active in using social networks to post job announcements and to recruit job applicants. Yet, as previously mentioned, more than half of the respondents (many located in the northeast) are not conducting job searches online and the vast majority has minimal contact with professionals and employers.

It is likely that if college students use social media to: 1) brand themselves with more professional images; 2) maintain stellar online reputations; 3) proactively seek job opportunities; and 4) proactively increase interaction with more professionals and employers, they would become more competitive job candidates. These techniques should not replace traditional professional networking skill development, but would prove most beneficial when used in concert. Essentially, the fusion of these tools could position student job seekers to invite job interviews and offers.

References

Barrett-Poindexter, J. (2012). How Facebook can help you win the job-search war. *USNews.com.* Retrieved from http://money.usnews.com/money/blogs/ outside-voices-careers/2012/03/12/how-facebook-can-help-you-   win-the-job-search-war

Britt, B. and Matei, S.A. (2011). Virtual sociability: From community to communitas. Indianapolis, IN: InterAcademic Press/ Ideagora.

Bullhorn Reach. (2012). An inside look at social recruiting in the USA: The Bullhorn Reach rankings report. Retrieved from http://reachlb-851626069. us-east-1.elb.amazonaws.com/content/social-recruiting-in-the-usa

Carr, C. T., Vitak, J., & McLaughlin, C. (2013). Strength of social cues in online impression formation: Expanding SIDE research. *Communication Research*, 40(2), 261-281.

Chan, M. (2010). The impact of email on collective action: a field application of the SIDE model. *New Media Society*, 12(8) 1313–1330.

Chandler, D. (1998). Personal home pages and the construction of identities on the Web. Retrieved from http://www.aber.ac.uk/media/Documents/short/ webident.html

Donath, J. (1998). Identity and deception in the virtual community. In Kollock, P. and Smith, M. (Eds.) *Communities in cyberspace*. London: Routledge.

Ebersole, S. (2000). Uses and gratifications of the Web among students. *Journal of Computer Mediated Communication*, 6(1), 1-17.

Ellison, N.B., Steinfield, C., & Lampe, C. (2007). The benefits of Facebook "friends:" Social capital and college students' use of online social network sites. *Journal of Computer-mediated Communication*, 12(4), 1-29. Retrieved from http://jcmc.indiana.edu/vol12/issue4/ellison.html

Hill, K. (2011). Will Facebook destroy your job search? *Forbes* magazine. Retrieved from http://www.forbes.com/forbes/2011/0718/features-facebook-social-media-google-destroy-job-search.html

Jobvite. (2011). *Social Job Seeker Survey 2011*. Retrieved from http://web.jobvite.com/SocialJobSeekerSurvey.html

Jobvite. (2012). *Social Job Seeker Survey 2012*. Retrieved from http://recruiting.jobvite.com/resources/social-recruiting-reports-and-trends/

Katz, E., Blumler, J. G., & Gurevitch, M. (1974a). Uses and gratifications research. *The Public Opinion Quarterly*, 37(4), 509-523.

Katz, E., Blumler, J. G., & Gurevitch, M. (1974b). Utilization of mass communication by the individual. In J. G. Blumler, & E. Katz (Eds.), *The uses of mass communications: Current perspectives on gratifications research* (pp. 19-32). Beverly Hills: Sage.

Kelly Services. (2011). *Kelly Global Workforce Index: Social Media/Networking: The Evolving Workforce*. Retrieved from http://www.kellyocg.com/Knowledge/Kelly_Global_Workforce_Index/Social_Media_-_Networking/

LaRose, R., & Eastin, M.S. (2004). A social cognitive theory of internet uses and gratifications: Toward a new model of media attendance. *Journal of Broadcasting & Electronic Media*, 48(3), 358-377.

Lea, M., Spears, R. & de Groot, D. (2001). Knowing me, knowing you: Anonymity effects on social identity processes within groups. *Personality and Social Psychology Bulletin*, 27(5), 526-537.

Ledbetter, A.M., DeGroot, J.M., Mao, Y., Mazer, J.P., Meyer, K.R. & Swafford, B. (2011). Attitudes toward online social connection and self-disclosure as predictors of Facebook communication and relational closeness. *Communication Research*, 38(1), 27-53.

LinkedIn Insights. (2013). Retrieved from http://www.linkedin.com/company/linkedin/employee-insights?trk=top_nav_insights

Mahmoud, A.E. & Auter, P.J. (2009). The interactive nature of computer-mediated communication. *American Communication Journal*, 11(4). Retrieved from http://www.academia.edu/847408/The_Interactive_Nature_of_Computer-Mediated_Communication

Marmaros, D. & Sacerdote, B. (2002). Peer and social networks in job search. *European Economic Review*, 46(4-5),870-879.

McKenna, K.Y.A., Green, A.S., Gleason, & M.E.J. (2002). Relationship forming on the Internet: What's the big attraction? *Journal of Social Issues*, 58(1), 9-31.

McLuhan, M. (1964). Understanding media: The extensions of man. New York, NY: McGraw-Hill. Meister, J. (2012). Forbes. Facebook and the job interview: What employers should be doing. Retrieved from http://www.forbes.com/sites/jeannemeister/2012/04/09/facebook-and-the-job-interview-what-employers-should-be-doing/

Moral-Toranzo, F., Canto-Ortiz, J. & Go´mez-Jacinto, L. (2007). Anonymity effects in computer-mediated communication in the case of minority influence. *Computers in Human Behavior,* 23(3), 1660–1674.

O'Gorman, M. (2006). *E-Crit: Digital media, critical theory, and the humanities.* Toronto: University of Toronto Press. Oracle. (2013). ROI of social media in the enterprise: A benchmarking survey. Retrieved from http://www.oracle.com/us/products/applications/taleo/enterprise/social-sourcing/resources/index.html

Park, N., Kee K,.F., & Valenzuela, S. (2009). Being immersed in social networking environment: Facebook groups, uses and gratifications, and social outcomes. *Cyberpsychol Behavior*, 12(6):729-33.

Petric̆, G. (2006). Conceptualizing and measuring the social uses of the Internet: The case of personal web sites. *The Information Society*, 22: 291–301, 2006.

Postmes, T., Spears, R., Sakhel, K., & de Groot, D. (2001). Social influence in computer-mediated communication: The effects of anonymity on group behavior. *Personality and Social Psychology Bulletin*, 27(10), 1243-1254.

Raacke, J., & Bonds-Raacke, J. (2008). MySpace and Facebook: Applying the uses and gratifications theory to exploring friend-networking sites. *CyberPsychology & Behavior*, 11(2), 169-174.

Rubin, A. M. (2009). Uses-and-Gratifications perspective on media effects. In J. Bryant & M.B. Oliver (Eds.), *Media effects: Advances in theory and research* (pp. 165-184). New York, NY: Routledge.

Ruggiero, T. (2000). Uses and gratification theory in the 21st century. *Mass Communication & Society*, 3(1), 3-37. Valdez, M. & McFarland, S. (2012). Job seekers getting asked for Facebook passwords. The Associated Press. Retrieved from http://news.yahoo.com/job-seekers-getting-asked-facebook-passwords-071251682.html

Wright, A.D. (2012). Your social media is showing: A candidate's online presence may say more than a resume. *HR Magazine*, 57(3). Retrieved from http://www.questia.com/library/1G1-283983157/your-social-media-is-showing-a-candidate-s-online

Chapter 10
Social Media, Law, and Practice
Angela D. Minor, Esq.

The recent trends of social media websites and the emergence of a culture of digital communication have placed a tremendous impact on the practice of law. This virtual space has created an issue of whether digital communication is in fact protected or unprotected speech according to the rules of admissible evidence in our current judicial system. Issues arise when unchartered territory is discovered in our judicial system, such as the use of social media sites as valid testimony and admissible evidence to prove or disprove a rule of law. Thus, unprecedented legislation is just waiting to be promulgated over the use of social media as evidence. The explosion of Facebook, Instagram, Twitter, LinkedIn, and even MySpace rapidly changed communication. Further, one single electronic device — the cell phone — has impacted how we communicate. This is not to overshadow the undeniable impacts of iPads, laptops, notebooks, and tablets. The digital era has forced many humans to exist in an unlimited virtual world. However, the law and the American Judicial System is now adapting to the customs and habits of people, which has always been the case. However, when the law is forced to adapt quickly to the demands of social change and behavior as it relates to social media website usage, the judicial system often publishes varied opinions on a case-by-case basis until a legal precedent is established. The legal system is adapting to the customs and habits of people and technology in order to balance the law and the ever increasing threat to the public's invasion of privacy.

Technology has placed all of us in a world where communication becomes power. How we communicate has drastically changed. We are not simply using a telegram or a telephone with caller identification. We are learning to express ourselves through the many venues of social media. The instant gratification of a reply from a text message, or "likes" from Instagram, or the number of friends on Facebook are becoming an addictive measure of our self-worth. When people communicate through social media, it creates some form of interaction. Interaction can lead to conflict; conflict often leads to litigation. The legal system is fairing remarkably well in this new trending wave of communication and human behavior.

Hearsay and Admissible Evidence

The law has a methodology for communication. That methodology is described as the process of admitting evidence and it is governed by the Code of the Federal Rules of Evidence. The rules concerning hearsay become paramount when determining what is admissible evidence on social media websites. According to the Federal Rules of Evidence, hearsay is defined as any out-of-court statement offered for the truth of the matter asserted (Federal Rules of Evidence 801). Hearsay is a statement of communication made outside of the courtroom, in other words, all statements made when a witness is not testifying on the witness stand is considered hearsay. Hearsay is heard or spoken. It is presumed to be truthful, whether offered from the person who said the statement or a person who heard the statement. In a court of law, hearsay governs the admissibility of evidence, because the pursuit of justice demands truthful statements that are free from biasness, incrimination, and falsity. Thus, the pursuit of truthfulness remains the same, even in the virtual world.

In a court of law, if the plaintiff heard the defendant say, "I stole the $50,000," then the plaintiff has to testify to the statement in court. Although the statement is hearsay, the admissibility of the statement has to be argued then ruled upon by the presiding judge. Administrators of social media sites are now cooperating with local and federal police as well as the Federal Bureau of Investigation (FBI). Moreover, some law enforcement officers are being trained to monitor social media sites, and they are called cyber police. Cyber police are trained to track criminal conduct as well as statements of incrimination, whether used in a civil or criminal hearing. In order for statements to be admitted into evidence they must fall under the terms and conditions of the Federal Rules of Evidence hearsay and hearsay exceptions. The Federal Rules of Evidence governs all evidentiary exceptions (Federal Rules of Evidence, 2012-2013). Any statements made out of court that are oral or written can only be admitted as evidence if they fall within the purview of the exception that is being argued before the court. Most statements on social media websites offered as evidence in courtroom litigation can be proved with some intent to communicate to the public, whether that intent is truthful or false. The judicial court system has yielded to the demands of expanding evidence to consider antics uttered on social media, because of the frequent use of these websites by the public at large. The rationale behind using communication from social media sites is that a person would not have said something on a public site, if they did not intend for it to be published. The word published here is defined as a communication to at least one or more persons (Calvert and Pember, 2012). Therefore, all communication on public sites is viewed as a publication by legal standards.

A glimpse of hearsay will aid in the understanding of why social media websites have become a focus for valid admissible evidence by most trial lawyers. During a trial and barring no objections, evidence is proffered between attorneys that must be authenticated before being admitted. Once an email account is authenticated by the plaintiff or the defendant, in a lawsuit, then whatever content published on these social media sites such as: Facebook, Twitter, LinkedIn, MySpace can be used against them in a court of law. The authentication process is simply identifying the owner of the email account.

In many cases, social media becomes a conduit for communication that infringes upon ethical and legal standards. Facebook is often used more than any other site. The problem is most people do not believe that statements on Facebook and other social media sites can be used against them in a court of law. One student made a threatening post regarding his school on his Facebook page and was convicted for said comments (*I.P. v. State of Arkansas*, 2012). The student appealed but lost his argument in the Appellate Court. Another example was a young woman on jury duty who posted the following on Facebook about the defendant: "I can't wait to find him guilty!" It was in reference to a criminal case, yet she was sworn-in to be an impartial juryman. Consequently, cyber police on Facebook reported her comments and she was held in contempt of court, found guilty, and fined $1,000.

Social media sites are simply the source of choice for communicating thoughts and expressions; however, I contend that it is not just these sites that are causing the judicial system to take a second look. More importantly, it is the behavior of people on these sites. Many social media users assume their activities are private. In a general sense, they are, but when communication violates the law, the right to free speech is compromised. The remainder of the chapter explores the legal liability and use of social media as evidence in courtroom litigation.

Social Media Sites and Admissible Evidence

Case law serves as an indication of how judicial lawmakers are interpreting and viewing social media's impact on the law. In the Superior Court of Sacramento County, a juror posted his comments on Facebook regarding the case he was currently serving as a juryman (*Juror No. One v. Superior Court of Sacramento Cty.*, 2012). Social media websites are public domains in which all information communicated on those sites are stored pursuant to the Stored Communications Act of 1986, (SCA) (18 U.S.C. § 2701 et. seq.), formerly known as the Electronic Communications Privacy Act. This means postings, whether on Facebook, Twitter, LinkedIn, and MySpace, are always stored, making those writings accessible to federal and state governments, as well as law enforcement. In the matter of *Juror No. One*, he posted his comments on his Facebook wall and invited his friends to respond (*Juror No One v. Superior Court of*

Sacramento Cty., 2012). The role of the courts was to assess whether the juror's communication breached the confidentiality of the defendant's right to have his case private from the public, whether that communication unduly prejudiced the defendant's case and whether the juror was untruthful about his ability to be impartial in a criminal case involving a jailable offense. The juror was reprimanded, fined, and removed immediately from civil service for his Facebook posting. Facebook is a public domain and postings are considered publications in a court of law.

In another matter, *Evans v. Bayer*, the argument of Free Speech and First Amendments rights became an underlying issue (*Evans v. Bayer*, 2010). Since social media sites are considered public domains from a legalistic point of view, users who state negative comments or false statements can be held liable for a Tortious offense known as Libel Defamation. Libel, in contrast to slander, is the written form of defamation, whereas slander is oral. Disparaging and false postings on social media sites can prove to be a quick, easy, and often successful defamation case. On the other hand, postings that are a matter of public opinion or the pure comments of the user can sometimes be ruled as protected speech. The courts have often found that postings on social media sites fall under the gamut of protected speech by our First Amendment Right to Free Speech. For example, a student posted derogatory remarks; in fact, the student formed a Facebook group of her and the sole purpose for her classmates to discuss how she disliked their high school teacher. The Facebook group created by the plaintiff Katherine Evans was called, "Ms. Phelps is the worst teacher I ever met" (*Evans v. Bayer*, 2010). Most of the group's participants supported the teacher and attacked the student. The court of appeals stated the Facebook group was a matter of pure opinion and protected speech, and there was no violation (*Evans v. Bayer*, 2010). The court of appeals found that this charter high school student exercised her right to free speech even when the remarks posted online were not in the most favorable light for the teacher, the school, or her peers (*Evans v. Bayer*, 2010). Additionally, the court considered the following factors in determining there was not a case of libel: all postings were done outside of school and on the student's home computer and all postings were done after school hours (*Evans v. Bayer*, 2010). This ruling follows the direct Supreme Court ruling over student speech set forth in *Tinker v. Des Moines Independent Community School Dist.*, 393 U.S. 503 (1969). The *Tinker* case established if the material or online speech substantially disrupts the work or discipline of the school, then it is necessary to justify suppression of student expression (*Tinker v. Des Moines Independent Community School Dist.*, 1969).

In the aforementioned cases, both matters dealt with online postings and all communications were used against them in a court of law. The functionality of the court system has no filter for what is admissible as evidence. Facebook communication postings are kept and recorded by the Stored Communications Act (1986). They are viewed by Facebook's cyber security team members and are deemed admissible evidence when illegal conduct is occurring or as precautionary measures.

The subject matter of online school postings reveals that the court system will most likely view all postings as admissible evidence but that some postings are protected speech. Protected messages are speech deemed to be simply matters of public opinion. A matter of public opinion is a defense in a court of law entitled "pure opinion," which means a statement of opinion is protected speech (Calvert and Pember, 2012). Moreover, in the matter regarding the juryman that violated the law, it is proof of the regulation of cyber security being upheld in the virtual world.

Even in the matter where a lawyer stated to the judge that he was unfamiliar with Facebook as a response to why he did not hand over his client's messages from a social media site, it was considered to be an action sanctioned by the court (*McConnel v. Red Robins International*, 2012). The judge ruled that the Facebook messages must be handed over in the case and ordered the attorney's client to pay more than $15,000 in sanction fees for not handing over discovery, which included Facebook postings and messages.

However, if the admissible evidence is deemed as communication with an element of illegal behavior and violations of existing rights and laws, then there are consequences. It is established in case law that admissible evidence is needed to prove or disprove the truth or falsity. The fact that it is posted online suggests that human behavior and conduct must be regulated — now, more than ever, in the digital realm. To date, the truth and the ideology of George Orwell's book *1984* have equipped the court system with easy accessible evidence to aid in the regulation online human behavior.

Social Media, Evidentiary Arrests, and Convictions

In some instances, social media used as admissible evidence can lead to arrests and convictions. In the case of *Michael Bradley v. The State of Texas*, the evidence used was not a communication posting but a picture uploaded on Facebook, which aided the victim of an armed robbery in the photograph identification process. The judge recognized the court's unprecedented approach to the admission of this evidence, stating:

> Admittedly, however, the way in which the photo arrays were put together place this case on the frontier of a largely unexplored legal wilderness: the role of social media in criminal prosecutions. Sometime after the robbery in this case, complainant saw the two men who had robbed him, and he asked someone with them for their names. He looked up the brothers' Facebook pages. There he found, among other things, a picture of Bradley posing with two guns — including one that looked remarkably similar to the gun stolen from complainant during the robbery. Complainant emailed these photos to the investigating detective and later identified both brothers in separate photo arrays (2012).

In the instant case, the court stated the photograph on Facebook constituted admissible evidence as long as the witness' prior observation of the accused was sufficient to serve as an independent origin of photo identification (*Bradley v. The State of Texas*, 2012). The court separated the traditional notions of face-to-face screening through a police lineup or viewing a picture album of criminals in a law enforcement database. In fact, the judge stated that the "vast online photo databases — such as Facebook — and relatively easy access to them will undoubtedly play an ever-increasing role in identifying and prosecuting suspects (*Bradley v. The State of Texas*, 2012). In the aforementioned case, there were no words or communications that moved the court to take action. In essence, it was the pictures used on Facebook to identify the assailants in the armed robbery. Facebook offers unfettered access and exposure of information regarding persons that use the site. Although the site offers privacy and protection, the more information the user relinquishes, the more his or her privacy rights are potentially lost.

The law is changing, in so far as technology has now become a hub for admissible evidence and a source for aiding law enforcement to combat criminal activity. The ability to identify two assailants on Facebook has drastically equipped law enforcement in making pointed and timely arrests. This is driving the U.S. judicial system to continue to allow information from social media sites to be used against citizens in court. The Fourth Amendment of the United States Constitution states in part that:

> "The right of the people to be secure in their persons, houses, papers, and effects, against unreasonable searches and seizures, shall not be violated, and no warrants shall issue, but upon probable cause, supported by oath or affirmation, and particularly describing the place to be searched, and the persons or things to be seized." (U.S. Const. amend IV)

The Fourth Amendment affords protection to every citizen for reasonable expectation of privacy. An argument can be made that postings and communications can be handed over to the government or if there are random checks without notice on private virtual space, then the public's fourth amendment right to privacy is diminished or compromised. Where is the line drawn? The line of demarcation becomes clear when the activity, behavior, and the communication oversteps legal boundaries. For instance, the use of social media sites for the purposes of communicating hate or harm, such as cyber-bullying postings are undoubtedly human behavior that constitutes an illegal act. As it relates to admissible evidence from social media sites, the law considers the constitutionality of the citizens. After all, your Fourth Amendment right to privacy is a paramount factor while using social media sites. Arguably, lawmakers have committed themselves to the understanding that the law has to change due to the use of smartphones and social media sites. Begging the question does the law really have to change, or does the law simply need to be reconstructed to include digital searches? I argue the latter.

In summary, social media sites afford users liberal and unfettered access to communicate in a limitless space. Users can connect internationally within seconds. However, users should, at all times, view it as a public domain. The privacy settings are maintained to protect the user from keeping unwanted persons from viewing their postings, pictures, and connections, but they do not protect them from having what they communicate being used against them in legal proceedings.

Twitter and Virtual Liability

Practicing attorneys across the country admit evidence from Facebook and Twitter for the benefit of both the plaintiff and defendant. Twitter is one of the most influential social media websites. Twitter became popular largely because of its celebrity usage. Ashton Kutcher, an American actor, producer, and writer, began to highly publicize the fast-paced social media site that allows thousands of people to follow you in one connected social group. According to ZDNet.com as of September 2011, Twitter had more than one hundred million users, while Facebook had more than eight hundred million. Like Facebook, Twitter is also an unfiltered public domain. As a matter of fact, users can reach celebrities directly through tweets. Even the U.S President Barack Obama has a Twitter account and encourages American citizens to follow his postings.

Twitter has raised important issues of privacy, copyright, free speech, and censorship. Amanda Bynes, a young American actor who received fame on Nickelodeon (in the late 1990s and early 2000s), has been arrested several times in recent months and is believed to be having a mental breakdown. Her parents are seeking to use her Twitter rants in a court of law to prove her mental state of mind, which could possibly exonerate her if she's found guilty of drug possession. Twitter and Facebook are social sites with a plethora of public information that could be used in a court of law. Without having to go through the hassle of obtaining a warrant or subpoena, law enforcement can just seek information found on Facebook or Twitter. However, law enforcement is often subjected to filing a subpoena after a certain period of time has passed and considering the contraband in question.

Accordingly, the Stored Communication Act grants law enforcement an undisclosed right to obtain messages, postings, and pictures from Twitter and Facebook, even if the data or account has been deleted. The Stored Communication Act allows the federal government to have unfettered access to what the public considers private communications. As we can observe, Twitter is no different than Facebook as far as admissible evidence. Whether the evidence is sought between counsels in the discovery stages before the trial or a state prosecutor or the federal government to secure a conviction, it comes down to question of truth and justice. One long-standing issue with social media sites as admissible evidence is the violation of the Fourth Amendment. Herein is the question of the millennium: have social media sites altered our Fourth Amendment fundamental right to privacy? One answer to that question is "no," since postings on social media sites are considered public forums. Thus, as published material, every user should understand that their postings, communications, and pictures are fair game to be used against them in a court of law. For example, a picture posted with the caption, "I'm enjoying the view here in Honolulu, Hawaii." Meanwhile, the user was supposed to be in court on that date and time, then the date stamp on the picture is bound to be the best evidence and make a good case of user's failure to appear and substantiate a court of law issuing a warrant for arrest or a contempt of court charge. In short, social media as admissible evidence is moving the court system to a place of control and structure rather than disorder.

When Social Media Postings Are the Cause of Action

When social media is used as part of the facts causing a legal action to arise, instead of evidence used to prove a fact, this becomes another interpretation of how courts view social media postings as evidence. For example, if a family law attorney alleges a defendant is an adulterer, then evidence from Facebook, Twitter, or MySpace can be used to prove that allegation. Here, the focus is the action that is caught on Facebook, Twitter, or MySpace that must be reprimanded, because it violates the law and is prohibited behavior or conduct. The actual conduct or behavior is the violation and issue of the litigation.

In the matter of *Shaun Brown v. Montgomery Co.*, the plaintiff, a platoon supervisor, had a holiday gift exchange party amongst his co-workers (*Brown v. Montgomery Co.*, 2012). The gifts exchanged consisted of alcoholic beverages and sex toys (*Brown v. Montgomery Co.*, 2012). A more critical factor to the case was the gifts were exchanged on the job, and pictures were taken with the gifts, while the employees were at their cubicles. Brown, a subscribed user to MySpace, uploaded the pictures on his page causing his behavior to be subjected to legal scrutiny. After the posting was discovered, Brown was terminated from his job, and newspaper articles were written describing his unethical behavior, resulting in bad publicity for the company. Brown's actions of having alcohol and adult toys at a holiday party, while on the job, alerted cyber security to an illegal activity and was the issue of the lawsuit. His postings subjected him to arrests and a criminal or civil conviction (*Brown v. Montgomery Co.*, 2012).

In another matter, Reuben Lack sued Shannon Kersey of Alpharetta High School because he was removed as Student Body President after he made a speech regarding the Prom King and Queen and his interests in the school debate team. He held conversations off-campus on his Facebook page regarding the same subject matter (*Lack v. Kersey*, 2012). He claimed the speech was constitutionally protected. He asserted a defense entitled "First Amendment Retaliation Claim" (*Lack v. Kersey*, 2012). The court found that he was not entitled to receive his seat as Student Body President, but his speech was protected according to *Tinker v. Des Moines Independent School District*.

The Supreme Court stated in *Tinker v. Des Moines Independent Community School District* that the "First Amendment rights, applied in light of the special characteristic of the school environment, are available to teachers and students. It can hardly be argued that either students or teachers shed their constitutional rights to freedom of speech or expression at the schoolhouse gate" (*Lack v. Kersey*, 2012).

In short, the court in *Lack v. Kersey* found that the student's speech on Facebook was protected because it was not lewd, vulgar, offensive, or school-sponsored speech that related to pedagogical concerns (2012). Brown's speech on Facebook did violate the court's factors of determining whether the speech was protected. His speech encouraged the student body to creatively find their interests and activities as well as develop the skills necessary to obtain their goals. Reuben Lack's Facebook posting read in part, "Find your activity to get involved. Stay with it. Be passionate about it. This will make your experience here all the better. Teachers can only do so much – but with this you need to take the active role. For me, my activity was debate. Nothing more gives you the critical thinking skills and fun of meeting new people at new places. It even looks good for colleges" (*Lack v. Kersey*, 2012).

If the speech in question encourages users, rather than discourages them, then more likely than not, the speech will be protected by the First Amendment. Here, the presiding judge focused on the content of the speech and deemed it to be encouraging and not lacking any educational value. Therefore, the speech was given a safe haven of protection afforded by the First Amendment.

In another matter, litigation ensued when a mother in a custody battle posted on her Facebook page that she was considering moving with the minor children out of state (*Metz v. Steele*, 2012). Whether the posting was published directly to the father or was sent to the father through a third party is irrelevant. As a result, the father filed a Motion to Modify Custody using her Facebook posting as evidence, which proved to be valid testimony. The courts have long settled decisions regarding communication that is voluntarily authored by a party in a legal dispute. Here, the posting had no First Amendment Retaliation Claim, but it clearly involved action that needed to be taken, as the move would affect the father's visitation rights. Based on the evidence presented on Facebook, the parties were granted a hearing before the judge.

Conclusion

Social media sites such as Facebook, Twitter, LinkedIn, and MySpace serves the purpose of connecting old friends, meeting professional acquaintances, and keeping up with the daily lives of family and friends. Social media sites are now considered to be the new form of electronic monitoring and digital surveillance. However, as a precautionary measure, users should refrain from making comments that relate to the following: litigation, celebrities, threats, comments that are directly related to job performance, threats to corporations or schools, as well as other vulgar and lewd acts. The transformation of legal cases through the admission of social media evidence proves that private domains have become fair grounds for admissible evidence.

References

Michael Bradley v. The State of Texas, No. 14-10-01167 Court of Appeals Houston, Texas (14th Dist.).

Shaun Brown v. Montgomery County, No. 11-2130 (E. Dist. Pennsylvania filed March 21, 2012).

Calvert, C. and Pember, D.R. (2012). *Mass media law.* New York, NY: McGraw-Hill.

Calvert McConnel v. Red Robins International, Inc., Slip Copy 2012 WL 1668980, 2012 U.S. Dist. LEXIS 66476 (N.D. Cal. 2012).

Evans v. Bayer, 684 F. Supp. 2d 1365 (2010).

Federal Rules of Evidence 801 (2010).

Federal Rules of Evidence Handbook (2012-13 Ed.)

I.P. v. State of Arkansas, Ark. App. 273 (2012).

Juror No. One v. Superior Court of Sacramento County, 142 Cal. Rptr, 854-858 (206 Cal. App. 4th 8542012).

Lack v. Kersey, No. 1:12-CV-930-RWS (N. Dist. Georgia (Atlanta Division) filed March 30, 2012).

Metz v. Steele, Ark. App. 373 (2012).

Stored Communications Act of 1986, (SCA) (18 U.S.C. § 2701 et seq.)

Tinker v. Des Moines Independent Community School Dist., 393 U.S. 503 (1969).

Section III Social Media and International Practices
Chapter 11
Participatory Media Impact on the Arab Spring
Adam Klein

"This is happening right now in Cairo, Egypt," a narrator's voice conveys to the viewers of a CNN Breaking News Report (CNN Newsroom, 2011). As a live camera zooms in from high above, capturing the thick plume of black smoke rising in the center of the city, a CNN foreign correspondent begins to describe the dramatic developments of a national revolution unfolding before a world audience. He identifies the black smoke as tear gas that has just been released into a crowd of late night protesters in an attempt, by Egyptian police, to enforce a citywide curfew that had just gone into effect. As the correspondent talks about the unwillingness of the protesters to return to their homes, we hear determined chanting from the crowd, along with the sound of tear gas bombs and bullets being fired somewhere in the distance. To us, the bullets sound like firecrackers. The camera zooms away from the streets, where now, people look like shadowy figures moving frantically across a game board. Like the view below, the story is also condensed by the narrator who recaps these events for those at home, "The protesters don't seem to be backing down from their single biggest demand — that President Hosni Mubarak leave power, now!" Elsewhere that same day, a different broadcast would emerge.

This report, however, would stream globally, having been posted by an unnamed author to YouTube.com. The title of the uploaded video is "Tear gas bomb — Egypt protest 2011" and it has no narrator (Hashem, 2011). Instead, a silent cameraman captures the scene of his fellow protesters marching toward their opposition in Tahrir Square. When tear gas is released into the streets, men can be seen gasping, choking, and vomiting while holding handkerchiefs to their faces. The protester capturing the real-life experience turns the camera around momentarily to document his own bloodshot eyes. A short time later, a new video surfaces on the web showing a dramatic standoff between police officers and protesters in downtown Cairo (Worldpeace2u2, 2011). From the tight view of a low-rise balcony, one can hear the pandemonium of the crowd immersed in tear gas, and the constant snap of bullets being fired from only a few feet below. From here, the bullets sound like bullets. Later that day, another video is posted to YouTube documenting the aftermath of a bloody demonstration (Youssefmomen, 2011). The wounded are being treated along a city wall by their fellow protesters. One man stands over another, whose white sleeve is blood-soaked. He motions to him, "how many fingers am I holding up?" The man on the ground does not respond. Another upload, posted just days later, captures a lone protester walking down an empty street, his arms outstretched as he approaches two police officers at the crossing (Fakarfaker, 2011). The women recording the quiet surrender from their rooftop might know this young man, who now slowly removes his jacket indicating that he is unarmed. After several seconds, a single pop echoes through the street as the protester drops to the ground, having been shot in the head. One woman begins to scream hysterically as the camera drops from her hand.

The contrast of these two examples of a national revolution happening before an international audience is much deeper than presentation alone. At face value, the differences between the cable news organization's coverage of the national uprising and that of local citizens' can be seen and heard in the editing and exposition of the events on the ground, or lack thereof. However, in these separate examples, audiences around the world have also received two entirely different forms of communication. The pivotal distinction emanates from the storytellers themselves, who, in the case of the YouTube videos, have perhaps forever transformed the presentation of an international event into an intercultural experience. This distinction is not to suggest that the news coverage of the foreign correspondents in Egypt were somehow cautiously removed from the "real" revolution. On the contrary, journalists from every major news network bravely put themselves into harm's way throughout the 2011 uprisings in order to relate the factual happenings of the Egyptian demonstrations — and in several instances were themselves met with violent consequences as a result of the journalistic roles they played. However, on YouTube, Facebook, Twitter, and other social networks, once thought of to be the chief domain of distant friends and college kids, we have begun to witness a digital transformation occurring in the nature of global communication.

To understand this transformation and the nature and progression of social media as a new intercultural platform, this research investigates the role of YouTube in helping tell the story of the protester, from Iran's Green Revolution to the Arab Spring uprisings in Egypt and Syria. The central focus of this chapter will examine the Arab Spring, when, as this study will show, social media's presence in the regional conflicts reached a critical mass such that the protests from cities like Cairo and Damascus were now being viewed on YouTube by the millions, and replayed globally on cable news networks.

Guiding this central investigation were two questions that aimed to reveal both the scope and communicative character of the YouTube broadcasts:

RQ1: How did the impact of YouTube evolve in the Arab Spring uprisings compared to its earlier presence in Iran's Green Revolution?
RQ2: What are the defining characteristics of the YouTube broadcasts as a communicative vehicle for impacting world affairs?

To approach an understanding of the significance of social media as a platform for communicating international events and experiences, it is important to begin by establishing how this phenomenon is as much about new voices as it is about new media. Through the Internet, the everyday citizen has entered onto a world stage with communicative capabilities that, until a few years ago, had been reserved for two dominant institutions of global affairs — government diplomats and major news outlets. The impact of social media in the realm of foreign affairs can perhaps best be understood by first examining the traditional communicative role of these two institutions that have in many ways been challenged, and even bypassed, by the participatory media movement.

Traditional Voices in the Global Arena

In 2009, on his first diplomatic trip to the region, President Barack Obama delivered a speech in Cairo, Egypt, titled "On a New Beginning." Speaking before a crowd of thousands of students and a state-televised audience, President Obama declared:

I do have an unyielding belief that all people yearn for certain things: the ability to speak your mind and have a say in how you are governed; confidence in the rule of law and the equal administration of justice; government that is transparent and doesn't steal from the people; the freedom to live as you choose. (Remarks, 2009)

As a political representative, President Obama's words were not intended for the Egyptian politicians, but rather for the people they governed, and the greater Muslim community. In the months that followed, however, President Obama's speech had little effect in changing the national policies of the political establishment in Egypt — that credit would lie exclusively with the Egyptian people. In many ways, however, it was not the speaker but the very perception of foreign diplomacy that has changed since the days of Woodrow Wilson's historic Fourteen Points speech, which has been credited with partly inspiring the 1919 Revolutions in Egypt, India, and China (Anderson, 2011).

Traditional diplomacy has typically been associated as originating from the state, whose representatives can range from world leaders to diplomatic officials to national media agencies. Pigman (2010) notes that "early modern usages of diplomacy were largely concerned with a process: the art of negotiation, and how to use negotiating effectively to achieve objectives of state" (p. 4). Pratkanis (2009) identifies some of the more common objectives of diplomacy used today as they pertain to matters of foreign conflict. Among them, he cites an underlying intention to "change the mind and behavior of enemies, neutrals, or those who might enter alliances," "win support for ideals," "destroy an enemy's morale," or to "induce an enemy to surrender" (p. 114). Undoubtedly, all of these and other functions of traditional diplomacy share an underlying manipulative thread, which is why this form of international communication has so often been associated with state propaganda.

In fact, over the last decade, efforts to institute foreign diplomacy have almost become counter-productive with the new global Internet generation that can easily identify the source of most messages. One recent example can be found in the 2003 Shared Values Initiative (SVI), in which the U.S. State Department broadcast commercials throughout the Middle East depicting positive images of Muslim life in America. The diplomatic program failed in that the SVI campaign was largely perceived as propaganda, in many cases, before it even left the gate. According to one report cited by Fullerton and Kendrick (2006), "Egyptian TV refused to air the ads because they were [seen as] political advertisements" (p. 107). It was as if the modern world had become too media savvy for traditional political diplomacy to have any cultural effect.

This brings us back to the storytellers, and the question of who then has the power today to best communicate world events, issues, and causes? The news media, no doubt, have played their own important role in shaping the global community's understanding and beliefs about foreign affairs and global issues as they arise. But, as many international communication scholars have found, the same news media often fall short in their coverage of a foreign conflict by focusing their reporting primarily on the potential or the spectacle of war, rather than investigating its underlying causes or possible resolutions (Kamalipour, 2005; Kellner, 2004; Thussu, 2004). Furthermore, among the most common practices associated with the news coverage of an international conflict is how the "wartime press" typically "reduce the number of conflict parties to two and the number of issues to one," thereby simplifying what are, in fact, very complex matters (Galtung and Vincent, 2004).

The news media are also often accused of being late to the scene of a foreign conflict that is usually several years in the making. Yet, until the actual moment of crisis, those stories largely go unreported by the mainstream press. A February 2011 Pew Research Center study found that, since 2007, when "they started measuring weekly news coverage, the single biggest international story was the Iraq War, garnering 43% of coverage during the week of September 9-14, 2007" (Rayfield, 2011). The next major international story to receive global news coverage, according to the report: the Egyptian Revolution of 2011. That absence in vital foreign news coverage, coupled with a broad and growing distrust in state-delivered diplomacy, has left a growing vacancy in who communicates the stories of global importance to the rest of the world. And that brings us back to Facebook.

The Rise of Participatory Media in Global Affairs

The "Facebook Revolution," as it has been called, is the story of a stunning Arab Spring of democratic revolutions collectively shifting the balance of power in nations like Egypt, Tunisia, Libya, Syria, Yemen, Bahrain, Saudi Arabia, and Iran. However, this period also represents a definable moment in human communication, in which the world community has begun to see emerging media outlets, like social networks, employed by everyday citizens as a means of bypassing traditional forms of global expression (i.e., government barriers on free speech and Western media monopolies). Perhaps nowhere in recent memory was this phenomenon more dramatically pronounced than during the 2011 Egyptian protests, in which citizens responded to their government's global media blackout of their peaceful demonstrations by posting regular updates and videos to Twitter and YouTube so that the world could know and see their story through their eyes. This particular event is a telling transformation in global communication, because it really represents a public's gateway to engaging their own diplomacy, and sharing it with other citizens around the world. In a very profound way, these revolutions foreshadow what could be the next evolution in international relations. The participatory media allow international conflicts to become more than just distant events that are represented in the sound bites of world leaders, or interpreted for us by news giants, but rather, they are shared with us now, as they happen, by everyday people.

In terms of functionality, we have already seen profound uses of social media by the public in nations like Iran in 2009, and even Burma in 2007, in ways that have also effectively delivered the traditional objectives of diplomatic communications. The 2007 Burmese anti-government protests chronicled how the Burmese people were able to connect "to the world relentlessly, using short message service (SMS) and emails, posting daily blogs, notices on Facebook, and videos on YouTube. The mainstream media rebroadcast and repackaged these citizen journalists' reports, made from the front line, around the world" (Castells, 2010, p. 42). These connections allowed the Burmese people to relate their mobilization against the oppressive military junta, and thereby, "induced the United States and the European Union to increase diplomatic pressure on the junta." Likewise, during the Iranian post-election protests of 2009, leaders of the Islamic Republic instituted a national media blackout in an attempt to conceal the anti-government demonstrations from the world's eyes. And yet, the Iranian citizens began to use their cell phones to capture the vicious, and sometimes deadly, clashes with their own military, allowing them to later stream those graphic images across the World Wide Web.

The near success of these two national uprisings, and the realized potential of new media in helping to facilitate those events, were, perhaps, precursors to the successful revolution of the Egyptian people in 2011. By then, the blueprints for utilizing cell phones, social networks, and a new digital platform of global communication had been drawn. Howard (2011) emphasizes how information and communication technologies had increasingly been used to "coordinate and publicize massive mobilizations, unite opposition movements through social networks, attract foreign media attention, and transport strategies and success stories from one nation to the next" (para 17). With regard to the Egyptian revolution and greater Arab Spring, Benn (2011) writes:

> The masses could gather in Tahrir Square in Cairo because texting, Facebook, and Twitter freed them from dependence on the official sources of information, such as state-controlled television and newspapers ... the Arab world revolts remind us of the power of free-flowing information and its role in the development of society from the time of Caxton through to Google. The result in Egypt, Tunisia, and Libya has been to make possible popular revolutions that would never have taken place had this information not been available. (p. 12)

While it is important to maintain that the uprisings throughout the Middle East and North Africa — though collectively dubbed the "Arab Spring" — are separate movements deriving from individual struggles, one cannot deny the role the digital media have played in igniting and uniting the spirit of these revolutions throughout the region. Writing on the "cascading effects" of the Arab Spring, Howard (2011) explains:

> Protesters in Tunisia and Egypt used social media to link up. Telling stories about their shared grievances and sense of desperation became much of the content flowing over these networks. Eventually, such content spilled over the social networks that transcended national boundaries. (para. 3)

"Transcendence" is perhaps the most appropriate word in our attempt to define the meaning of this fully matured social media phenomenon that was realized during the Arab Spring uprisings. Beyond the functionality of the new media landscape and how citizens utilized it, there is a potent human element in these communications that transcends traditional forms of international discourse. Through the complexity of cyberspace, citizens can engage their own diplomacy with other citizens around the globe in the most basic form of human communication — a first-person account. What kinds of political breakthroughs or exchanges can emerge from this raw form of a public discourse? Are we, as an evolving global community, moving toward a new era of citizen-based diplomacy through social media? To answer these and other questions, this study would examine the impact, style, and content of 150 YouTube videos that illustrated the common narrative of a people sharing the firsthand experience of a national revolution.

Three Revolutions

To measure the impact of the YouTube broadcasts in communicating the experience of the Arab Spring, the research began by comparing scenes of protests that emerged from Egypt in 2011 and Syria in 2012 to an earlier version of a "social media uprising" that developed in Iran in 2009. The Green Revolution, as it has been called, was a spring of nationwide protests that extended across Iran in response to the re-election of President Mahmoud Ahmadinejad, which many citizens deemed to be a stolen, and therefore invalid, election. A defining moment of the uprisings occurred on June 20, 2009, when a 26-year-old aspiring musician named Neda Agha Soltan was shot and killed by a member of the government paramilitary as she watched a nearby demonstration. Neda's murder was captured on camera by fellow protesters, and though Iran's leaders sought to keep the violent military crackdown of the protests from international eyes, the video of Neda's tragic death went viral on YouTube in the days that followed.

In many ways, the Persian Spring that preceded the 2011 Arab Spring uprisings established the first full-scale phenomenon of a live revolution being captured by citizens on their digital devices, and disseminated globally within hours via the World Wide Web. In this way, the Green Revolution presents an ideal marker on the timeline of participatory media's place in the global arena, against which we can measure the dramatic progression and evolution of social media in the Arab Spring two years later.

The revolutions that began in Egypt and Syria in 2011 were selected among approximately eight national uprisings that unfolded in nations across the Middle East and Northern Africa during that time period, each representing what appeared to be a growing democratic movement collectively known as the Arab Spring. By most accounts, the Egyptian revolution began on January 26, 2011, when thousands of citizens gathered in Tahrir Square in organized fashion to demand the end of the three-decades-long presidency and governance under Hosni Mubarak, whose leadership was viewed as a corrupt dictatorship. As dramatically and unexpectedly as the uprisings emerged, Tahrir Square quickly became the center stage of the world's attention. Like the protests in Iran, the nationwide demonstrations were met with a violent response from the Egyptian police and military forces, though several generals and soldiers notably refused to act upon their fellow citizens. All the major news networks broadcast the revolution globally. However, in terms of the media, it was YouTube, Facebook, and Twitter that would ultimately tell the story of this revolution from the protester's hands, between January 26 to February 11, when Mubarak finally resigned from office.

The Egyptian revolution represents perhaps the most recognized uprising of the Arab Spring because of the undeniable role that social media played there in sharing the hour-by-hour events through websites like YouTube.com. In analyzing the progression and nature of the YouTube footage emerging from this 2011 international story, the research was able to identify the characteristics and notable evolution of this global medium in its most realized form.

As of this writing, the Syrian revolution continues to march into year three, seemingly on the breaking point of becoming a true civil war. Like the Egyptian revolution, Syria's uprising began in 2011, but then dramatically escalated in 2012, as citizens of that nation banded into rebel forces to oust the leadership of another dictator, President Bashar al-Assad, and five decades of rule under the Ba'ath Party regime. Unlike the Egyptian revolution, the mainstream media has not been afforded the same degree of open access to cover the protests and violent clashes between rebel and government forces in Syria. In many ways then, as was the case in Iran, the role of YouTube has been paramount in informing the world about the events happening on the ground in cities like Damascus and Daraa. While countless protests have occurred across the country, Syria's revolution has been marked by a series of armed conflicts between citizens and military forces on street corners and across rooftops.

In terms of this research, Syria's story also represents the next evolution of YouTube in the Arab Spring. However, as an ongoing three-year struggle, the Syrian revolution also offers an important evaluation of the prolonged phenomena of a social media uprising. That is, it addresses the question of whether the movement would be sustained in terms of maintaining a global following. In the next section, this research will explain how YouTube expressly provided key data in analyzing such questions of scope and impact on the world stage.

Methodology

Using the successive revolutions in Iran (2009), Egypt (2011), and Syria (2011-13) as the subjects of social media-fueled uprisings, this study set out to collect the firsthand accounts of these events from the YouTube uploads of the citizens who experienced them. For the comparative nature of the study, Iran's Green Revolution was treated as the initial model of online activity against which the Arab Spring, represented by the Egyptian and Syrian video accounts, was separately measured. The search parameters for attaining a sample of YouTube videos began with the keyword search for each respective national revolution. In order to collect footage of the protests and surrounding action, and within a consecutive time frame, the terms "Iran Protest 2009," "Egypt Protest 2011," and "Syria Protest 2012" were entered into the YouTube search engine. Though the research sought to closely examine a sample of 50 videos for each respective nation, it is revealing to note that the search of Iran's 2009 YouTube videos yielded "About 81,300 results," compared to the 2011 Egyptian sample that generated "About 177,000 results," and the 2012 Syrian sample that produced "About 416,000 results. Using only the volume of search results as a basic barometer, one can see early on how YouTube has grown as a democratic platform for presenting, sharing, and commenting on these global events.

However, this research specifically sought to examine videos that relayed the experiences of the protests from the private citizen's point of view, which would best represent the "forum for people to connect, inform, and inspire others across the globe" for which YouTube.com was initially created ("About," para 1). Ironically, YouTube has also become the shared domain of professional organizations as well, such as mainstream news outlets and non-governmental organizations that likewise use this public space to reach the global audience. As such, any search of the Arab Spring yields a significant amount of professional footage, mainly news clips of the protests from networks such as CNN, BBC, Russia Today, and Al Jazeera. Therefore, this collection of YouTube videos included only the first 50 uploads that were provided by individuals, as evidenced by the footage itself, which had the distinct amateur qualities of shaky, typically unedited shots of a local protest scene. Those YouTube posts that were uploaded by identified authors such as CNN, BBC, Al Jazeera, etc., were automatically discounted, as were any videos that depicted a news correspondent, and/or organizational sponsor of any sort.

Once the 150 total videos had been collected, the study turned to the viewership volume, content, and style of each individual upload. YouTube conveniently provides the exact number of views for each video uploaded to its site. The total and mean number of views was tabulated for each respective nation as of the last week in January, 2013, when the videos were collected. For this study, YouTube viewership signifies audience impact the same way that television ratings or newspaper circulation can reveal the reach of those mediums. One could characterize those videos that received only hundreds of views as having a marginal impact, while those that received tens of thousands, and in some cases, hundreds of thousands of views, may be classified as having a "viral" response, denoting the sizable impact they made in this digital field.

To determine the nature of the content, the study focused on the action being captured by the individual, identifying it first as either peaceful or violent in character, and then recording the specific event that unfolded. For the coding process, the researchers documented the approximate size and form of the peaceful gatherings. For the violent scenes, coders identified one or more events from what ultimately became six reoccurring categories that included police/military forces physically attacking the protesters; the protesters retaliating against the police/military force; tear gas bombs released on the protesters; police/military forces shooting protesters; official vehicles running down protesters; and the documenting of wounded or dead protesters.

In addition to volume and content, the style of each YouTube video was also recorded according to the proximity of the storyteller to the footage being captured, and the finished product of the video if it bore any amateur produced qualities, such as music, editing, or subtitles. The proximity of the protester to the scene was divided into two categories of "On the Scene" or "Shot from a Distance," with the former signifying that the camera operator was a part of the protest, while the latter portrayed a vantage point that was removed from the action. Likewise, the second stylistic category was also separated into two categories of "Raw Footage" or "Partially Produced Footage." While the raw footage plainly showed the event happening as it unfolded, the partially produced video suggested an added element of enhancement on the part of the filmmaker aimed at influencing how viewers should interpret the event.

Before the full sample was analyzed, an inter-coder reliability test of 10% of the total 150 videos was conducted to assess the level of agreement in identifying only those elements of content and style, since the measure of volume simply involves recording YouTube's published number of views. The two coders observed 45 separate elements from the videos and agreed upon 40 of them (88%). Using Scott's Pi as an additional measure to factor in the random chance of agreement, the coders yielded a 77% level of agreement.

Finally, this study also sought to identify some of the defining qualities of YouTube as an emerging platform for relating the experiences of these revolutions. For this, the research took a step back to consider the thematic visual text of the videos themselves. The study paid close attention to the most reoccurring forms of content and style that emerged from the initial analysis, as well as other cinematic qualities that presented a common feature of the sample of as a whole. A guiding question that helped to focus this observational approach into identifiable categories was, "What distinguishes this video from a news broadcast of the very same footage?" Using that comparative standard, the study identified three distinct qualities that help to define the larger role of participatory media in global communication.

Analyzing the YouTube Broadcasts

From a broad perspective, the total and mean numbers of views of the 150 videos that captured the protests in Iran, Egypt, and Syria each represent the audience's attention to these international events. It is true that YouTube viewership does not denote the number of viewers, but rather the total amount of times that the video has been seen. However, for the purpose of this study, which is to measure impact, a video that has been viewed more than once by the same individual can be said to have produced the same, if not a greater impact, in terms of connecting these events with a given audience. As an online community, YouTube is ultimately about "trending" events and issues from around the world; a phenomena that is expressed by videos that are watched several times, often forwarded on as links among friends and family via email, social networks, and cell phones, and even increasingly reported upon in the news media, as each video's worldwide circulation grows.

The events of the 2009 Iranian uprisings, followed by the 2011 Egyptian and 2012 Syrian revolutions, collectively illustrated a telling timeline of YouTube's presence as a storyteller on the international stage from the Green Revolution to the Arab Spring. In Table 1, it is evident from these samples that the three revolutions each received a viral-like response as illustrated by the mean number of views for each uploaded video, which drew tens of thousands of views.

However, the total number of views from 2009 to 2012 reveals a sharper trend in the online impact of each international event.

From the 2009 Green Revolution to the 2011 Egyptian Arab Spring, the viewership between the samples rose from 847,104 to 2,087,852 views, representing a 147% growth in measured impact. It is apparent then, that while the Iranian uprising did make a sizable impact with audiences on YouTube — perhaps setting the stage for the next major international event to follow — the Egyptian revolution was that event that reached the critical mass of followers such that it became synonymous with a social media revolution. Srinivasan (2012) writes, "Social media, perhaps thanks to the international and domestic hype, has a cache in Egypt that it did not have before the events of 2011" (para 4). As evidence, he cites the influence that social media had in 2011 on "infiltrating the media elites," noting how activists reached the mainstream news "from the "outside in" by documenting videos of protests, creating credible blogs, and tweeting stories to influence both international and domestic journalists" (para 5).

National Focus	Total No. of Views	Mean No. of Views
Green Revolution		
Iranian Uprisings (2009)	847,104	16,942
Arab Spring		
Egyptian Revolution (2011)	2,087,852	41,757
Syrian Revolution (2012)	1,193,040	23,860

n = 150 total YouTube videos reviewed – the first 50 results for each respective search (nation).

Table 11.1 A Comparative Sample of YouTube Viewership from Three National Uprisings

Further evidence of the saturation of YouTube into the global media landscape could be seen in this study by the heavy presence of mainstream news sources in the search results for "Egypt Protest 2011." Whereas the vast majority of video uploads related to the Iranian protests were the work of private citizen journalists, the professional news media were equally as represented in the Egyptian sample as the amateur voices. This would suggest a threshold that has been crossed in which the mainstream news not only acknowledges the role of YouTube in co-telling the story, but they also have actually joined that community in efforts to reach mass audiences now going online to get their information. A 2012 Pew Research study on "YouTube & News" analyzed 260 YouTube videos surrounding global news events and found that "51% bore the logo of news organization" versus the 39% that were "clearly identified as coming from citizens," noting further that stories about the "unrest in the Middle East" were among the most popular subjects (Mitchell and Hitlin, 2012).

Like Egypt's Arab Spring, the Syrian revolution also demonstrated a significant increase in viewership from 2009, with the entire sample receiving more than 1.1 million hits (41% more than Iran's Green Revolution). Likewise, the collection of representative sources also revealed a broad mixture of mainstream news authors with the firsthand accounts of citizens, signaling again the arrival of this medium on the global stage. However, a noticeable drop in viewership can also be observed between the 2011 Egyptian revolution and 2012 Syrian sample. With 50 videos receiving 1,193,040 views, the Syrian sample does demonstrate a sustained interest on the part of audiences in YouTube's coverage of the events. However, the approximate 900,000 fewer views could account for the sudden high-profile coverage of Egypt's 2011 revolution versus the gradual and prolonged multiyear Syrian conflict that continues into 2013.

One notable addition to the Syrian videos that was not nearly as prevalent in the Egyptian or Iranian samples was the strong international presence of protest rallies uploaded from cities like London, Vancouver, Rome, Los Angeles, and Washington, DC. Though these globally staged protests were not accounted for in this study, they do possibly represent the growing outcry of support for the Syrian rebel cause, and, the notable decision to return that sentiment through the channels of YouTube, as if to say, "We heard you."

From global impact, the research next took a closer look at the videos themselves to discover the nature of the content and style of the footage being uploaded across the three revolutions. Underscoring this analysis were the questions "what did these protesters want us to see?" And, "how did they want us to see it?" Of course, the revolutionary scenes unfolding in cities like Tehran, Damascus, and Cairo determined much of the nature of the content that was then shared by citizens who carried cameras and cell phones as they protested or observed the uprisings from afar. In Table 11.2, it is evident that the protesters sought to share their violent experiences of the uprisings as much as they did the peaceful gatherings and marches that saw anywhere from hundreds to thousands of citizens demonstrating on city streets, bridges, and town squares. Few of the peaceful gatherings were small in size, featuring speakers or local picketing. Instead, the citizen journalists overwhelmingly presented the sheer enormity of their cause in scenes that displayed the massive crowds of protesters, implying the message of unity.

Nature of the Footage	Iran (2009)	Egypt (2011)	Syria (2012)
Peaceful protest, No. (%)	**24 (48%)**	**17 (34%)**	**25 (50%)**
Local speakers and picketing	7 (14%)	4 (8%)	3 (6%)
Organized gathering of 100s	12 (24%)	10 (20%)	15 (30%)
Organized gathering of 1000s	5 (10%)	11 (22%)	11 (22%)
Marching	7 (14%)	10 (20%)	5 (10%)
Violent protest, No. (%)	**26 (52%)**	**33 (66%)**	**25 (50%)**
Police beating protesters	12 (24%)	12 (24%)	6 (12%)
Protesters fighting police	7 (14%)	10 (20%)	4 (8%)
Tear gas bombs released	3 (6%)	10 (20%)	0 (0%)
Protester(s) shot by police	6 (12%)	4 (8%)	12 (24%)
Vehicle runs down protesters	1 (2%)	3 (6%)	1 (2%)
Showing the dead/wounded	1 (2%)	3 (6%)	12 (24%)

n = Percentage of total videos reviewed for each respective nation (% out of 50).

Table 11.2 A Contextual Comparison of the YouTube Protest Footage

But, of course, not all of the footage shared an optimistic sentiment. The violence video footage was a predominant theme in the Egyptian uprisings, comprising 66% of the entire sample, while both the Iranian and Syrian uploads featured approximately 50% of scenes in which the protesters clashed with police forces in some way. What is most notable about the content of these graphic videos is the underlying message that is sent around the world when people see government officials, military, or police forces shooting, beating, and even running over citizens on the street. The message is: "See what our government is doing to us."

Traditionally, the accounting of government acts of violent on its own people is the domain of United Nations summits or hearings held at international tribunals, both of which are official settings in which the atrocities are addressed weeks, if not months, after they have happened. But in the YouTube broadcasts, the world was able to see the brutal actions of a government attacking its citizens in real time, and with the knowledge that it continues still. More important, rather than a diplomatic body receiving the report, it is the global court of public opinion that is witnessing these scenes of violence on YouTube. It becomes clear that the citizens in Egypt and Syria, in particular, were aware of this fact when many of their videos included descriptions of a scene by its author.

One such author, who had captured the chaos unfolding on Qasr al-Nil Bridge near Tahrir Square, described the footage for YouTube viewers:

> Qasr al-Nil Bridge witnessed violent clashes between the Central Security Forces, and the rebel Liberation Fri in anger. Security tried to disperse demonstrators in every way, using rubber bullets and tear gas, and even armored vehicles that were going to intimidate the demonstrators. But the rebel Liberation managed to defeat the security forces and crossed the Bridge Kasr El Nil, to Iatsamua in Tahrir Square in waiting to overthrow the regime.

In total, the most common form of violence documented by these filmmakers were government forces beating protesters with clubs, followed by scenes of police/military firing their weapons at the activists. But the protesters also sought to share the true cost of a revolution with audiences, which is seen in the footage of the severely wounded activists being treated by fellow citizens, or the dead protesters being carried through the streets. A video from Syria depicting thousands of citizens marching in silence as they carry enshrouded bodies over their heads is accompanied by the following description: "The funeral of martyrs killed by government personnel turns into freedom and anti-government protests in the Syrian city of Homs on 9th April 2011" (Free Knight, 2011a). Another graphic video uploaded by the same author shares, "Footage of the random shooting towards civilian protesters on the road between Inkhil and Al Sanameyn. You can see at least one person seriously injured and another one dead" (Free Knight, 2011b).

In terms of style, the latter two scenes were shot up close by an active protester, as was the case with 74% of the videos that were uploaded from Syria (see Table 11.3). Likewise, approximately half of the footage captured from the Iranian and Egyptian uprisings were each filmed "on the ground," often by a protester in the midst of a demonstration or engulfed in a violent clash with military forces. The close-up style of these videos revealed more than just the cinematic details that would otherwise be lost in the wide shots. In terms of the storyteller, the on-the-ground filming tells the version of events that the protester is seeing and living. This is the firsthand account that shows the realities, confusion, chaos, bloodshed, and even morbidity of a full-scale revolution in ways that the mainstream news media cannot. There are scenes that depict the retaliatory efforts of demonstrators throwing stones at police/military forces who shoot them with rubber bullets and tear gas bombs, and one video that captures four teenagers using nothing but fireworks against a nearby military squad. For these videos' authors, the decision to film such events is not only a bold decision, it's a dangerous one.

If the on-the-ground footage carries the ability to show the gritty realities of a revolution, then the scenes shot from afar best revealed the size and scope of the demonstrations, and lent a profound bird's eye view from which to observe the positions and movements of the military and citizen brigades. Other videos that were removed from the action even filmed events that would perhaps otherwise go unseen. For instance, several videos shot from behind curtains, inside cars, or on rooftops, covertly captured the scenes of police officers shoving random protesters into vans, or suddenly shooting an unarmed woman or man. Such videos would probably be confiscated by the perpetrators had they been recorded within proximity of these crimes.

Style of the storyteller	Iran (2009)	Egypt (2011)	Syria (2012)
Proximity to the protest, No. (%)			
Footage shot from the ground	26 (52%)	25 (50%)	37 (74%)
Footage shot from a distance	24 (48%)	25 (50%)	13 (26%)
Raw / Edited Footage, No. (%)			
Raw, uncut footage	46 (92%)	34 (68%)	47 (94%)
Edited footage w/ cuts and/or music	4 (8%)	16 (32%)	3 (6%)

n = Percentage of total videos reviewed for each respective nation (% out of 50).

Table 11.3 A Stylistic Comparison of the YouTube Protest Footage

In addition to the author's closeness to the action, the research also considered the finished product of the videos uploaded to YouTube. In this category, a distinction was made between the raw uncut footage and that which had the amateur produced features, such as subtitles, soundtrack music, or edits, between scenes of the same protest. In Table 11.3, it is apparent that the collected footage of the original Green Revolution was almost entirely raw, unedited scenes (92%) that were directly uploaded by their authors. The same was true for the 2012 Syrian revolution in which 94% of the 50 videos observed were uploaded as they were captured directly from camera to YouTube. In terms of underlying message, the raw footage conveyed the sense of realism that is indicative of these citizen-based YouTube broadcasts.

However, the Egyptian protest videos demonstrated a notably higher percentage of produced works (32%), which could account for several individual factors such as the authors' collective media savvy or their access to editing software. The increase in production value could also reflect the Egyptian citizens' growing acknowledgement of their worldwide audience coupled with the realized potential of YouTube as a vehicle for reaching that audience. The inclusion of subtitles to translate the chanting sentiments of the crowd, or selected musical theme for a desired dramatic effect, each share the same function as those descriptions of the video scenes that were noted earlier. In each of these examples we can see the authors' awareness of the audience, and the expressed desire to educate and emotionally connect with that global community.

Defining Characteristics of Participatory Media

In identifying some of the qualities that define the social media platform, the research considered this communication process comparatively against other international storytellers, primarily the news media that would cover the same events. It is true that the historic events of the Arab Spring are no different when told through the lens of a foreign news correspondent's camera than when conveyed by an amateur filmmaker capturing the scenes from their cell phone. Likewise, in terms of coverage, the journalists who reported the events in Cairo and Damascus were sometimes just as close to the action as the protesters who digitally shared that experience on YouTube. So how then are the YouTube broadcasts significantly different from a news report? The answer to that question is not exclusively found in the message, but rather in the transaction that is occurring between the sender and the receiver — the global audience — who, through social media, receives an intercultural discourse. In other words, in viewing these broadcasts, the global citizenry becomes a part of a more personal, direct, and basic form of communication than was intended for them.

This study noted three distinct modes of expression through which intercultural discourse is achieved within this unique visual platform. One of the main communicative elements that activate the intercultural dialogue is the first-person storyteller. Certainly, a journalist can cover the same visual information about a dramatic standoff unfolding between protesters and police forces. For the viewing audience, however, the images seen through YouTube also communicate the story of the filmmaker who has uploaded them. By removing the filter of news analysis from the scene, no matter how expressive or informative the analyst, the story itself becomes a firsthand account; a personal piece of history and culture that is offered candidly through social media. In this way, the YouTube videos could more aptly be compared with mediums such as pen pal writing between foreign students, or an autobiographical book that shines an international light on a particular lived experience. Both of these examples, like the YouTube uploads, demonstrate the same mechanism of an intercultural communication that is intimately shared by participants. On the effects of this viewing experience, one journalist and YouTube user writes:

> I see a boy, maybe 16-years-old, crumpled over the road median, one leg folded calmly over the other. I catch a quick look at his head and wonder if there is life in his half-closed eyes. Then I notice the bullet wound in his neck, jagged pink tissue under his chin. The panting voice begins to chant hurried phrases. The only word that I can understand is "Allah". I chose to be here and now I want to leave. But I'm actually already at home, sitting in my living room. Yet what I saw was real. I just saw a Syrian protester moments after he'd been shot in the neck... Thanks to YouTube, the Syrian Uprising is real for me and I check it just as I would my emails or stock portfolio. (Kuran, 2012, para 1)

In addition to the person-to-person communication that is supported by YouTube, the research also noted a recurring effect in the absence of narration during the videos. Once again, the impact is experienced by the viewer, who watches the scenes of protest free of journalistic interpretations, and, perhaps with an even greater level of engagement allowing him to discern these events on the screen for himself. As with much news coverage, the international correspondent's reporting of events has the potential to shape the viewer's opinions of the actors or narrative in the story. Better known as news framing, Entman (2003) describes this common journalistic practice as the ability of the storyteller "to promote a particular interpretation, evaluation, and/or solution" of an event, which can slant the interpretation of the everyday citizen (p. 417). But when the additional layers of explanation and supposition that are typically offered by the news narration have been removed, viewers are free, if not required, to draw upon their own conclusions and understandings of the event.

The last element that helped to facilitate the intercultural impact of the YouTube broadcasts was the raw format in which the majority of footage was captured. Like the absence of the narrator, the unedited quality of the videos immediately conveyed the work of a bystander, thereby signaling these accounts to be first-person experiences. The uncut footage also presented the viewer with a true-to-life uncertainty of the coming events as the camera moves across the panoply of human drama. This, in effect, becomes their live window through which to view any action, clue, or event that suddenly appears within the frame, and then work out its meaning. In his work on the Arab Spring and social media, Iskandar (2013) writes, "the rise of testimony and unvarnished and unedited personal narratives as privileged forms must be treated with both appreciation and scrutiny" (p. 246).

In the countless videos from the Arab Spring that depicted fervent activists demonstrating in the presence of armed police officers, the YouTube viewer, unlike the news watcher, must hold their breath in anticipation of not knowing what will happen next to a protester in the crowd, or for that matter, to the filmmaker himself. The unedited scene essentially becomes a visceral experience for the audience that watches the violent footage with little or no disclaimers, thereby sharing the jarring events from one moment to the next:

> Many videos are less crisp — jerky, fleeting images of crowds chanting, of people darting to safety as shots ring out. But always, the excited, frightened, panting voice of the camera-phone filmmaker...But when it comes to bringing events into outsider's living rooms, nothing can yet beat the grainy, usually unscripted, You Tube upload of a camera-phone video. (Kuran, 2013, para. 8)

The impact of these three combined elements — the near silent, unedited, first-person accounts of a revolution unfolding before the viewer's eyes — is a straightforward and candid portrayal of the scenes that allow for open interpretation, and a potentially stronger connection to be made between sender and receiver.

Through social media, it can be said that the tone of international communications has begun to transform into an intercultural discourse among peoples, not nations. The Egyptian Revolution, in particular, crystallized that moment when global communications became the domain of the everyday citizen, circumventing those political gatekeepers who have long presided over it, or the mainstream media that helped facilitate that mechanism by marginalizing the civic response to foreign affairs. The mainstream coverage of the Arab Spring revolution has, in fact, also revealed the news media's definitive acknowledgement and acceptance of social media's role in co-telling the story, as seen in the regular reliance on YouTube, Facebook, and Twitter content in television news reports. The video posts that emerged from Egypt and Syria have become pivotal news sources in relaying the stories of those revolutions, thereby affirming the legitimate place of social media on the international stage.

Conclusion

The historic events of the Arab Spring have, to date, produced three new governments that are more reflective of the people rather than the state, though such new regimes are still developing along what appears to be a jagged pathway toward democracy. Beyond the political fallout of these national revolutions, the cross-cultural uprisings across the Middle East and Northern Africa have also bared major revelations about the impact of social media as both a storyteller and an organizer of world-changing events. Many scholars, as well as social media experts, have debated the true influence of websites like YouTube and Twitter on the Arab Spring, with some arguing that the success of these uprisings must be attributed in part to the presence of social media, while others contend that the so-called "Facebook Revolution" only had a marginal effect by merely amplifying, but not inspiring, the widespread rebellions. Goldman (2013) writes, "Academic researchers and think tanks published papers on the subject, with most concluding that Twitter and Facebook had played an important role in amplifying conversations and reporting information, but not in actually fomenting revolution" (para 1).

However, much of the present research has been based upon the most-publicized Egyptian Revolution that occurred in 2011. This study sought to take a broader approach by surveying the impact factor of YouTube across three revolutions that developed over different time periods. In returning to the initial question of this chapter on impact, it became clear that there was a sharp increase in the viewership and posting of amateur videos from Iran's 2009 uprising to Egypt's 2011 revolt, that was followed then by a noted drop in viewership during the Syrian uprisings, although that sample still received 350,000 more views than the Green Revolution. This pattern seems to reflect the enduring presence of social media in global affairs that became most pronounced during the Egyptian Revolution, and ultimately sustained at a lesser, but nonetheless strong level in the unfinished story of Syria's uprising, the regular video accounts of which still receive an average 24,000 views on YouTube. These findings would challenge those scholars that have suggested, with regard to the telling of the story, that a level of "fatigue [has] set in — for both activists and the passive viewers" (Goldman, para 4). Instead, this research seems to fall more in line with other studies that show a peak in social media activity during the 2011 uprisings followed by a moderate decline, and eventually a steady level of activity (Crimson Hexagon, 2013; Howard et. al., 2011). In other words, social media's domain in international affairs was not a single-event phenomenon, nor is it a passing phase, but rather an established channel of new intercultural communication.

As to the second question, the defining characteristics of YouTube, these features have begun to take shape in the form of raw accounts of history that are unfolding without a narrator, but instead, a guide who is able to show us events through his eyes, and in doing so, elevates the viewer's role from passive observer to front seat passenger. It could be theorized here that, as a vehicle for impacting world affairs, YouTube delivered a new kind of social media diplomacy that the global community had never before experienced, because never before had world events been mass communicated firsthand by those citizens who lived them. In her work on the changing nature of diplomacy, Mueller (2009) reminds us that, "the concept of citizen diplomacy predates that of public diplomacy" (p. 101). In her definition, she writes that the citizen diplomat will "build person-to-person relationships — the web of human connections that later serve as the context for official dialogue and negotiations." This principle concept of global communication suggests that in order for true diplomacy between nations to occur, the public voice and the human experience must be shared first — it should precede the government's. In the Arab Spring, we saw that principle illustrated in the direst of circumstances. The extraordinary and successful uprisings against the longstanding dictatorships in Tunisia, Libya, and Egypt in particular, were shared in the public's domain of social media, and rebroadcast in the mainstream media. The images of an impassioned people demonstrating for their rights were cemented in the minds of everyday people around the world watching online:

> In clip after clip of footage from the street protests that have been sweeping the region, demonstrators – mostly young men – can be seen among the crowds holding mobile phone cameras aloft to document the scenes. The shaky footage of peaceful protests – and images of horrific carnage – have been uploaded to Facebook, Twitter, Flickr, YouTube, and other sites. (Social Media, 2011)

Instinctively, those at home watching the shaky footage of the protesters on the ground know that what happens next is unedited, unscripted, and authentic. Rather than the news media setting up the dominos, and predicting the direction in which they will fall, this form of social expression is not formulaic, which makes the life-threatening revolution of an actual people feel as it should, frighteningly real. Online, people can decide what is critical to relate and share with the world, and they can capture those events in the first person. The omniscient perspective of the news media, though more objective, tends to deliver a disconnected world audience. In other words, we watch what the news is watching, and over time, become twice removed from its deeper meaning. But in the Arab Spring, we saw exactly what the protester wanted us to see — what they were going through. This was not an "international situation, coming to us live," but instead, an intercultural experience shared digitally between citizens.

References

About YouTube (2013). Retrieved from http://www.youtube.com/t/about_youtube

Anderson, L. (2011). Demystifying the Arab Spring. *Foreign Affairs*, 90:3, 2-7.

Benn, T. (2011). The Flowers of the Arab Spring grow from buds of free information. *New Statesman*, 140:5048.

Castells, M. (2010). The new public sphere: Global civil society, communication networks, and global governance. In Daya K. Thussu's *International communication: A reader*. New York, NY: Routledge.

Crimson Hexagon (2013). What happens to social media After a Twitter revolution? Retrieved from http://www.crimsonhexagon.com/mashable-what-happens-to-social-media-after-a-twitter-revolution/

CNN Newsroom (CNN television broadcast, January 28, 2011). New York, NY: Time Warner.

Entman, R. M. (2003). Cascading activation: Contesting the White House's frame after 9/11. *Political Communication*, 20, 415-432.

Fakarfaker (2011, February 7). Innocent and unarmed Egyptian man gets shot by police while protesting. Retrieved from http://www.YouTube.com/watch?v=uw7-nCFqC3A

Free Knight 2011 (2011a, April 9). Martyrs funeral in Homs turns to freedom protest. Retrieved from http://www.youtube.com/watch?v=i3EVPmM18b8

Free Knight 2011 (2011b, April 1). Killing of freedom protesters by the Syrian Army near Al Sanameyn. Retrieved from http://www.youtube.com/watch?v=lP15DRrBob0

Fullerton, J., & Kendrick A. (2006). Advertising's war on terrorism: The story of the U.S. State Department's shared values initiative. Spokane, WA: Marquette Books.

Galtung, J., & Vincent, R. (2004). U.S. Glasnost: Missing themes in U.S. media discourse. Cresskill, NJ: Hampton Press.

Goldman, L. (February 15, 2013). Social media has been a mixed blessing for the Arab Spring. Retrieved from http://techpresident.com/news/wegov/23510/social-media-harming-arab-uprising

Hashem987654321 (2011, January 28). Tear gas bomb – Egypt protest 2011 – Manifestation. Retrieved from http://www.YouTube.com/watch?v=RBs6kAPiSNA

Howard, P.N. (February 23, 2011). The Arab Spring's cascading effects. Retrieved from http://www.miller-mccune.com/politics/the-cascading-effects-of-the-arab-spring-28575/

Howard, P.N., Duffy, A., Freelon, D., Hussain, M., Mari, W., & Mazaid, M. (2011). Opening closed regimes: What was the role of social media during the Arab Spring? Retrieved from http://pitpi.org/wp-content/uploads/2013/02/2011_Howard-Duffy-Freelon-Hussain-Mari-Mazaid_pITPI.pdf

Iskandar, A. (2013). Teaching the Arab uprisings: Between media maelstrom and pedantic pedagogy. *PS: Political Science & Politics*, 46:2, 244-247.

Kamalipour, Y. R. (2005). Introduction. In L. Artz & Y. R. Kamalipour (Eds.), *Bring 'em on: Media and politics in the Iraq War* (pp. 1-6). Lanham, MD: Rowman & Littlefield.

Kellner, D. (2004). Spectacle and media propaganda in the war on Iraq: A critique of U.S. broadcasting networks. In Y. R. Kamalipour & N. Snow (Eds.), *War, media, and propaganda: A global perspective* (pp. 69-78). Lanham, MD: Rowman & Littlefield.

Kuran, K. (2012). The revolution on a laptop: YouTube journeys through the Arab Spring. Retrieved from http://www.internationalpolicydigest.org/2012/04/12/the-revolution-on-a-laptop-youtube-journeys-through-the-arab-spring/

Mitchell, A., & Hitlin, P. (2012, July 16). YouTube and news. Retrieved from http://www.journalism.org/analysis_report/youtube_news

Mueller, S. (2009). The nexus of U.S. diplomacy and citizen diplomacy." In Nancy Snow and Philip M. Taylor's (Eds.) Routledge *Handbook of public diplomacy*. New York: Taylor & Francis.

Pigman, G.A. (2010). *Contemporary diplomacy: Representation and communication in a globalized world*. Cambridge, UK: Polity Press.

Pratkanis, A. (2009). Public diplomacy in international conflicts: A social influence analysis. In Nancy Snow and Philip M. Taylor's (Eds.) *Routledge handbook of public diplomacy*. New York: Taylor & Francis.

Rayfield, J. (February 8, 2011). Egypt protests got most news coverage of any international story since '07. Retrieved from http://tpmlivewire.talkingpointsmemo.com/2011/02/egypt-protests-got-most-news-coverage-of-any-international-story-since-07.php

Remarks by the President on a new beginning (June 24, 2009). Retrieved from http://www.whitehouse.gov/the-press-office/remarks-president-cairo-university-6-04-09

Social Media, cellphone video fuel Arab Protests (2011). Retrieved from http://www.independent.co.uk/life-style/gadgets-and-tech/social-media-cellphone-video-fuel-arab-protests-2227088.html

Srinivasan, R. (2012). Taking power through technology in the Arab Spring. Retrieved from http://www.aljazeera.com/indepth/opinion/2012/09/2012919115344299848.html

Thussu, D. K. (2004). Murdoch's war: A transnational perspective. In Y. R. Kamalipour & N. Snow (Eds.), *War, media, and propaganda: A global perspective* (pp. 93-100). Lanham, MD: Rowman & Littlefield.

Worldpeace2u2 (2011, January 28). Amazing Egypt protest violence footage in downtown Cairo. Retrieved from http://www.YouTube.com/watch?v=Ov5z8Sc9GSc

Youssefmomen (2011, January 28). Egyptian protest 28/1/2011 part 4. Retrieved from http://www.YouTube.com/watch?v=z-sCXV5Qo2k&feature=related

Chapter 12
Social Media and Participatory Communication: The UNDP and
the Diffusion of Empowerment
Nickesia S. Gordon

From the diffusion of innovations to more contemporary approaches to
information dissemination, communication and communication technologies
have consistently played a role in the development process. Former practices
emerging from the dominant development paradigm often see individuals as
targets of communication and not partners in the process. These top down
communication practices have actually worked to increase the communication
divide than bridge it. One of the most significant criticisms leveled at such an
approach to development communication has been the limitations inherent in the
conceptualization of power and power structures that contextualize the
environment in which development occurs (Wilkins, 2000). In this regard, social
media offer less centralized ways of engaging in communication and more
participatory discursive practices that are pluralistic and fluid, thereby contesting
institutional or hierarchical approaches to communication.

   In development contexts, there is a movement to develop more participatory
models of communication, given the recognized connections between social
change and communication. In this regard, development organizations and
practitioners are trying to establish ways of engaging with communities that
facilitate sustainable social change as well as encourage long-term cooperation.
Based on social media's almost inherent deregulation of the communication
environment and potential for democratic modes of engagement among the
global   citizenry,   many   nongovernmental   organizations   (NGOs)   and
development organizations incorporated social media platforms into their
communication strategies. Since social media platforms offer collaborative
mechanisms for communication (Kaplan & Haenlein, 2010), they allow the

communication plans of development organizations that utilize such platforms to have the appearance of participatory and inclusive ways of engaging with their publics. Certainly, based on the idea that social media presuppose an active audience and more subjective frameworks for meaning making, organizations that do utilize these platforms achieve a semblance of engaging in participatory communication. However, as Miller (2009) points out, faith in the active audience can sometimes reach "cosmic proportions" (p. 6), and while social media have the potential to facilitate inclusion, it does not mean this potential has been realized. Deployment of social media communication strategies does not always equate to actual realization of this potential.

By conducting a content analysis of two public social media pages established by an international development organization, namely the United Nations Development Program (UNDP), this chapter examines the probability of social media for participatory development communication. The author is primarily interested in answering the following question: Does the use of social media platforms by the UNDP facilitate two way or participatory communication between the agency and its constituents?

The analysis focuses on UNDP's Facebook and Twitter pages, which seem to have the most reach in terms of audience and members. The UNDP was selected, because it is the United Nations (UN) agency charged with supporting and implementing development projects in the global south. The analysis is grounded in the theoretical framework of participatory development communication. Specifically, it uses a participatory communication for social change model proposed by Figueroa Kincaid, Rani & Lewis (2002). Finally, the chapter offers a critique of the idea of participatory communication/development implicit in the usage of the above-mentioned social media platforms by UNDP.

UNDP

The UNDP is the United Nations' global development network. It is a multilateral organization advocating for social change and seeks to connect countries to knowledge, experience and resources to help people build a better life. The UNDP is active in 177 countries across the globe (www.undp.org). The unit is responsible for implementing and monitoring the progress of the eight millennium goals developed in September 2000 and agreed to by all 191 UN member states. This agreement is known as the United Nations Millennium Declaration and commits world leaders to combat poverty, hunger, disease, illiteracy, environmental degradation, and discrimination against women by the year 2015. The MDG goals include Building democratic societies, preventing crisis, enabling recovery, protecting the environment, halting and reversing HIV/AIDS, empowering women and growing national capacity.

In addition to its mandate to oversee the achievement of the MDG goals, UNDP is generally responsible for developing strategies and policies to combat global hunger and poverty. It has created various development indicators, which are used to monitor the achievement of certain targets in various countries. This was UNDP's response to criticisms leveled at its technocratic and neo-capitalist economic approaches to measuring development by scholars and practitioners (Escobar, 1995; Dervin and Huesca, 1997; Mody, 2000; Wilkins, 2000). The use of social media by the organization to communicate with its constituents about its operations can be read as an effort to align their practices with more participatory and collaborative methods.

Communication and Development

The term "national development" is often used interchangeably with the word "development." It is a concept steeped in much controversy given its origin and political application. It emerged during the postcolonial era when many European countries were forced to grant independence to their colonial territories (Biccum, 2002; Stiglitz, 2003). Traditional theories about national development often associated it with modernization, with or without its common modifiers such as economic, political or social development (Gordon, 2008). Development communication seeks to identify the role of communication and communication technologies in creating and disseminating information about development issues. As such, communication platforms such as mass media are seen as powerful tools for information dissemination and the shaping of public opinion. They are seen as having a role to play in helping national governments to achieve national development goals as well as encouraging social change behavior among local citizens (Brown, 1976; 1981; Waisbord, 2004; Gordon, 2009). Scholars, such as Singhal and Rogers (1999), argued the media in developing countries have the potential to educate the public about social problems, such as HIV prevention, family planning, maternal and child health, more equal status for women. These are all issues UNDP is charged with addressing.

Early development communication theory often centered on a model of diffusion, a framework usually associated with the concept of diffusion of innovations. Diffusion of innovations is a model of information dissemination aimed at encouraging behavior change and implementing social change policies or ideas developed by reputed development scholar, Everett Rogers (1995). In its initial stages, the model was heavily reliant on Shannon and Weaver's idea of a two step flow of communication and the power of influence held by informal groups or elite members of a community. This model saw individuals as targets of communication as against partners and mirrored the then dominant paradigm of development that engaged in particular discourses that associated Euro-America with progress and ex-colonial territories with stasis. This framework emulated a top down communication approach, and development scholars and practitioners argued for a more egalitarian method that would be more inclusive and collaborative (Escobar, 995; Tomaselli, 1997; Mody, 2002).. Former practices have actually worked to increase the communication divide than bridge it.

Participatory Communication

As the connection between communication and social change are further explored, alternative models have been suggested by development scholars and practitioners alike. Top down impositions of messages about development related issues only seemed to lead to the alienation of intended audiences. Therefore, models that favored audience ownership of messages as well as referenced their lived experiences were proposed (Tomaselli, 1997; Melkote, 2000; Wilkins, 2000; Figueroa etal, 2002). As Tomaselli (1997) noted, "subject generated expression and messages are argued to be much more effective in changing social attitudes among specific communities and groups than...glossy, and audience-remote messages of the mass media" (p. 4), and arguably development organizations themselves. Participatory models of communicating for social change position community members at the centre of dialogue and construe them as agents of their own change. Subsequently, participatory communication shifts focus from the previous paradigms emphasis on persuasion and transmission of information from external technical experts to dialogue, debate and negotiation on issues that connect with community members (Figueroa et. al, 2002, p. ii).

For the purposes of this chapter, the model of participatory communication proposed by the Johns Hopkins University Centre for Communication Programs will be used as the primary theoretical framework to assess the nature of the communication found on UNDP's Facebook and Twitter pages. The model is known as the Integrated Model of Communication for Social Change (IMCFSC) and focuses on the process by which dialogue as a participatory form of communication is related to collective action (Figueroa et. al, 2002, p. iii). IMCFSC was chosen for this study because it offers a very useful framework for examining participatory communication; that is, it offers established evaluative criteria that help a researcher determine the degree or actual presence of participatory practices in various development communication strategies. IMCFSC is a very extensive model that also incorporates assessment tools for determining whether or not social change has actually occurred as a result of implemented participatory communication strategies. Given that this chapter is limited in its scope of investigation to just examining the nature of the communication present on UNDP's Twitter and Facebook pages to determine whether or not it represents participatory exchanges, it will only utilize the section of the model that evaluates community dialogue.

IMCFSC posits that for social change to occur, a model of communication that is cyclical and relational in nature is necessary, meaning that community members engage in a communication process that is continuous and in which they take turns creating and sharing information with each other and then "interpreting and reinterpreting its meaning until a sufficient degree of mutual understanding and agreement has been reached" (Figueroa et. al, 2002, p. 4). Further, this model must lead to outcomes that depict mutual exchange rather than one-sided, individual change. In addition, a key component of this model of communication for social change is an iterative process that starts with a catalyst or stimulus. While this catalyst/ stimulus can be external or internal to the community, it must trigger dialogue within the community and among its members equally, to the point where collective action and resolution to social problems is the outcome (p. iii). An important thing to consider regarding this model is that participatory communication is conceived of as community dialogue. As part of this dialogue, community members themselves identify particular social problems and then take collective action to resolve them.

Communication as Community Dialogue

The view of participatory communication as community dialogue recognizes ten steps that describe a somewhat sequential process in which participatory exchanges takes place. As the authors of the model point out, all steps may not happen as the process is context driven. However, these descriptive identifiers are useful for evaluating if activity on the social media platforms being examined qualify as being participatory. The ten steps comprise: Recognition of a problem, Identification and involvement of leaders and stakeholders, Clarification of perceptions, Expression of individual and shared needs, Vision of the Future, Assessment of current status, Setting objectives, Options for action, Consensus on action and Actual plan.

These steps outlined above provide guidelines for reviewing exchanges on UNDP's social media pages and help to determine if community dialogue is actually taking place. Social media sites are regularly thought of as comprising online communities where dialogue between and among members or groups supposedly unfolds. Many organizations turn to these sites to engage with their publics, "increasingly using social media [platforms] as a way to inform interested individuals of ongoing developments, while allowing the public at large to instantly provide their own feedback" (Maggiore, 2009, p.628). The UNDP's utilization of Facebook and Twitter may be read as the organization's effort to connect with its various publics and communities in the above described way. The technology and tools available on the sites allow users to respond to posted communication messages as well as to initiate communication themselves regarding development issues UNDP may be engaged. In essence, social media, such as Facebook and Twitter, give UNDP tremendous interactive potential with its publics and communities. Social media presents an opportunity for participatory communication and mass collaboration.

Social Media as "Mass Collaboration"

Social media may be described as digital communication platforms that allow nontraditional (usually) online mediated communication networking that enables the creation, dissemination and exchange of content by member users. Membership is often times required but not always necessary for users to participate in the content building and proliferation on these sites. There are many definitions of what social media are, most seeming to fall into two basic categories, i.e. functional (what they do) and structural (type of platform). The above mentioned definition is a criterion related definition coined by the author that seeks to bridge both categories. It will be the definition used for the purposes of this research.

Social Media's potential for mass collaboration rests with its unequalled appeal, massive reach and rapid growth across the global population. For example, as of May 1, 2013, Facebook had 665 million daily users, indicating an increase of 26% from the year before (techcrunch.com), while Twitter had an estimated 288 million active monthly users as of December 2012, reflecting an astounding 714% growth since its inception in July 2009 (globalwebindex.net). In April of 2010, 22% of all Internet usage time was used to engage with social media, and 75% of Internet users worldwide visit a social network or blog when they go online (Nielsen, 2011). In addition, over 110 billion minutes on social networks and blog sites. This growth in social media usage has also coincided with a substantive leap in mobile phone usage, especially among citizens of the developing world. Between 2000 and 2008, mobile phone usage in Africa increased by 875% and by 920% in the Middle East. Eighty seven percent of the world's population uses cell phones and are using them to access the internet. In 2011, 50% of all pages visited by those mobile users were social media pages (Kumar, 2012). The majority of the global population that access social media sites from mobile phones emanate from developing regions, such as Asia-Pacific, the Middle East and Africa and Latin America (Nielsen, 2012), suggesting that, in terms of sheer numbers, the ability of organizations such as UNDP to use social media to engage populations with development issues on a large scale is quite high.

Along with breadth of reach among populations of developing countries, social media sites also have several "interactive" tools that heighten their potential to facilitate dialogue and create "living" communities online. Kumar (2012) sees social media as creating a "global virtual community hall" (p.2). Puri (2007) envisages these sites as creating "virtual social spaces and communities that transcend geography" (p. 1). Both descriptions point to the mass scale collaborative nature of social media and their potential to act as communities. These descriptions resonate with the concept of community dialogue as they point to the idea of inclusion and participation by members/ users whose voices constitute this virtual sphere. They also allude to the opportunities for information exchanges, feedback and even dissent among community members. In this vein, Facebook has several interactive tools that users may employ to have their voices heard. These include, but are not limited to, buttons such as "Like," "Friend," "Post," "Share," "Report," "Tag," "Delete," and "Comment." Similarly, Twitter has buttons such as "Tweet," "Retweet," "#Hashtag, "@Tag," "Follow," "Mention," "Share a Link," and "Reply." These tools along with others allow users to initiate, join as well as direct "conversations" or dialogue creating real time communication in many instances.

Based on the argument among development communication scholars for more inclusive approaches to development practices including development communication strategies, social media platforms offer great potential to help agencies, such as the UNDP achieve objectives. Social media have shown their potential to empower citizens at the grassroots and effect social change during such movements as the Arab spring. Through the various interactive tools, ordinary citizens have an opportunity to "talk back" to organized systems of power and achieve results creating what Appadurai (2000) refers to as grassroots globalization. Their emphasis on user-generated content (many to many concept), challenge hierarchical management structures of messaging and foreground community dialogue and civic engagement (Obar et.al., 2012).

Methodology

This study uses a webnographic approach in looking at the nature of participatory communication on the UNDP's Facebook and Twitter pages. Webnography is a qualitative methodology often used in exploratory research that allows a researcher to conduct ethnographic studies in online environments (Evans, 2010; Puri, 2007. Webnography is particularly suited to this study, since it is research that examines the online interactions among users of two particular social media sites. This kind of methodology has several advantages, the first of which is researcher invisibility, an important feature in conducting any kind of ethnographic study (Rubenstein, 2011). As Puri (2007) point out, "the ethnographer's ideal is to become 'a part of the furniture'" (p. 5) the extent to which he or she blends into the environment they are studying so as to minimize corruption of the data. Since Facebook and Twitter are considered to be public pages, the researcher's unannounced presence presents minimal ethical issues as they do not even have to join any of these sites to access the content on the pages. The second advantage offered by webnography is the archival features present on social media and other online sites that give researchers access to historical data. It is, therefore, possible to study trends over time as well as revisit sites at different points in time to do rigorous checks for consistency (Puri, 2012). The third and final advantage is the ability to observer real-time trends. By looking at timelines as well as the network or web of postings, the researcher can readily identify patterns and precedents. As Puri observe, " [the] online ethnographer has access to width as well as depth of data at a moment in time, making it far quicker to pick up on repetitive patterns and identify trends" (p. 5).

The author utilized content analysis to examine the exchanges on UNDP's Facebook page. Content analysis is an efficient means of investigating the content of media for purposes of quantification (Wimmer & Dominick, 2006). It is a method of analyzing written, verbal or visual communication messages (Cole, 1988). The study specifically uses summative content analysis, a method that translates the frequency of occurrence of certain symbols into summary judgments and comparisons. It works on the assumption that the greater that space and/or time that a symbol occupies the greater the meaning or significance (Fink & Gantz, 1996; Hsieh & Shannon, 2005). This type of content analysis offers a useful way of analyzing how participatory the dialogue found on the UNDP's Facebook page is. The content generated by users can be "quantified" to determine whose voice is dominant by virtue of the amount of space it occupies on the page.

The study additionally employed NodeXL, a social media research tool, to analyze the information found on the UNDP's Twitter page. NodeXL allows researchers to extrapolate data from social media platforms such as Twitter unto an excel worksheet for analysis. The tool allows for analysis from a network perspective (Hansen, Shneiderman & Smith, 2011) so that the researcher may measure, map and model connections among followers. This graphical presentation of network connections provides a view of reciprocity in communication among followers and helps the researcher to determine the degree and nature of the connection among the members of particular networks. This is a practical and valuable way for the author to understand how the users/followers on the UNDP's Twitter page engage in dialogue. Are they relegated to the periphery or are they closer to or at the center of the communications.

The researcher examined UNDP's Facebook and Twitter page activities over a six-month period between December 2012 and May 2013. A sample of postings from the most populous or active month for each page during that time period was selected for detailed analysis. It was necessary to focus on a specific month, because of the sheer volume of data, an examination of which was beyond the scope of this chapter. For the Facebook page, the month of January 2013 was selected for closer examination. This selection was made based on the observation that January was the most popular month for the UNDP's Facebook page between the period of December 2012 and May 2013. This month had the most "likes" as well as overall traffic during the selected time period and, therefore, provided a satisfactory sample from which to observe patterns or trends. The postings also contained comments that spanned several months, given that users can respond to posts in an asynchronous fashion. As a result, the data gleaned from January represents a cross section of commentary over the course of several months, which made it fairly representative of trends present on the page. For Twitter, NodeXL randomly selected 100 users and their networks from UNDP page for analysis over a three-year period between 2011 and 2013.

Findings and Discussion

At the time of this study, the UNDP's Facebook page had over 171,000 likes with more than 10,000 persons talking about the page. According to the page's insights, the largest group of people talking about it was between the ages of 25-

34, most of who were from Dhaka, Bangladesh. The following findings reflect observation of the communication exchanges on UNDP's Facebook page during the month of January 2013, the page's most active month as previously mentioned. Posts from the page's timeline were examined and their content analyzed according to ownership (i.e., who posted), frequency, depth (i.e., likes versus comments), subject matter, as well as directionality.

In January, there were approximately 37 main posts on the UNDP's Facebook page. All were initiated by UNDP. These main posts initiated secondary messages mostly in the form of "likes," "comments" and "shares." Other popular interactive Facebook buttons, such as "friend," "post," "delete," "tag and "unlike" among others, were noticeably absent or were not used on the page. Of these, secondary posts, "likes" totaled 8,616, "shares," 3,340 while "comments" added up to 860. Since "likes" and "shares" far outweighed the number of "comments," it could be read that the majority of messages posted on the page lacked depth and perhaps provided limited opportunity for engagement given the sparseness of commentary allowed by the most utilized buttons. The "like" and "share" buttons are among the least interactive and expressive tools, as they do not provide users with space to express thoughts and ideas or to reply to each others' posts. The communication offered by these buttons is essentially one-way and linear at best, not dialogic or conversational.

The "comment" button, which was the least utilized button on the page, presents users with an opportunity to participate in discussions as a community. Users can give extended feedback not only to main posts but to secondary posts made by other users as well. They can respond directly to specific comments and engage in full dialogue with multiple users at any given time. Additionally, the extended space for expression offered by the "comment" button allow users to find out what their shared interests might be, identify problems together as well as offer solutions to these identified problems. Most importantly, the "comment" button has the potential to transform users of the page into members of an online community based on the capacity for dialogue and communication exchange.

According to the IMCFSC model of participatory communication, for community dialogue to occur, members of a community must have an opportunity to exchange and clarify different points of view regarding an issue. This means that substantive and multiple cycles of feedback has to occur, what the model refers to as a feedback loop. The "like" and "share" buttons do not allow such exchanges as users are not privy to the thoughts and ideas of other "likers" of a message. When they "share" a message, they are merely passing it on without any input of their own. Given that the UNDP owned all main posts on its Facebook page, users were mostly passing on a corporate message instead of one informed by the community.

In terms of ownership of messages, the UNDP owned all main posts as previously stated. This suggested that the primary and most visible content on the page was that of the establishment and not the community. The UNDP, therefore, established itself as the catalyst for discussion at all times on the page.

A catalyst, as described by the IMCFSC model is a dynamic, iterative process, which leads to dialogue within the community (Figueroa et. al, 2002, p. 6). A catalyst may be external as in the case of policy or internal coming from the community itself. On the UNDP's Facebook page, the trigger for community dialogue was always the institution, a predominantly external force. In this regard, community dialogue was hampered since the community had less of a chance of identifying problems for themselves. Their problems were often articulated for them as may be deduced from this particular post and others like it:

On Democracy Saturday we'd like to know: which of these areas of   democratic governance do you think is most important?
- Access to Information and E-Governance
- Access to Justice and Rule of Law
- Anti-Corruption
- Civic Engagement
- Electoral Systems and Processes
- Human Rights

The issue of democratic governance had been problematized in very specific ways for the community without their input. Not only did the post suggest to users what they should consider as important or problematic regarding democratic governance, it also assumed that there was universal agreement on what this type of governance looks like. The a priori established categories that made up the survey also inherently elicited support for the way in which democratic governance was being spoken about by the UNDP. That is to say, the categories were fixed and left little room for alternative conceptions. Users were therefore obliged to agree by making a selection from the established categories or couldn't participate in the discussion if their voices were not reflected in the survey's selections.

The second most visible form of content in terms of sheer numbers were likes. The most number of "likes" received by a main post in the month of January totaled 945. A survey of those "likes" revealed an ownership pattern that favored college and university students and staff as well as formal career professionals. The latter two categories combined accounted for 69.4 percent of the "likes" while NGOs made up 11.7 percent. According to world population statistics, these demographics do not necessarily make up the world's poor, i.e. those living on less than two dollars a day. Given the UNDP's mandate, its primary constituents are the world's poor. Yet their voices were hardly represented on the organization's Facebook page. The world's poor were being spoken about but their vision of the future, a critical component of the IMCFSC model of participatory communication, was absent. For example, the post below asked a question that was related to a community's ability to prepare for and respond to hardships and unforeseen disasters. It is a question that sought to understand the conditions under which the world's most vulnerable coped and survived: "On Resilience Sunday, we want to know-what does resilience mean to you?" (Facebook post, January 7, 2013).

However, the majority of the responses, particularly comments, reflected the positions of individuals who were not from this group. Many comments were from individuals associated with international NGOs and universities. While it is plausible that members of the elite and better off segments of the global community may have an understanding of and can articulate the needs of the less fortunate, social change is less likely to occur if members of the affected communities are not involved in defining and solving social problems. This begs the question, to whom is the UNDP speaking through their Facebook page? The directionality of the messages on the page gave some clue.

The communication flow on the UNDPS' Facebook page was vertical and top down in nature. All discussion topics were initiated by UNDP which meant that the organization effectively set and controlled the communication agenda. The UNDP also did not repost content unless it was from another UN organization or an international NGO, nor did it respond to comments made on the page by users. This linear organization of communication leads to limited participation from users and creates what Sassen (2003) refers to as a "democratic deficit" in terms of community articulation of goals and needs. In other words, communities do not get an opportunity to articulate their social, cultural and political agendas. For participatory communication to occur, community leaders and stakeholders must be identified and consulted to have these needs voiced and eventually addressed (Figueroa et. al, 2002, p. 8). Since UNDP did not use any of the interactive tools that would allow this to occur, it is safe to say that participatory communication was not unfolding effectively via the organization's Facebook page. To whom the UNDP is not talking was perhaps most apparent, to answer the question posed above. The organization did not "friend" nor accept "friends," only "likes." Liking other pages was the extent to which the UNDP interacted with others on Facebook and a list of pages that the UNDP did 'like" was very telling regarding with whom it wished to connect. For example, the organization liked Anderson Cooper, CNN TV show host, Beyoncé, Pop Star and Forbes Magazine, to name a few.

The members of the Facebook community that the UNDP chose to "like" are not necessarily the stakeholders when it comes to issues of poverty, HIV AIDS reduction, equality of education and the other social problems the UNDP is mandate to address. The nature of the content on UNDP's Facebook page seemed to correlate with its vertical communication strategies. During the month being examined, the subject of the communication generally pivoted around seven themes created by the UNDP, each associated with a particular day of the week. These were equality, resilience, progress, HIV awareness, ending poverty, democracy, and green awareness. Themes appeared to be randomly selected and associated with specific days and several themes appeared more frequently than others. For example, "Equality Monday" appeared on average, three times for the month while "Progress Tuesday" appeared just once during the same period. Themes were not constant in their association with specific days of the week: for instance while there was "Democracy Sunday," there was also "Resilience Sunday" at some point. These themes essentially drove the evolution of the content on the page and often appeared in the form of a quiz or questionnaire for example; "Equality Monday/ Empowering women is essential to development because_____" (Facebook post, January 14, 2013).

That the themes did not seem to vary suggested a tightly controlled communication agenda that had little to no input from community members. The objectives of the discussions were clearly outlined by each theme and the expectations about what could be done about the particular social problem already pre-established. While the questions seemed to elicit feedback regarding a particular social issue, there was no indication on the UNDP's Facebook page that any comments in response to questions were considered in any decision making process. In fact, there was no acknowledgement that comments were even read as there were no responses to them from the organization. Therefore, community members were treated as targets of communication messages as against participants in a dialogue concerning what to do about identified social problems. The content was prescriptive and interrogative, leaving little room for consensus building and collective action.

Not surprisingly, after examining the comments posted by users in response to UNDP's main posts, the content of the comments seemed to fall in two general thematic categories, namely "assent" and "praise." Assent is used in this case to mean general agreement with or support of a particular position while praise refers to admiration or lauding of that position. Secondary posts tended to show overwhelming agreement with UNDP's position on a range of issues raised on its page. For example, in response to the organization's post about how to go about ending violence against women, many comments mirrored the following: ""I fully agree u b khulsum..violence is evil. Sympathy to victims and I am sorry really that I am not so helpful to them "(2013, January 22, Facebook post). Reponses to another post featuring two little boys and the tag line 'what does development look like?' netted similar results; take for example this comment: "looks like the future we want for our children" (2013, January 25, Facebook post). Comments across a range of issues also predominantly offered praise for UNDP development strategies shared on the page, an observation illustrated by the proceeding comment responding to a post about the tour of the 177 countries in which UNDP is present by its CEO, Helen Clarke : "great work...............respect respect respect" (2012, May 12, Facebook post) or "Kudos UNDP for the good work u r doing" 2013, January 12, Facebook post), which was made in response to a UNDP update on the 2010 earthquake in Haiti. The main posts made by UNDP on its page were not only top down in nature but were also leading and encouraged consensus: "It's Green Wednesday today | Even a crow knows how to keep the environment clean!!! Let's learn something and do our share. We shouldn't just throw our garbage anywhere... SHARE & LIKE if you agree!" (2013, January 16, Facebook post).

Did you know development is a human right? "The right to development is an inalienable human right by virtue of which every human person and all peoples are entitled to participate in." – UN Declaration on the Right to Development, Article 1. http://bit.ly/UlZug1 via United Nations Human Rights LIKE or SHARE if you agree! (2013, January 17, Facebook post).

Do you agree it's time to end violence against women once and for all? Show your support & 'like' this photo of our friends DFID - UK Department for International Development, "It's time to end violence against women once and for all! This can be the year of change: http://bit.ly/EndVAW Share it with your friends to help us make it a thing of the past, and tag yourself to show your support" (2013, January 21, Facebook post).

The lack of neutrality in how the above posts are framed gives a clear imperative for users to agree with the position taken by the organization. The structure of the messages did not invite dialogue but rather assent to or agreement with the position taken by the organization on the particular issues raised. While there were comments that voiced disagreement or critique, they were not the dominant voices on the page.

UNDP's Twitter Page

At the time of this study, UNDP's Twitter page had approximately 20, 600 tweets and more than 204,000 followers. The organization was also following 4, 499 other Twitter accounts. Twitter is considered a conversational microblog (Barash & Golder, 2011) as the size of the messages are limited to 140 characters or less. The messages are very brief and more like texts in nature. Twitter users have several tools at their disposal to help maximize the reach and impact of 140 characters or less. The most popular are the @sign, which facilitates symmetric connections, meaning that the flow of information and attention moves in a unified direction (Barash & Golder, 2011) and the retweet and #hastags, which essentially diffuse information. They help users follow specific messages and often contribute to the emergence of trends. They also help identify relationships among users and determine whether they are strong or weak, linear or webbed.

NodeXL offers a visual representation of individuals in a network by mapping ties along nodes or vertices on a graph. Nodes or vertices often appear as dots or discs of varying sizes, while ties are represented as edges. NodeXL does this by using matrices which measure activity based on the tools, such as those mentioned above, that users employ while on Twitter networks. In order to determine the nature of the communication among users on the UNDP's Twitter page, the analysis will focus on issues of centrality (who is important or has a prominent position on the network) symmetry of connections (direction of communication attention), diffusion of information (organization and spread of tweets) and topic trends (what is being spoken about the most on the network). Using the NodeXL software, data from the UNDP's Twitter network was retrieved and imported into Excel. Because of the sheer volume of data on the page, a sample of the activities of 100 users was randomly selected for analysis.

Once imported into Excel, the data was analyzed using several available NodeXL metrics and formulas in order to determine the nature of relationships as well as information flow among users on the network.

In terms of measuring degrees of centrality among users on the network, attention was paid to the directionality of the vertices that connect nodes. Social network analysts use various metrics to calculate how 'central' or important each actor   (node)   is   inside   a   network (http://socnetv.sourceforge.net/docs/analysis.html). If a researcher wishes to know how important an actor is inside particular network then centrality is observed to determine this information. In-degree centrality in particular, measures the 'activity' of each node, meaning, the direction in which activity is flowing from that particular node. In-degree central nodes might be considered more prominent than others and is an indicator of the "importance" of that particular node/ user. As Barash & Golder (2011) note, important users have a lot of followers. This is how they spread information of importance to them and gain influence on the network. Followers may be important or unimportant in and of themselves based on whether or not they themselves have large followings.

Based on the data, UNDP was the most important actor on the network, since it had the most followers. The UNDP also had other important actors following its page, which also heightened the organization's degree of importance on the network. What this meant was that the organization was being followed by a large group of individuals who themselves had significant followings. For example, the UNDP was being followed by @Noora888, who had 1,969 followers. The UNDP had an important link through this user and others like him or her. These links also drove the focus of attention toward the UNDP. Based on the Graph 1 (label it), one can observe that on the network, most of the attention was flowing inward to the UNDP from its followers while none was necessarily flowing in the opposite direction i.e. outward from the organization to its followers (See Graph 1). What this implied was that UNDP did not reply, retweet or interact with messages posted by followers. The communication flow was unidirectional, not unlike the pattern found on the UNDP's Facebook page. In essence, the centrality measures of the communication flow on the UNDP's Twitter network revealed a one-way communication pattern, which is not reflective of participatory communication.

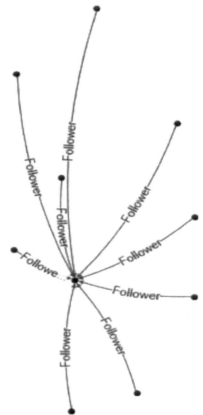

Figure 12.1 A random selection of every ten users out of the universe of 100
reveals the unidirectional flow of the communication messages

The symmetry of attention or communication flow observed in the network also
confirmed the unidirectional nature of the activity found on the UNDP's Twitter
page. The attention was asymmetrical, meaning that the user receiving attention
was not replying or sending attention back to followers. In other words, the
relationship was not reciprocal. This asymmetry was evident throughout the
network as users were also not connected to each other. They were only
connected through their link to the UNDP, which was positioned at the centre of
the network, and had limited ties to each other. One could therefore deduce that
users were not replying to each other's messages or corresponding in any
significant way. The conclusion drawn was that users were not talking to each
other on the network since they were not receiving information from each other
via the @reply network. This is significant since sending @replies to each other
is evidence of strong social ties among users. Participatory communication
depends on social connections as this is the only way to garner consensus on

actions geared toward solving social problems. The graph below shows the lack connections among users on the UNDP Twitter network:

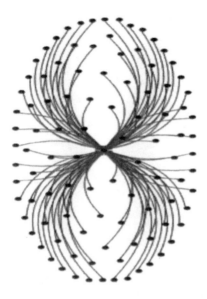

Figure 12.2 Asymmetrical attention showing lack of connections among users on network. Attention flow toward the UNDP located at the centre. The graph also indicates the lack of significance most users of the network have given that most of the nodes appear at the periphery of the graph. This is a strong indication of a lack of inclusion in the communication process.

Asymmetrical attention or communication patterns on social networks allow platforms such as Twitter to be an extension of other forms of mass media (Barash & Golder 2011). When Twitter is used in this manner it becomes a tool of information diffusion and not a conversational medium. Information gets passed on from a primary source through a particular medium and quickly spreads to the masses. In this sense, individuals and groups become targets of communication. They are not necessarily invited to share their individual and shared needs, only to pass on a particular message initiated by an institution. This pattern is reminiscent of the Shannon and Weaver model of information dissemination as well as Roger's diffusion of innovation framework. The graph below gives a visual representation of this diffusion process where in individuals are predominantly targeted with messages. The majority of the vertices emanated from the centre of the graph where the UNDP was located, then filtered out to other important users who also targeted their followers with the messages they received from the organization. These other important users acted as opinion leaders in the way of the Shannon and Weaver Model, who used their influence to target followers. Of note, the pattern of the graph is that of a "star," a configuration that generally emerges when the mention of a #hashtag for instance, by a particular user triggers its mention by many of that user's followers. This pattern suggests that adopters of a message may be easily influenced or that the early adopters of the message are very influential (Barash & Golder 2011). The emergence of this pattern reinforced the idea that the nature of the communication mirrored the two step flow model of messages. A grid pattern on the other hand, suggests that social influence is a big factor in the adoption of a message as messages are being retweeted multiple times and in multiple directions. The latter is a stronger indication of community dialogue where members are constantly interacting with each other through a feedback loop and have multiple opportunities to seek clarification of perceptions or voice agreements or disagreements.

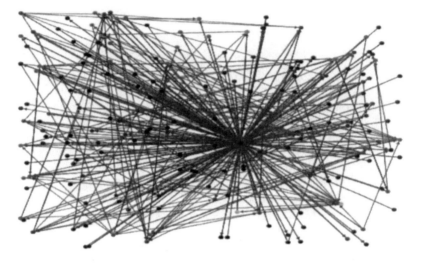

Figure 12.3 Star patterned graph showing targeted communication. This is a more detailed graph, which maps those following the UNDP as well as those the UNDP follows. The UNDP rarely follows any of its followers as the graph indicates.

The graphical representations delineated the nature of the communication relationship between UNDP and its publics, indicating that it was linear and predominantly unidirectional. There was little engagement with the community and minimal opportunity for participation. The comments themselves also supported these observations in several ways. First, a significant portion of the comments seemed peripheral to the development issues that UNDP has as its mandate. Of the 256 tweets extrapolated by NodeXL, only two directly addressed issues of poverty, five related to women and gender while only two directly referenced the term development all. Other social issues directly related to UNDP's mandate such as reversing HIV/AIDS, building national capacity, protecting the environment and building democratic societies did not have any direct references in the twitter conversations examined. Take these tweets for instance: "RT @Forbes: Adjusted for nearly a century of inflation, Daisy Buchanan's pearl necklace would be worth at least $4.7M today http://t.co/oIt..." and "How much competition in mobile device market? http://t.co/2bnen0nbAk #mobile #tech," as well as "Jolly Ranchers: good candy or best candy? http://t.co/dinF3UicIQ." These issues are not germane to UNDP's mission nor do they concern social change is any fundamental way.

Geographically, most tweets seemed to emanate from the Global North, another indication that communication was characteristic of the dominant development paradigm which characterizes progress as "naturally spring[ing] from Europe and the West" (Biccum, 2002, p.9). Most of the tweets originated in New York City, which was perhaps not surprising given that UNDP is headquartered in New York and was responsible for a significant portion of tweets on its page. The two other most popular locations were Washington, DC and London, cities from where a large number of development organizations operate. These locations are centers of global power that dominate global power relations. They are also major cities in the Global North and are associated with progress and modernity. That these cities were also dominant players in the communication dynamics on UNDP's Twitter page revealed that the exchanges unfolding on the organization's page was a microcosm of the larger global politics which features hierarchies of power grounded in the concepts of developed and underdeveloped. This dichotomy positions developing countries as 'naturally' requiring the assistance of the West. These countries then set the agenda for development as well as the tone of the conversation related to achieving development goals.

Tweets that originated from these locations tended to be instructive as was illustrated by the following tweet that originated in Washington, DC; "#WorldBank gives #Rwanda Rwf32bn grant to improve decentralisation of govt services http://t.co/OufsHqLvLx." Not only did this tweet illustrate that communication is seen as a behavior change mechanism, it was also not indicative of a participatory approach. The figure of authority here, the World Bank, was making clear what was wrong with the Rwandan system of governance, that is, it needed to be decentralized. Not only had the World Bank identified the problem in this piece of communication, it had also created a solution, i.e. money in the form of a grant. There was no suggestion of collaboration or feedback from the Rwandan community that they had agreed to or had participated in this decision. Based on the trajectory of the communication via the NodeXL graphs as well as the content analysis of the tweets themselves, it was apparent that participatory communication grounded in community dialogue did not characterize UNDP's communication strategy on its Twitter page.

Limitations

The study offers a critical examination of the communications practices employed by of the United Nation's major agencies, UNDP, on two of its social media pages. In doing so the author encountered one specific limitation. In order manage the quantity of data available on UNDP's Facebook and Twitter pages, the study limited its data collection to specific time periods. For Facebook, data was only collected for the month of January 2013. By limiting the data to just this month, specific trends that may have evolved before or after this time period would not have been included in the analysis. A more longitudinal approach may have revealed varying patterns of responses from UNDP, especially during special events months such as International Women's Month, which occurs in March or World Aids Day, which falls on a December 1 each year. For Twitter, although the data spanned a three-year period, only the tweets of one hundred users were examined. Similarly, patterns may have not have been accounted for due to the restricted number of tweets looked at. However, given that this is an exploratory study, it is not unusual to limit data sets to specific time periods.

This kind of research is valuable in establishing the present state of a phenomenon and to help researchers gain a better understanding of the key issues or variables that may be at play. The results usually offer important insights that could be used as the basis of further research. In the case of this study, the researcher was interested in looking at the current state of the communication flow in UNDP's two social media pages examined. Further, the researcher wanted to investigate whether or not the current communication patterns matched participatory and democratic models of communication that are often associated with the use of social media platforms. The results indicate that there instances of non-participatory modes of communication on both UNDP's Facebook and Twitter pages. This is an important insight as it indicates that communication via social media is not by nature democratic or inclusive. Organizations such as UNDP interested in developing more dialogic communication approaches may want to find out how they could better harness the power of social media to achieve these goals. The results of this study can form the basis of further research that could help identify better ways of making communication less linear and more egalitarian via asocial media platforms.

Conclusion

The above analysis of the activities on UNDP's Facebook and Twitter pages suggests that the scope for community dialogue and collective action is limited on these social networking sites. Participatory communication as modeled by the IMCFSC framework does not seem to guide the communication exchanges on the networks and users are predominantly peripheral actors to whom messages are targeted. Information is centralized and tightly controlled.

Ironically, it may be social media's very democratic nature that lends itself to the top down communication patterns observed on the UNDP's social media sites. Since social media have the capacity to challenge hierarchical management structures of messaging, users can generate alternative messages that oppose or threaten the positions of the dominant group. From a marketing and public relations standpoint, this is could be a disaster for organizations that wish to maintain a uniform identity and consistent message. A marketplace of ideas, therefore, becomes undesirable, if organizations have no control over messages that are posted on their social networking sites. As a result, information flow has to be centralized to achieve company objectives. This seems to be the case with the UNDP and its social media pages. In fact, the organization has a disclaimer on its Facebook page that says as much, i.e. it reserves the right to "delete or edit any comments that it considers inappropriate or unacceptable" (https://www.facebook.com/UNDP/info).

While it is a nonprofit organization, the UNDP maintains a corporate structure, which places limitations on how it conducts its communications. It is limited in its capacity to create a participatory communication culture on its social media pages since it is most interested in information dissemination via these platforms. As a result, the organization relies on strategies of diffusion to accomplish its information dissemination goals. Social media platforms inherently lend themselves to such strategies since they are powerful tools for communication related to issues of mobilization, providing informational updates and giving directives. A large portion of the messages on the UNDP's Facebook and Twitter pages reflect these types of communications, i.e. they are geared toward mobilization, dissemination of policy information as well as reporting on UNDP successes with various development projects. These strategies create weak ties with the users who are generally treated as recipients of information and not stakeholders where social issues are concerned.

The fact that access to social media sites is dependent on access to the Internet limits their capacity to be tools of mass collaboration. The current technological ecosystem is still plagued by connectivity issues as well as persistent digital divide. While it is true that Internet penetration is growing at a rapid pace in developing regions, the gap between those who are connected and those who are not is still very wide. For example, in 2011, the rate of Internet penetration for North America was 78.6% while that for Africa was 13. 5% (www.internetworldststs.com/stats.htm). In total, only 32.7% of the world's population has access to the Internet. Connection to social media was even less. In 2012, Facebook global penetration stood at only 12.1%. It is difficult to imagine that those who are connected represent the world's poor who live on less than two dollars a day, especially given the high costs sometimes associated with internet connectivity in some regions of the world. Additionally, places such as North America and Europe are structurally advantaged in the technological ecosystem. This state of affairs further limits the potential for participatory communication to unfold on UNDP's Facebook and Twitter pages. It does not seem likely that the UNDP would be engaging with key stakeholders of and community members most affected by social problems such as poverty and HIV on its pages. They are simply not connected and are therefore not participating in any dialogue. This lack of connection reiterates an ongoing issue; that is, "the rift between those who see communication as behavioral change and those who support a more participatory approach has still not healed" (Quarry, 2012, http://www.comminit.com/polio/print/9300440).

Finally, participatory communication seems to be less about the medium at hand and more about the larger structural/political frameworks within which development operates. The analysis of the UNDP's use of Facebook and Twitter reveal old communication patterns associated with the dominant paradigm of communication and development. The primary media then were television and radio. However, despite the evolution of information communication technologies that makes it possible for more democratic approaches to idea exchanges, old patterns still persist. This suggests that perhaps issues of participation and community dialogue are grounded in the power dynamics that direct global politics and not in the use of any particular medium.

References

Ali, A. H. (2011). The power of social media in developing nations: New tools for closing the global digital divide and beyond. *Harvard Human Rights Journal*, 24, 185-219.

Barash, V. & Golder, S. (2011). Twitter: Conversation, entertainment, and information all in one network! In D. L. Hansen, B. Shneiderman & M. A. Smith (Eds.), *Analyzing social media networks with NodeXL: Insights from a connected world*, 143-165. Burlington, MA: Morgan Kaufmann.

Brown, A. (1976). The mass media of communications and socialist change in the Caribbean: A case study of Jamaica. *Caribbean Quarterly, 22, 4*, 43- 49.

Brown, A. (1981). The dialectics of mass communication in national transformation. *Caribbean Quarterly, 27, 2&3*, 40-46.

Biccum, A. (2002). Interrupting the discourse of development: On a collision course with postcolonial theory. *Culture, Theory and Critique 43, 1*, pp. 33-50.

Chau, C. (2010). Youtube as participatory culture. *New Directions for Youth Development, 128*, 65-74.

Escobar, A. (1995). *Encountering development*. Princeton, NJ: Princeton University Press.

Evans, L. (2010). *Authenticity Online: using webnography to address phenomenological concerns.* [Abstract]. In: A. Mousoutzanis, & D. Riha, (Eds.), *New Media and the Politics of Online Communities: Critical Issues* 11-20. Oxford: Inter-Disciplinary Press. Retrieved from http://orca.cf.ac.uk/40705/.

Figueroa, M., Kincaid, D. L., Rani, M., Lewis, G. (2002). Communication for social change: An integrated model for measuring the process and its outcomes. *The Communication for Social Change Working Paper Series,* 1, 1-42. Retrieved from http://www.communicationforsocialchange.org/pdf/ socialchange.pdf

Fink, E. & Gantz, W. (1996). A content analysis of three mass communication research traditions: Social science, interpretive studies, and critical analysis. *Journalism and Mass Communication Quarterly, 73,(1),* 114-134.

Global Web Index (January 28, 2013). Twitter now the fastest growing social platform in the world. Retrieved from http://www.globalwebindex.net/twitter-now-the-fastest-growing-social-platform-in-the-world/#Tom

Gordon, N. (2009). Globalization and cultural imperialism in Jamaica: The homogenization of content and Americanization of Jamaican tv through programme modeling. *International Journal of Communication, 3,* 307-331.

Gordon, N. (2008). *Media and the politics of culture: The case of television privatization and media globalization in Jamaica (1990-2007).* Boca Raton: Universal Publishers.

Hansen, D., Shneiderman, B., & Smith, M. (2011). *Analyzing social media networks with NodeXL: Insights from a connected world.* Burlington, MA: Morgan Kaufmann. Internet World Stats (September, 2012). World Internet penetration rates by geographic regions-2011. Retrieved from http://www.internetworldstats.com/ stats.htm

Hsieh, H. F. & Shannon, S. E. (2005). Three approaches to qualitative content analysis *Qualitative Health Research,* 15, 1277-1288,

Internet World Stats (2012, September). World internet penetration rates by geographic regions- 2011. Retrieved from http://www.internetworldstats.com/stats.htm.

Internet World Stats (September, 2012). Facebook penetration in the world between   2011   Q1   and   2012-Q1.   Retrieved   from http://www.internetworldstats.com/stats.htm

Kaplan, A., & Haenlein, M. (2010). Users of the world, unite! The challenges and opportunities of social media. Business Horizons, 53,(1) 59-68.

Kumar, N. (2012). Social media: A virtual global community hall. Indian Streams   Research   Journal,   2   (10),   1-5.   Retrieved   from http://connection.ebscohost.com/c/articles/86683407/social-media-virtual-global-community-hall Litt, E. (2012).

Litt, E. (2012). Knock, knock. Who's there? The imagined audience. *Journal of Broadcasting and Electronic Media, 56, 3,* 330-345.

Maggiore, P. (2012). Viewer discretion is advised: Disconnects between the marketplace of ideas and social media used to communicate information during emergencies and public health crises. *Michigan Telecommunications and technology Law Review*, 18, 627-660.

McCormack, R. (2012, March 13). Lessons learned from the Kony 2012 campaign.   Communication,   Media,   Policy.   Retrieved   from http://www.comminit.com/policy-blogs/content/lessons-learned-kony-2012-campaign-0

Melkote, S. (2000). Reinventing development support communication. In K.G. Wilkins (Ed.), *Redeveloping communication for social change: Practice theory and power*, 39-53. New York: Rowman and Littlefield.

Melkote, S. & Steeves, L. (2001). Communication for development in the third world: Theory and practice for empowerment (2nd Ed.). Thousand Oaks, CA: Sage.

Miller, T. (2009). Media studies 3.0. *Television and New Media*, 10 (1), 1-6. Retrieved from http://tvn.sagepub.com/content/10/1/5.extract

Mody, B. (2000). The contexts of power and the power of the media. In K.G. Wilkins (Ed.), Redeveloping communication for social change: Practice theory and power, 185-195. New York: Rowman and Littlefield.

Nielsen (2012). State of the media: The social media report 2012. Retrieved from   http://www.nielsen.com/us/en/reports/2012/state-of-the-media-the-social-media-report-2012.html

Nielsen (2011). State of the media: The social media report Q3. Retrieved from http://www.nielsen.com/us/en/reports/2011/social-media-reportq3.html

Obar, J. et al (2012). Advocacy 2.0: An analysis of how advocacy groups in the United States perceive and use social media as tools for facilitating civic engagement and collective action. *Journal of Information Policy*, 2, 1-25.

Olanoff, D. (May 1, 2013). Facebook's monthly active users up 23% to 1.11b; daily users up 26% to 665m; mobile use up 54% to 751m. Retrieved from http://techcrunch.com/2013/05/01/facebook-sees-26-year-over-year-growth-in-daus-23-in-maus-mobile-54/

Perez-Latre, F., Portilla, I. & Blanco, C. S. (2010). Social networks, media and audiences: A literature review. *Comunicación Y Sociedad, 24, 1,* 63-74.

Puri, A. (2007). The web of insights: The art and practice of webnography. Retrieved from http://nz.nielsen.com/reports/documents/WebofInsights PaperMay07.pdf

Rogers, E. (1995). *Diffusion of innovations.* New York: The Free Press.

Quarry, W. (2012, November 12). Polio: Is it too late for participation? [Web log post]. Retrieved from http://www.comminit.com/polio/print/9300440.

Rubenstein, P. (2011). Why (and How) the growth of social media has created opportunities for qualitative research in organizational development. *The Industrial-Organizational Psychologist*, 49 (2), 19-26.

Sassen, S. (2003) The participation of states and citizens in global governance. *Indiana Journal of Global Legal Studies*, 10 (1). pp. 5-28.

Sharma, V. et al (2012). The revolution in digitized ICTs and emergence of social networking sites transformed traditional media to new mass media: a rise of new age media. *Indian Streams Research Journal*, 2, 4.

Singhal, A. & Rogers, E. (1999). *Entertainment education: A communication strategy for social change.* New Jersey: Lawrence Earlbaum Associates.

Srinivasan, R. (2012). Rethinking digital cultures and divides: The case for reflective media. *The Information Society: An International Journal*, 28, (1), 24-36.

Stiglitz, J. (2003). Globalization and its discontents. New York: W. W. Norton Company.

Tomaselli, K. (1997). Action research, participatory communication: Why governments don't listen. *Africa Media Review.* Retrieved from http://archive.lib.msu.edu/DMC/African%20Journals/pdfs/africa%20 media%20review/vol11no1/jamr011001002.pdf

UNDP (2013, May). Messages posted to http://www.facebook.com/UNDP.

UNDP (2013, May). Messages posted to https://twitter.com/UNDP.

Usher, W. T. (2012). Australian health professionals' social media (web 2.0) adoption trends: Early 21st century health care delivery and practice promotion. *Australian Journal of Primary Health*, 18, (1).

Waisbord, S. (2004). Media, and the reinvention of the nation. In Downing, A., McQuail, D., Schlesinger, P., Wartella, E. (Eds.) *The sage handbook of Media Studies, 375-392.* Thousand Oaks: Sage.

Chapter 13
Cock-Crow in the "Electronic Republic:" Social Media and Kenya's 2013 Presidential Elections
Kehbuma Langmia

Social media are not only social; they are political in many respects. They are the arsenal to the disenfranchised who want to air their views publicly and win support, where necessary. For instance, the ubiquitous presence and influence of social media as an instrument of political activism is proving to be a necessary evil in Africa. The recent presidential election in Kenya drew the attention of the international community, since the past election resulted in violent clashes between rival ethnic tribes. Another important reason for the high stakes in this past election was the fact that activists used the social media platform to reach out to the masses. There was no more monopoly of the state media. Unlike the Arab Spring where social media were used to galvanize the youth in North Africa to politically chase away their dictators from power, Kenya was different. This chapter examines the role of social media in the recent Kenya presidential election by examining YouTube video postings by Kenyan citizens.

The Arab Spring phenomenon ushered a new dawn in North Africa and parts of the Middle East, mostly due to the influence of social media. It sent political shockwaves to most developing countries. The power of social media, as a force to assemble dissenting voices that can help bring down some North African dictators, has been noted (Allagui and Kuebler, 2011; Stepanova, 2011; Lotan, Graeff, Ananny, Graffney, Pearce, and Boyd, 2011). As a result, some politicians have become "weary" of the power of social media (Crawford, 2009; Sheedy, 2011; Kraidy, 2011; Dick, 2012; Newham and Bell, 2012). Attempts are being made to either suppress it or recruit spies to monitor the activities of users, because they reconfigure the people's public sphere. Unlike in the past, the public sphere communicative interchange now starts electronically, then moves gradually to "in-person" exchanges in the physical environment. During the Habermassian era, where "in-person" meetings at salons and coffee houses constituted the main democratic space, the emergence of new media made virtual public sphere a possibility. Now, activists recruit followers on Facebook, Twitter, YouTube, and many other platforms for online public discussions and commentaries. In the case of North Africa, it moved from virtuality to "in-person" groupings at a specially designated place, such as "Tahrir Square" in Egypt, but the ignition was triggered in the electronic world.

This new form of galvanizing the disenfranchised, the downtrodden, the oppressed, and others in need is causing political sleepless nights for those who hold firmly to power, especially in sub-Saharan Africa where dictators are causing untold economic, educational, and political havoc on their own people. Social media interactions have redefined political outreach as they have become an instrument to empower the oppressed and the downtrodden.

The social media world ushered a new kind of freedom of expression; an expression that enables one to hide behind anonymity, as the case may be, to challenge power wielders. With respect to politics where lives can be lost and personal characters attacked, users appear comfortable when they can attack the power mongers anonymously and not suffer any reprisals. This is exactly what enables social media to gain momentum in Africa and across the world.

Betot, Jaeger, and Grimes (2010) outline some of the benefits of social media in today's world, especially as they relate to curbing corruption and providing transparencies. This chapter examines the YouTube platform as a unit of analysis where postings of political activities by Kenyan citizens are disseminated to the rest of the world. A snapshot of how YouTube contributes at home and abroad to democracy in Kenya is examined through the analysis of YouTube postings on the election preparation, election campaigns, candidates' debates, voting procedures, and other segments of the electoral process.

YouTube postings are often triangulated: audio, video, and text. It is what Kavoori (2011) calls "digital flow" through a force of "chaining." A simple click can ignite interrelated semantic videos links that endlessly unravels. Unlike film or television where the subject matter is fixed from the beginning to the end, YouTube subject matter can be expanded with ancillary videos on similar subjects placed on the left screen that can easily be viewed with one click.

The aim of this study is to select targeted videos from the YouTube chain using a keyword search to get as much data as possible that could possibly answer two research questions (see methodology) related to how social media played a significant role in the election.

There are other platforms of social media, such as Facebook and Twitter, that constitute communication channels, however, this study particularly looks at the influence of YouTube, because it has been one that combines three modes of communications (i.e., text, audio, and video in one). Another reason to limit this analysis on YouTube is because it provides more latitude to anonymity postings, and viewers outside and inside Kenya can contribute anonymously as the case may be. This three-prong analysis also provides rich data to make inferences and conclusions on what part social media can play in an election. In order to fully grasp the role of social media in Kenya, a brief discussion on the state of new media in general and social media in particular in sub-Saharan Africa is worth examining.

Social Media and Sub-Saharan Africa

Social media are relatively new to sub-Saharan Africa. When the Arab Spring began in North Africa in 2011, spearheaded by the forces of the social media, sub-Saharan Africa did not follow their lead. No one knows for sure why. The traditional media (radio, newspaper, and television) are still the dominant media channels for information dissemination. In addition, the radio, especially, plays a significant role in news dissemination in sub-Saharan Africa today (Amutabi, 2013; Mare, 2013; Alzouma, 2010; Gathigi and Brown, 2010). The difficulties arising from intermittent power failures and poor computer literacy skills in this region have also dealt a severe blow to new media growth. Telecommunication infrastructure, to say the least, has also been a factor in stalling the growth of new media revolutions in Africa (Langmia, 2006; Mbarika, Okoli, Byrd, and Datta, 2005). As such, sub-Saharan Africa has lagged behind.

However, recent studies (Carmody, 2013; Bratton, 2013; Maduku, 2012; Mehta, Maretzki, and Semali, 2011; Murphy and Priebe, 2011) have shown geometrical growth of digital mobile phone activities in Africa, and more countries have broadband Internet access primarily needed for social media to burgeon. Also, the increased presence of mobile telephones in the region is testimony to the bright future of electronic activities. Nonetheless, some countries like Kenya, Uganda, South Africa, Tanzania, and Nigeria are spearheading Internet growth in the region. Yet, a study by Walton and Donner (2011) underscores deep seated drawbacks to social media strengths in galvanizing the masses for a political cause. They found significant lapses in broadening this media due to rampant power outages, electronic illiteracies, ephemeral outreach, and authorship. This finding supports earlier findings about Internet capabilities that are limited to urban areas with mostly the rich having the upper hand in its use. With political activities that warrant the participation of diverse populations, this is certainly a limitation. But other studies have championed the arrival of social media to Africa. Braun (2013), while acknowledging some of the pitfalls that affect Internet accessibility, especially in Kenya, confirms statistics from the Ministry of Information that there are more than 14 million cyberspace users in the country, representing close to 30% of the country's total population.

Social media activities played an unprecedented and significant part during Kenya's first presidential debate. Ossiya (2013) maintains that even though the traditional media outlets covered the much anticipated debate between the incumbent Raila Odinga and Uhuru Kenyatta, there was what he called "social media traffic" during the debate (para 1). This strengthened the role the overwhelming force of new media could do to pave the way for a new kind of election coverage in the continent.

The millennium goal of the United Nations, as opined by the former United Nations Secretary General Koffi Annan underscores the importance of new media technology as an instrument for development: "New technology offers an unprecedented chance for developing countries to 'leapfrog' earlier stages of development. "Everything must be done to maximize the peoples' access to new information networks" (Steinberg, 2003, p. 45). In addition, the resolutions of the ITU (International Telecommunication Union) are in line with making the world a technological global village. This globalization of the media should not be a top down process, it should be bottom up. The needs of those in the rural areas, those who have never seen a computer, those for one reason or the other are facing all forms of the digital divide (education, culture, ethnicity, race, monetary, political), should be the driving force for meaningful change to occur. Manufacturers of new media gadgets should be aware of these limitations in order to design technology that caters to their needs. That way, we all will savor the juice of the new media technology goals (Langmia, 2011). Radio, television, and newspaper are the dominant mass media in Kenya, and with the high literacy rate in the country, readership and viewership have been high since independence in the 1960s. For instance, in 2008, during the post presidential election violence, some FM radio stations were particularly singled out as the main instigator of violence (Amutabi, 2013). But, that notwithstanding, social media acted in 2008 as the alternative voice for the citizens to actively participate freely (Mäkinen and Kuira, 2008). Although noticeable shift in plural media has been creeping to the nation's media landscape, such as social media (Facebook, YouTube, Twitter) in the last five years. This study intends to examine the role of YouTube only.

Methodology

A work of this nature necessitates a technique to select videos that capture the views of the citizens without any internal or external censorship. YouTube, another platform for user-generated content (UGC), provides the freedom to upload unedited or edited materials for quick and easy consumption. In order to understand the role of this platform during the presidential election, the following two research questions were posed: 1) How did Kenyan citizens utilize verbal and nonverbal elements within YouTube postings during the presidential election? 2) How did Kenyan citizens utilize the "texts/comments and likes" features on their YouTube postings during the presidential elections?

A keyword search using "Social Media and Kenyan 2013 Presidential Election" returned more than 57,800 results as of May 20, 2013. A majority of the uploads were from foreign as well as national television stations, such as K24TV, KTN Kenya, TV2 Africa, and UKENTV, etc. Two coders purposively selected ten videos on YouTube, specifically dealing with the Kenyan presidential election to code and analyze. Videos from governmental, national, and international agencies were not included. The videos were selected for anlaysis from a pool sourced from the citizens video, including KiPLANGAT MOI, GP Nairobi, Kenyanelection Petition, Smartmonkey TV, Kenyancitizen TV, and Middle Class KE.

Coding Scheme

Saldana's (2009) coding pattern techniques were used to code the selected videos into a pattern of related and unrelated themes. The source, views, posted comments, likes, and themes in each video constituted the pattern for each unit of analysis. The source indicates the author of the uploaded video, and views are "netizens" who watched the video, according to the statistical tracking data kept by YouTube. The views indicate the weight or importance accorded the message from the video or the quality of the video from the viewer's perspective. The likes icon at the bottom of each video also provided clues on how people identified with the content. Lastly, the ten videos analyzed had an intercoder agreement of 90%. The next section breaks down the ten videos according to the triangular strands for analysis.

Source	Likes	Themes	Views	Comments
Kenyanelection petition (Africogs Kethi K)	145	0	0	One person, one vote
Ukwelivideo (Presidential debate)	208	1	0	Campaign funding
GPNairobi (Youth voice Garang)	35	1	1	Youth and jobs
CJ Denies Bribery Claims (Kenya cititv)	302	9	1 (dislike)	Vote upheld by SC
MiddleClassKE (Take it and go!! Episode 8)	532	7	10	Kenyans & Patriotism
Njeri Kamau (Kenya 2nd Presidential debate)	619	0	2	Make peace not war
Tom Maruko (Kenyan	1811	2	1	The ICC

Presidential Debate)			(dislike)	question
Political Realignment (Kenyan citizenstv)	1297	4	3	Health care & education
Kenyan Citizen TV (Respect Supremecourt)	394	0	0	Respect gov't institutions
Kenyacitizentv (Facts Of The Cord Petition)	1873	9	5 (like) 2 (dislike)	Raila challenge

Table 13.1 Video Analysis

As seen in Table 13.1, these ten videos uploaded by Kenyan citizens on YouTube had various themes as outlined. Most of the theme had to do with peace, prosperity, and economic growth. Apart from the last video that had a contentious theme dealing with the challenge of the result by Raila Odinga (the incumbent), the rest were upholding state institutions and advocating for social, political, and economic well-being of the Kenyan citizens.

According to Kavoori (2011), YouTube videos constitute a viral space made up of what he calls a participatory culture between users in a chained contextual system. An overriding theme, as indicated above, permeated the adjacent videos in a subset of chains from a simple click of the intended targeted unit of analysis. The number of viewers showed the impact or the significance of the video. For instance, Tom Maruko's video above received the second highest viewership. But on the contrary, it received one dislike and only two commentaries. But "Facts of the cord petition" by the Kenyan citizen TV received the highest viewership (1873), 9 comments and 4 likes and 1 dislike. But since likes in social media indicate passionate following by users, "Take it or Go!! Episode 8" video received 10 likes, making it the largest liked video among the 10 analyzed so far. This video was comic-style, featuring a male and a female sitting on the sofa of a living room and recapping the major stories of the day including the appointment of a new pope in Rome. But the overall content (analyzed in the audio/verbal section) was based primarily on the Kenyan presidential election. They used caricature, satire, and sarcasm to lampoon contestants as well as the hate messages that filled the air waves.

"Youth Voice Garang" video by GP Nairobi had the lowest viewership, but interestingly enough, it epitomized the role of the forgotten youth in the whole scheme of politicization in Kenya. As would be analyzed later, the main theme of this video was about youth and employment. Without jobs, youth participation can only be muted, he argued.

Watching a video upload from Njeri Kamau, whose overriding theme was "make peace not war," provided an equally interrelated videos on the right of the screen that treated similar themes from different video sources. That chaining system, as enunciated by Anandam Kavoori can continue endlessly to other similar videos on similar theme of "make peace not war" from a different country or continent. So this analysis did not include those chains for fear of getting caught up in an endless string of unrelated videos.

Three strands of analytical framework were adopted for analyzing the videos: the visual/non-verbal; audio/verbal, and the texts/written comments/likes that accompanied some of the videos.

Visual/Non-verbal Analysis

Most of the videos had images and symbols that were significant in understanding the role of the ordinary citizen during the election period. As the theme of the Kenyan election petition video was one person, one vote, there was a female lawyer seen before the Supreme Court in a room packed with mostly male faces, making the Kenyan woman another central figure in the election. This Kenyan election petition video was particularly geared toward annulling the election and she was surrounded by spectators and a sign language interpreter pegged on the bottom right of the screen demonstrating with fingers. The fact that the Kenyan authority made provision for a sign language interpreter in the courtroom was symbolic. It indicated that those with language impairment were not left out in the process of participation.

During the presidential debate, the "ukwelivideo" group uploaded a video with the candidates standing in a podium in a similar way to the United States presidential debate format as the moderator was facing the candidates and having active eye contact with them. There were male and female candidates on the podium. With respect to video title, "CJ Denies bribery claims," uploaded by Kenyan citizen TV, images of Facebook and Twitter contributors to the ongoing election were splashed on the screen before the gigantic Supreme Court building. The image of the judges in a British-style gown was equally seen as they walked majestically to the stage.

On the other hand, this other video title, "Take it and Go!!! Episode 8," featured two personalities (male and female) in a living room and a medium shot that remained unchanged for four minutes, twenty-two seconds. Their laughter and other gesticulation indicated they were comedians. The medium shot was able to portray their facial gestures and relaxed mood in the midst of a tense election. Their presence was reassuring to the rest of the viewers.

The video that also had more non-verbal messages was titled "Kenya second Presidential debate-meet Mohammad Dida" by Njeri Kamau. There were several still images of the candidate, Mohammad Dida, at the center of the screen in medium shots, long shots, and extreme medium shot, as well as his party logo as the music played in the background. The variety of shots in this video went a long way to show the mood and tempo during the election. They also symbolized the influence, they believed, Dida was generating among the Kenyan electorate. An intriguing symbol of a ballot box with 50 US dollars stuffed in the box in the video showed the role money was playing in the election. What was intriguing was the fact that the currency displayed on the video was foreign, thus influencing viewers to believe that there were elements of outside inspiration to the Kenyan election process. Other still images included: two fingers symbolizing peace, a picture of Dida, a picture of other candidates, a picture of the party's flag with a dove carrying a fig leaf and a voting card with presidential nominees on it, and another voting card with his party affiliations beside it. These were signs that even the party leaders were out to promote peace throughout the election period.

Visual effects played another cardinal role as can be seen in another video, titled "Kenyan Presidential Election Debate," uploaded by Tom Maruko. This video was filmed on the streets in Kenya as citizens, buses, and cars were busy plying the streets. Life seemed to be normal during this period, according to this video. There were no protests, violence, or disorder of any sort. There were a number of cut-away shots, but the most prominent was the one showing an intersection of Kenyatta Avenue and Uhuru Highway, which indicated a completely Westernized city void of African traditional touch. All these indicated normalcy and the state of excitement for the election.

The orange party showed its complete dominance as it highlighted the active role of male and female party members wearing their orange party regalia during campaign in the video "Political Alignment," as can be seen in Table 13.2. The theme of this video, with its overwhelming number of viewers, was centered around Health and Education. That was probably why one could see more female representatives in the party. It was probably these non-verbal messages in the video that triggered more likes and comments on YouTube. Indeed, therein lies the power of social media in this era of new media-driven political campaigns. Table 13.2 below categorizes the video according to shots, images, signs, and symbols, as discussed earlier.

The next section discusses the audio and verbal analysis in some of those ten videos. It should be noted that not all ten videos displayed significant audio and verbal features. Only a handful, as seen below, had audio and verbal content worthy of analysis.

Video	Images	Shots	Symbols/Signs	Others
Kenyanelec P	Court	MS	Female/sign language	Men dominate
Ukwelivide o	TV Studio	WS/LS/MS	Moderator/ earphone	Female role

GPNairobi (Youth)	Living room	LS	Twitter #	Dark room
CJ denies bribary	Court	LS/CU	UK-styled gowns	CJ still image
MiddleClass KE	Living room	MS/2 shots	Male/female	Laughter/ smile
Njeri Kamau (2nd D)	Dida, Vcard	MS	Victory sign	Bbox, money
Tom Maruko (Debate)	Streets	MS/LS	City, citizens	Interviews
Pol. Realign (citizenstv)	Orange	LS/WS	Party tour	Scarves/ hats
Kenyacititv (R S.Ct)	Press conference	MS	Cameras/Mics	Judges
Kenyacititv (Factcourt petition)	Military	LS	Crowd	Odinga

Table 13.2 Non-Verbal Categories

Audio/Verbal Analysis

In the "Youth Voice Garang" video, a single, ordinary voter stood in a dimly lit room wearing a white T-shirt with a Twitter address caption "#GPNairobi" on it. This meant those watching that video on YouTube could also follow him or his group on Twitter. The tone of his voice showed the state of the youth presence in Kenya. He was committed, alert, and informed, especially on the issues as he highlighted the concerns of the youth, which were employment related. The verbal texts on his shirt, as indicated above, showed the place of the youth today in Kenyan politics. The Twitter address was a sign that youth should meet virtually and discuss their concerns. They should strategize and create a common platform. It was no longer meeting at the physical gathering place; now was the time for electronic gathering on Twitter. On the contrary, in the next video, "ukwelivideo," as seen in table 13.3, there was a lone female on the floor of the Supreme Court in a physical setting.

Her main concern was that before electronic voting, ballot boxes were hand delivered and politicians found a way to stuff the ballot boxes. She also complained that in 2007, the law was changed and voters were required to handwrite their vote and return it to the constituency officer, but the constituency officers found a way to change it. So the law changed again to electronic voting. With all these reckless administrative mistakes, she believed, the presidential election result needed to be invalidated. Judging from the number of viewers and the lack of "likes" and "comments" on this video, it can be deduced that her argument failed to win support. Of course, the election result was never annulled and the incumbent leader Raila Odinga failed in his bid to maintain his grip on power, and Uhuru Kenyatta took over as the new leader of Kenya. A summary of the audio alongside the characters involved in the video can be seen in Table 13.3 below.

Source	Characters	Music/Sound	Texts
Kenyaelection Petition (Africogs Kethi K)	1 & spectators	Silence	N/A
Ukwelivideo (Presidential debate)	5 & 1 female	Bed music	Names
GPNairobi (Youth voice Garang)	1	N/A	Twitter
CJ denies bribery claims (Kenya cititv)	5 judges & 1 female	VO narration	Faceboo k Twitter
MiddleClassKE (Take it and go! Episode 8)	1 male & 1 female	Bed music	Advice
Kenyan Citizen TV (Respect Supreme Court)	1 (SC decision)	Noise	Set/dec

Table 13.3 Integrated Texts

As seen on Table 13.3, only a handful of videos had integrated texts synchronized with the audio. In the video uploaded by Njeri Kamau (see Table 13.1), the message from one of the party leaders was splashed on the screen with these captions: "Message from Mohamed Abduba Dida: Vote in Peace and Vote for Peace and Change in Kenya," "Make Peace Not War," "In each of us there is a little of all of us," "peace for me, for us, for everyone, for the planet." This re-emphasizes the importance of peace and love that all the candidates, including the incumbent and the opposition, accorded the election.

The video titled "CJ denies bribery claims" produced by Kenyan citizen TV, had snippets of social media effect on the election visible to the viewers. The narrator showed how people commented on Twitter and Facebook their feelings about the election. The camera zoomed in on their photos, as well as the texts. This actually demonstrated the extent to which people were involved in the election. They wanted to make sure their voices were heard across media platforms. Also in this particular video, Dr. Willy Mutunga's statement to rebut allegations of misconduct in his campaign posted a statement on Twitter that read: "We have been the target of attack, slander, libel, and outright indecent, vulgar, and unacceptable abuses." This statement appeared on YouTube as a caption and viewers unfamiliar with Twitter would be curious to register on that platform in order to get more information about the allegations. In essence, YouTube became another platform to channel messages from Twitter.

Other videos among these ten had similar characters — voice over (VO) and bed music (background audio). But "Take it and Go!!! Episode 8" made the most effective use of audio and text because the two personalities (comedians) started with an overview of world events before discussing the Kenyan election. During their discussions, they had intermittent texts above and below the screen on how they felt about the election process. They expressed fear for violence, but at the same time, advocated for peace and love because hate speeches between warring tribes were featured on social media. Their bed music was soft and cool for the listening pleasure of their audience. It was as a result of their skillful use of videography on YouTube that their postings had the highest viewership, as seen in Table 13.1.

The next section of analysis actually examined the other components of the YouTube platform, i.e., texts featured on the videos, as well as the written texts that accompanied some of the videos outside the periphery of the video window plane. The number of times viewers liked the videos were also recorded and analyzed below.

Text/Written Comments/Likes

This section covers the comment and text section created by YouTube that allows viewers to write and post comments on each video they have watched. Their views are always seen below any given video. With these ten videos, not all had comments. In fact, only a handful had written comments from viewers as seen in Table 13.1. Of all the videos, " Take it and Go!!! Episode 8" had the highest likes (10) and 7 comments, the second highest among those analyzed in this study. One comment from DM says, "2.02 this guy is just interesting:D black smoke?? They should have weed smoke. We blacks like making an impact." The word "interesting" in the comment summarizes the general feeling of the other nine comments. This, again, showed the love people attached to their country. The theme of their video was patriotism. They looked natural and relaxed in the video, and most importantly, they compared what was going on in Kenya to the struggle between lions and lionesses. This was an attempt to emphasize the theme of peace and love as they stretched the imagination of their viewers.

The video "Facts Of The Cord Petition" had the incumbent Raila Odinga petitioning the Supreme Court to nullify the election result that had given Uhuru Kenyatta a slim victory on grounds of voting irregularities. In this video, one of the viewers' comments was critical. The author, "the Republican Truthsayer" said:

> "If it's true, then UHURU does not deserve to be President. How could he do this to country so fragile at this point. If he won fairly, then I will be the first to congratulate Hon.Kenyatta...." (The Republican Truthsayer)

The second comment added another view to the Republican Truthsayer's comments:

> "Preliminary Response: Oraro prove how 85K votes rigged out Rao of a whooping 14M registered nationwide election. How did a computer hitch rig him out yet IEBC went manual? IEBC using IT services or sharing in coming data how did that cause petitioner to loose [sic]? ok prove IEBC deliberately willfully locked out Cord agents. Case Dismissed with Costs." (Siasabora)

But other comments insinuated tribal rivalry:

> "One man..... One man continues to hold this country hostage. The bad blood between Luos & Kikuyus will only end when he exits the political scene." (Lex Rango)

The Luos and the Kikuyus in Lex Rango's comment are the major tribes fighting for power in Kenya. Thus, it would appear hate speech was equally present during this election.

Conclusion

This chapter sought to answer two research questions regarding the role of social media in the presidential election process in Kenya. The first research question was about our understanding of how Kenyan citizens utilized verbal and nonverbal elements on YouTube that were posted during the presidential election. It is evident from the analysis that verbal elements—through the use of audio and texts within the video—contributed in one way or the other to inform people about the campaigns, the voting procedures, and, most importantly, the results of the election. A video posting from Mohammad Dida, for instance, drove the theme of peace and not war. One featuring Dr. Mutanga, using voiceover, rebutted unfounded claims about election practices by his party.

"Take and G!!! Episode 8," the video by the two comedians, provided comic relief and satire on the election process.

In sum, these videos used YouTube to signal their presence on the world stage by providing those not able or willing to follow the election on traditional media another outlet. They also made greater use of the non-verbal visual techniques, whereby viewers were able to gain election flavor and feel the ambiance from the colors, street activities, and door-to-door campaigns, as seen with the orange party.

With respect to the second research question on how Kenyan citizens utilized "texts/comments and likes" features on their YouTube postings during the presidential elections, this analysis was able to deduce that the videos with the highest number of likes were not necessarily the ones that had the greatest viewership. Thus, "likes" do not translate to content approval. Again, a video, such as the comic video clip highlighted above, had the greatest comments and the comments were different from person to person. In fact, it was through the analysis of this video that one could still see the extent of tribal bickering between the Luo and the Kikuyu tribes that derailed the main focus of the 2008 elections. This tension between the Luo and the Kikuyu tribes during the last presidential election caused uncontrolled violence that affected mainly these two tribes.

Ultimately, social media, through the analysis of YouTube postings during the Kenyan presidential election, created a sense of awareness, immediacy, and participatory democracy. For Kenya to televise and allow this election to be covered by ordinary citizens using social media is not only felicitous but worth emulating by other countries in the region. This ushers the dawn of a new era of e-government and participatory democracy in Africa. Most importantly, the fact that there was not a repeat of the genocide-like violence that characterized the 2008 presidential election is proof of democratic maturity demonstrated by the Kenyan people as a whole. They deserve recognition and respect by charting a new path for the rest of sub-Saharan Africa to follow.

However, this can be sustained only if the old order gives way to new innovations and new forms of shared governance, where the public is not docile or pushed aside, but allowed to participate freely. They will actively be engaged in choosing their leaders, as Kenya demonstrated in this year's presidential election. This means, also, that those who are elected into office through the democratic ballot boxes are accountable and ready to engage in meaningful dialogue through new media communication with the people to forge a positive way forward. This is also a call to governments in sub-Saharan Africa to invest heavily in new communications technology because that is the future.

Since topography and other geographical impediments and other weather-related causes are preventing telecommunication infrastructural growth in the region, the time has come to carry out meaningful changes to remove these roadblocks and embrace new forms of communication. Another obstacle is technology literacy. More and more schools in Africa need to inculcate social media in their curricula and train teachers or invite expatriates from overseas to train students, such that students who graduate with degrees in social media or new media can be able to act as informants to the government and the private sector to improve communication links with the rest of the world. Right now, the majority of the people eager to use social media, for one reason or the other have limited resources. Their only available choice is to crowd at cyber cafes and pay fees to get connected. This is not the way forward if technological revolution needs to be championed in Africa. Right now, only the rich elites and university students with smart phones that have wireless connections — where possible — engage in social media activities.

References

Amutabi, M.N. (2013). Media boom in Kenya and celebrity galore. *Journal of African Cultural Studies*, 25 (1), 14-29.

Betot, J. C., Jaeger, P. T and Grimes, J. M. (2010). Using ICTs to create a culture of transparency: E-government and social media as openness and anti-corruption tools for societies. *Government Information Quarterly*, 27, 264-271.

Bratton, M. (2013). Citizens and cell phone in Africa. *African Affairs*, 1-13.

Carmody, P. (2013). A knowledge economy or an information society in Africa? Thintegration and the mobile phone revolution. *Information Technology for Development*, 19(1), 24-39.

Crawford, K. (2009). Following you: discipline of listening in social media. *Journal of Media & Cultural Studies*, 23, (4), 525–535.

Dick, A. L. (2012). Established democracies, Internet censorship, and the social media test. *Information Development*, 28 (4)259-260.

Kavoori, A. (2011). *Reading YouTube: The critical readers guide.* New York, NY: Peter Lang.

Kraidy, M. M. (2011). Media reform in Lebanon: New media, new politics? Retrieved from http://repository.upenn.edu/asc papers/249

Langmia, K. (2011). Traditional cultures and their effects on globalization: An African Perspective. In A. Kirk & S. Olaniran (Eds). Globalization and Digital Divide. New York, NY: Cambria Press, pp. 23-39.

Langmia, K. (2006). The role of ICT in the economic development of Africa: The case of South Africa. *International Journal of Education and Development, Using ICT*, 2 (4),144-156.

Lotan, G., Graeff, E., Ananny, M., Gaffney, D., Pearce, I., and Boyd, D. (2011). The revolutions were tweeted: information flows during the 2011 Tunisian and Egyptian revolutions. *International Journal of Communication*, 5, 1375-1405.

Maduku, D. K. (2012). Understanding retail bank customers' attitude towards and usage of cell phones and Internet banking services in Gauteng, South Africa. Online Dissertation, University of Johannesburg.

Mare, A. (2013). New media, pirate radio, and the creative appropriation of technology in Zimbabwe: case of Radio Voice of the People. *Journal of African Cultural Studies*, 25 (1), 30-41.

Mbarika, V.A., Okoli, C., Byrd, T. A., and Datta, P. (2005). The neglected continent for IS research: A research agenda for sub-Saharan Africa. *Journal of the Association for Information System*, 6(5), 130-170.

Mehta, K., Maretzki, A and Semali, L. (2011). Trust, Cell phones, social networks, and agricultural entrepreneurship in East Africa: A dynamic interdependence. *AJFAND*, 11(6), 5373-5388.

Murphy, L.L. and Priebe, A.E. (2011). My co-wife can borrow my mobile phone! Gendered geographies of cell phone usage and significance for rural Kenyans. *Gendered Technology and Development*, 15(1), 1-23.

Newham, J. and Bell, P. (2012). Social network media and political activism: a growing challenge for law enforcement. *Journal of Policing, Intelligence and Counter Terrorism*, 7 (1), 36-50.

Saldana, J. (2009). *The coding manual for qualitative researchers*. Los Angeles, CA: Sage.

Sheedy, C.S. (2011). Social media for social change: A case study of social media use in the Egyptian revolution. Unpublished Thesis, American University.

Steinberg, J. (2003). Information technology and development either/or. *The Brookings Review*, 21(2), 45-48.

Walton, M. and Donner, J. (2011). Mobile-mediated publics in South Africa's 2009 elections. In J. E. Katz (Ed.). *Mobile Communication: Dimensions of Social Policy*, 117-132.

About the Editors

Dr. Kehbuma Langmia is an Associate Professor at Howard University within the Department of Strategic, Legal, and Management Communications. He teaches research and other media-related courses in the department, as well as in the graduate program. His research interests are in social media, Information Communication Technology(ICT) and their implications on culture and identity. He has authored textbooks, research articles, book chapters, and non-fiction books. His books and articles have been cited by many scholars in the field of Information Communication Technologies (ICT).

Dr. Pamela C. O'Brien is an Associate Professor and the Chair of the Department of Communications at Bowie State University. She is the creator of the Emerging Media concentration for undergraduate students within the Department. She teaches courses in communication theory, quantitative methodology, communication law and policy, and broadcast advertising and sales. Her research interests include social media as a counter-hegemonic force, remediation of communication technologies, and the critical-cultural study of animation, especially adult-oriented television animation and Walt Disney. She has published articles on animation, social media, and politics, and a television production textbook.

Dr. Tia C. M. Tyree is an Associate Professor at Howard University within the Department of Strategic, Legal, and Management Communications. She teaches several graduate and undergraduate courses. Her research interests include African American and female representations in the mass media, hip-hop, rap, reality television, film, and social media. She has published articles in several journals, including *Women and Language, Howard Journal of Communications, Journalism: Theory, Practice & Criticism and Journal of Black Studies*. She is also co-author of *The HBCU Experience*. Her website is www.tiacmtyree.com.

Ingrid Sturgis is an Assistant Professor/New Media in the Department of Media, Journalism, and Film at Howard University. She teaches multimedia storytelling, copy editing, and other new media-related courses. She has earned coveted fellowships from the Fulbright-Hays Program and the Society for New Communications Research. She has worked online as editor for Essence.com and for AOL's Black Voices; consequently, social media has become the focus of her research. Her other research interests include mobile money, black media entrepreneurship, the digital divide, digital literacy, and analytics. Her most recent book is *Are Traditional Media Dead: Can Journalism Survive in the Digital World*. Tweet her at @isturgis.

About the Authors

Dr. Jennifer Brannock Cox is an assistant professor in the Department of Communication Arts at Salisbury University. She teaches courses in print, mobile, and online journalism; public relations; and social media. Her research interests include online media, social media journalism, newsroom culture, and community journalism. She has authored several research papers and articles for academic publications.

Dr. Todd Shurn is Associate Professor of Systems and Computer Science at Howard University and a former University of Southern California visiting researcher. His research interests are heterogeneous communication networks, multimedia streaming and storage, multi-modal computer applications, interactive media, and computer games. Dr. Shurn has served on review teams for the National Science Foundation Engineering Research Centers, and National Institutes of Health Bioinformatics program. He has provided consulting services to Disney, Time-Warner, Microsoft, *The Washington Post*, Steve Harvey, Sinbad, Tavis Smiley, and others. He is an ongoing technology editorial contributor to the *Chicago Defender* newspaper.

Stella-Monica N. Mpande is pursuing her Ph.D. from Howard University, with a focus on Mass Communications and Media Studies. Her research interests include the use of social media by the African Diaspora and African governments in cultural socio-economic development, film and television, and human rights. Mpande has presented her research in various conferences, including the Yale Bouchet Conference on Diversity, National Communication Association, and African Studies Association.

Dr. William B Hart is an assistant professor in the Department of Mass Communications and Journalism at Norfolk State University. He teaches a variety of courses, including research methods and media technologies. He also does research in a wide variety of areas, including video games and social media. He has presented dozens of conference papers, including a paper on social media use while watching TV and a paper on the use of social media in mass communication departments. In addition, he has published more than a dozen book chapters and journal articles on a range of topics using a variety of research methods. His website is www.williamhartphd.com and his Twitter handle is @WilliamHartPhD.

Dr. Erica C. Taylor is an assistant professor in the Department of Strategic, Legal, and Management Communication at Howard University. She previously taught strategic communication courses on the undergraduate and graduate levels at Norfolk State University, where she also served as faculty adviser of the campus Public Relations Student Society of America (PRSSA) chapter. Her primary research interests include social media best practices and strategic and crisis communication at Historically Black Colleges and Universities (HBCUs). She has published and conducted various professional and peer-reviewed scholarly presentations in these areas. Her Twitter handle is @EricaCTaylor.

Jamie Cohen is the program director and instructor of Molloy College's new media program. He co-founded the program and major based on new media theory and practice. He was also formerly the Director of Web and Digital Media at the Hofstra University School of Communication, where he taught digital journalism and media studies. His research is based on web television, online tools, digital curation, and digital literacy. He is skilled in website development and management and has been published several times on media literacy and digital curation.

Paul Mihailidis is an assistant professor of media studies in the Department of Marketing Communication at Emerson College, and the Director of the Salzburg Academy on Media and Global Change. Dr. Mihailidis's research concerns the connections between media, education, and citizenship in the 21st century. He has published widely on media literacy, global media, and digital citizenship. He is the editor of *News Literacy: Global Perspectives for the Newsroom and Classroom* (Peter Lang), author of the forthcoming *Media Literacy and the Emerging Citizen* (Peter Lang, 2013), and co-editor of the forthcoming *Media Literacy in Action* (Routledge, 2013). Dr.Mihailidis sits on the Board of Directors for the National Association for Media Literacy Education (NAMLE).

Dr. Jayne Cubbage is a journalism and mass communication educator. She teaches broadcast journalism and mass communication courses, including media literacy, broadcast news writing, mass communication theory, and television production. Her research interests include non-majority communications audiences, media literacy, and social networking. She is the Founder and CEO of the African American Media Literacy Initiative, LLC, a media education company with a mission to ensure an empowered media audience.

Yanick Rice Lamb is an associate professor and interim assistant chair of the Department of Media, Journalism, and Film at Howard University. She teaches multimedia reporting, interactive editing, and magazine writing. She is also adviser to *101 Magazine* and the Howard University News Service. Her research focuses on diversity in coverage and the impact of social media and technology on news. Formerly editorial director of *BET Weekend* and *Heart & Soul*, she has also been an editor at the *New York Times*, the *Atlanta Constitution*, *Essence* and *Child*. She is co-author of *Born to Win: The Authorized Biography of Althea Gibson.*

Kendra Desrosiers is a marketer and digital strategist at Google with a passion for social media, content, and mobile technology. Before joining the Silicon Valley community, she worked in media as a multimedia journalist and founder of online arts and entertainment magazine, *25 Magazine*. An avid music enthusiast, Desrosiers also previously worked in marketing and programming at The Recording Academy, which produces the famed GRAMMY Awards. Desrosiers holds a Master of Business Administration from the Massachusetts Institute of Technology and a B.A. in Journalism from Howard University.

Dr. Jamila A. Cupid is a business etiquette coach as well as an Assistant Professor, teaching courses in strategic communications in the Center of Excellence in Mass Communications at Lincoln University of Pennsylvania. She has served as a public relations and digital media professional, with expertise in research and strategy, in New York City and Washington, DC, for several years. In addition to her industry experience, degrees, and scholarship in the United States, she has studied in the Caribbean and South America. Her research is focused in international and intercultural public relations, communications and digital media.

Dr. S. Lenise Wallace is a motivational speaker, college professor, and communication professional. She is an Assistant Professor, teaching communication courses at CUNY LaGuardia Community College in New York City. She has more than ten years' experience in public relations and image consulting. She has energized audiences across the country, turning her speaking engagements into overall interactive experiences. Her research interests include public relations and race, gender, and sexuality in mass media. Due to her prominent work in the field, Dr. Wallace was featured in *The Practice of Public Relations* by Fraser Seitel, one of the nation's leading public relations textbooks.

Angela D. Minor, Esq., is an Assistant Professor of the Department of Strategic, Legal, and Management Communication at the Howard University's School of Communications. Additionally, she serves as the Director, of the Martin Luther King, Jr. Forensics Program, which comprises of the award-winning Debate and Mock Trial teams. She is also a graduate of Howard University's School of Divinity. When she is not teaching and mentoring, she enjoys practicing law. Attorney Minor is the co-founder of the Law Offices of Minor & Willcox, LLC, which has offices in the District of Columbia and Maryland.

Dr. Adam Klein is an Assistant Professor in the Department of Communication Studies at Pace University. He teaches courses in media studies, propaganda, and communication theory, with a research focus in global communication and conflict. Dr. Klein has written articles on topics such as the Iranian nuclear showdown, the American antiwar movement, and the Israeli-Palestinian conflict. In 2010, he published the book *A Space for Hate,* exposing how racist organizations are utilizing the Internet to introduce hate speech into the mainstream. His book can be found in over 600 libraries internationally, including the FBI Academic Library in Virginia.

Dr. Nickesia Gordon is Associate Professor of Communication at Barry University. Her research interests involve looking at the intersections between gender, mass media, and popular culture. She also has an active research agenda in new/social media, communication, and development, as well as the political economy of mass media. She teaches courses in Mass Media Theory, Media Management and Programming, Communication Research Methods, as well as introductory communication courses.